S0-CFZ-722

"I have seen in my visions what I call the 'Children of the Blue Ray', those who are incarnating as the teachers of humanity's next evolutionary step. This book is a gift from Spirit to the 'Children of the Blue Ray' and their caregivers -- indeed, to all of us."

Gordon-Michael Scallion, Futurist and editor of *The Earth Changes Report*

"Caryl Dennis is an investigator of anomalies, and what she has found deserves attention. Because of her unique interview skills, she has happened upon a pattern of newborns who defy the classification of 'normal.' These gifted ones begin almost immediately displaying characteristics similar to those I have identified as being typical to near-death survivors; and they speak of other worlds and other lives as if being a 'human' was but one of many choices they could have made before birth. I truly believe Caryl has tapped into something here that the research community needs to address."

P.M.H. Atwater, Lh.D., author of *Coming Back To Life, Beyond The Light, Future Memory,* and *Goddess Runes.*

The Millennium Children

Tales of the Shift

Caryl Dennis
with Parker Whitman

Other books by Caryl Dennis:

Colorology: The Study of the Science of Color

The UFO Reference Book

What's Your Color? (Pamphlet)

The Millennium Children

Tales of the Shift

Caryl Dennis
with Parker Whitman

Copyright (c) January, 1997 Caryl Dennis & Parker Whitman

All rights reserved. The following document is the sole property of Caryl Dennis and Parker Whitman and is protected under the copyright laws of the United States of America. No part of this document may be reproduced or transmitted in any form or by any means, electronic or mechanical, including photo copying, without written permission from Caryl Dennis or Parker Whitman.

Cover illustration by Parker Whitman

Published by:
Rainbows Unlimited
1245 Palm Street
Clearwater, FL 34614
(813) 441-2270.

First Edition January, 1997

Printed in the United States

ISBN 0-9627845-1-6

Dedication

This book is dedicated to my youngest brother, Ted Scott Dennis. May the sharing of his life story awaken the memories for other single twins, so that they can integrate their loss before it's too late for them.

Table of Contents

Introduction

What "shift"? And what does the approaching Millennium change have to do with it? The year 2000, after all, is merely an artificial human construct, a number on society's calendar -- how could it have meaning in the actual process of humanity's development from whatever it once was to whatever it's going to be? Well, it couldn't -- except that if enough people attach significance to a symbol (in this case a symbol of time measurement closely linked to a cultural, spiritual archetype -- Jesus Christ), that symbol *becomes* significant.

And the shift? Nothing more or less than a fundamental transformation of human consciousness -- some say *all* earthly consciousness. A shift from dualism (the world is made up of scores of irreconcilably opposed forces: good and evil, body and mind, flesh and spirit, etc.) to the "Law of One" (all opposites are illusionary and are simply methods for making the Universe happen); a shift from competition to co-operation as the primary mode of behavior; from fear to love as the primary motivation of action. From one frequency to another, "higher" one -- like finding a TV channel that has much better programming than the one we've been watching! Ecstasy, bliss and deep joy rather than merely cheap laughs; universal, unconditional love rather than tawdry sentimentality. Voluntary cooperation instead of conflict and power politics. The shift that has been prophesied for many centuries by many seers in many cultures, and is now being heralded by events both internal and external, personal and social, geological and meteorological, technological and paranormal: *that's* what "shift"!

The date on a particular calendar may have little to do with the reality of an evolutionary process (which the shift certainly is), but many people of a particular mindset may well be -- and are

1

being -- propelled into transformative behavior by their convictions concerning the year 2000's importance. The return of Jesus Christ is imminent! The "End Times" are upon us! The advent of the New Age is upon us! The Ascension is happening now! Look out for the Photon Belt! A great comet is going to wreak havoc on planet Earth! The planet Nibiru is returning, as it does every 3,600 years! The Mayan calendar ends in 2012 and "history" will end with it! There is a third to fifth (or fourth) dimensional transfer underway involving planet Earth! Global warming and other human-caused damage is going to change our reality! ET's (or Visitors, or Watchers, or Time Travellers or Interdimensional Invaders) have grabbed ahold of human history and they're turning it inside out!

The prophets and scenarios are legion, but every scenario involves a shifting from one perceived reality to another, usually more profound one. Although there are those who feel we are doomed to extinction as surely as the dinosaurs, if only because the earth and the cosmos do what they do, how that shift manifests to any given individual is, very simply, a function of that individual's belief system.

Thinkers as diverse as Peter Russell (*A White Hole In Time, The Global Brain Awakens*), Alvin Toffler, Joseph Chilton Pearce (*Evolution's End*), Terence McKenna, Jose Arguelles, Zechariah Sitchin and P.M.H. Atwater, to name but a few, all see some sort of transformation in human consciousness on the horizon. Each interprets that vision in his or her own unique way and attributes it to varying causal factors, but they all see *something* coming!

Atwater, one of the premier researchers into the near-death experience (and a three-time experiencer herself!) points out in her book *Future Memory* that "millions of diverse and different peoples throughout the world" have undergone fundamental changes in consciousness over the last twenty years (whether because of a near-death experience, a spiritually transformative event such as an encounter with "ETs" or angels, physical trauma of some kind, or as a result of diligent spiritual practice). She finds that this "internal convergence", as she calls it, is accompanied by actual changes in physical brain structure.[18]

I'm one of the people who has experienced that fundamental change. In Part I of this book I'll relate how "the shift" has manifested and continues to manifest in my life -- in other words, what has happened in my personal life that leads me to believe I am a "Millennium Child." I'll also describe the investigational pathways along which my "shift" has led me. In Parts II and III, I'll share with you the results of my investigations into the phenomena of the Vanishing Twins and of the intuitive Millennium children. Parts II and III are the culmination of ongoing manuscripts that I have published in various forms over the last three years, revised and updated. We'll consider the miracles of birth and growth, in society as well as among individuals. We'll consider positive and concrete actions that we can all take to improve life on Earth. We'll consider what we're becoming, and how.

Many believe that the frequency, the unique vibrational rate, of our Mother Earth is rising as we go into the new millennium; she has begun a cleansing and healing process, necessitated at least partly by the damage inflicted upon her by humankind. Obviously, all life on Earth is experiencing this higher frequency, with varying results, at least among humans. Whereas some people are getting more in touch with their spiritual source (whatever they perceive that to be), others are becoming disoriented, self-destructive, even violent, reacting in fear to the ongoing and increasing changes around them. On the astral level (that is, the invisible world from which the

3

three-dimensional, "physical" world emerges), as dualism dies, its death throes are felt by all, and some are simply driven mad in the process. Again, it all depends, as they say, on who's riding the bicycle; it goes in different directions for different riders!

I must point out that few if any of the people whose works I have drawn upon and quoted in the creation of this book would agree with the hypotheses that I'm putting forth. Those opinions are my own and no one else's. The idea of some sort of non-human intelligence manipulating human reality is, at least publicly, quite repugnant to anyone involved in mainstream science. No one quoted in this book should be assumed to believe any such proposition, unless they say so themselves.

Having said that, let me add that I am firmly convinced that such interaction and manipulation is taking place. It is one of the reasons I was compelled to write this book. There are a number of ET "groups", with agendas that range across the spectrum from horrific through indifferent to beatific, operating in and on earth. One has only to investigate the subject with an open mind to come face to face with that reality. Although it is not an easy one to integrate, we have no choice but to do so if we are to survive and grow as a species. George C. Andrews, author of *Extraterrestrials Among Us* and *Extraterrestrial Friends and Foes* (two books that should definitely be read before attempting to dismiss the possibility of an ET presence on this planet) puts it as well as anyone in an unpublished paper titled *UFO Phenomena and The Self-Censorship of Science:*

> Those who insist on imposing four-dimensional frameworks on multidimensional phenomena in attempting to scientifically explain anomalous events

may be missing the point, in a way comparable to someone trying to explain quantum physics in Newtonian terms. . .Any group that assumes itself to have a monopoly on the truth is a danger to the well-being of the world at large, and that includes scientific as well as religious dogmatic belief systems.

Perhaps this book will help to point out some avenues of investigation that will lead all of us closer to open disclosure of the truth about these "visitors", whoever or whatever they may be.

An interesting perspective comes from "Sasha", channeled by Lyssa Royal in the book *Preparing For Contact:*

When a planet is getting ready for extraterrestrial contact and contact with new levels of reality, the brains of the species on the planet begin evolving rapidly. This is happening right now on Earth. As the brains begin evolving to another level, a new subspecies begins to emerge through a kind of subtle mutation. When this begins to happen, the brain-wave capacity of the human changes and therefore their ability to perceive other levels of reality begins changing. It is then that they realize the extraterrestrials are not going to suddenly appear to humans; rather, humans will begin to perceive the ET contact which has gone on all along.[6]

Is "the shift" part of humanity's preparation to join whatever sentient beings may be "out there" waiting for us to get our collective act together? Is this the *"Childhood's End"* envisioned by Arthur C. Clarke a half-century ago in his science-fiction classic of that name? Is the emergence of nothing less than a new archetype in the group consciousness

-- the big-eyed, seemingly omnipotent ET that has become, through media saturation, an integral part of Western culture -- is that emergence part of a group psychosis, or part of the birth of a new human reality? Or is it something more sinister, part of a plan for humanity by beings -- human and otherwise -- for whom your spiritual and physical freedom are irrelevant? The questions, at this point, are endless; what I intend to share with you in this book is my search for the answers to those and many other questions as they emerged in my life, and what I've found so far.

It's my impression, based upon years of travel, research and interviews, that what "Sasha" describes is indeed happening. Our world is changing because the way in which we perceive it is changing. Our perceptions are changing because the energy matrix out of which we create those perceptions is changing. Our brains, the meeting-place of the Infinite and the mortal, are perhaps responding to signals we will only understand in retrospect -- signals from something we cannot comprehend until we are truly at one with it. To that end, and as a necessary part of that process, appearing among us are an increasing number of children with heightened intuitive, intellectual, and even physical abilities. It's my belief that these children are the ones that will -- indeed, must -- emerge as humanity's future leaders if we are to move forward spiritually and avert -- or survive -- a global catastrophe of unimaginable proportions. I also feel that in order for these children to attain their seemingly almost limitless potential, their caregivers -- and indeed society as a whole -- must do everything possible to allow their gifts and abilities to grow unhindered by the misguided (albeit well-meaning) beliefs about child development that still prevail in the modern world. Many resources are provided in Part III of this book that can aid in that effort.

These "intuitive children", as I call them, are born retaining pre-birth memories (past-life and between-life, as well as life in the womb) and/or displaying marked psychic abilities (clairvoyance, clairaudience and clairsentience) as well as the ability to see beyond the visible light spectrum, which enables them to perceive auras, ghosts, extraterrestrials, devas, fairies, angels and various "light beings". Their other senses (hearing, taste, touch and smell) may also be hypersensitive, which may cause them to display behavior symptomatic of what is now called Attention Deficit Hyperactive Disorder (ADHD), Attention Deficit Disorder (ADD), learning disability (LD), autism or hyperactivity. Their intelligence level is usually in the genius range, and they display a variety of inventive and creative talents, being often quite "handy" with machines of all kinds. They frequently find living in this three-dimensional world rather limiting. Of course, all of the intuitive children do not necessarily demonstrate all of these abilities.

Most, if not all, of us are born with the "equipment" to be intuitive children. However, because family environment and cultural conditioning usually discourage behavior considered different from the norm, psychic abilities in particular are often allowed to atrophy in the absence of any encouragement. We are from a very early age highly sensitive to disapproval, expressed or not. The fact that apparently increasing numbers of these intuitive children are "making it through," so to speak, I see as a sign of hope for the future.

All of the tales of the Millennium Children -- young and old -- contained herein are true (to the best of my knowledge) and were told to me by a parent, grandparent, friend, therapist or the individual him- or herself. The names of the people involved, however, have been changed out of consideration for their privacy. While many of these stories stretch the current medical, scientific and psychological paradigms, I can

7

testify that the people telling them were sincere, seeking only validation or understanding (or help!).

Hearing so many of these stories in the last nine years, as I traveled throughout the United States researching and lecturing on the subjects of Colorology and UFOlogy, I recognized the need for information, resources and support for the caretakers of these special children, as well as for the children themselves. Both often feel isolated and unsupported by the traditional educational system, which, being neither equipped nor trained to assist these children in reaching their full potential, tends to put them in learning-disabled or "special" classes, or simply ignores them. These precious spirits are being branded ADHD, ADD, and so on, and are being medicated, ostracized or even institutionalized to force them to conform to an established definition of "normalcy".

If these children are indeed to be our leaders in the new millennium, we owe it to them (and ourselves!) to provide them with every opportunity to realize their full potential. It's essential that we listen with open minds when they tell us of experiences that may stretch our current view of reality. The reactions of the adults around them is critical to the attitude these children develop toward their experiences. I have seen the difference between a household in which "dreams", nighttime experiences and psychic phenomena are openly discussed with acceptance, understanding and love, and one in which fear, repression, anxiety and denial are the normal reactions. It is well-known that children absorb and reflect back the perceptions of the significant adults in their lives. We owe it to ourselves, our children and the future of planet Earth to obtain as much information as possible to assist these "special" people in their shift -- and ours. Knowledge is indeed power.

Futurist and visionary Gordon-Michael Scallion calls the intuitive children *The Children of the Blue Ray*. In his audio tape of the same name he states:

> These are the forerunners, they are those that come to prepare the way for the next race -- what may be termed the next root race. Their origin in the inner world has come from those planes of existence that you would call the mental levels. It is here that through their particular sojourning they have congregated, banded together under the ray that would be blue. Not so much that their skin color would be blue, but this indeed will be a portion of the next root race, but rather their vibratory soul group is of the blue vibration.....Their function or purpose, what may be viewed as their karmic desire, is to express themselves in peaceful manners and be able to utilize the earth in its original form. Original form is then cohabitant with the various elements and elementals. It would be better understood if you would view the blue children as predominantly teachers.....Having abilities at birth to excel in music, art, writing and psychic communication between all kingdoms. All of these are latent in their consciousness and awaken early.[8]

My experience and research have led me to the conclusion that the solution to our problems lies in the heart of every single human on earth. The key requirement is the reconnection of mind and heart, so that the motivation for action changes. It's not survival of the fittest, "every man for himself", that is the "natural order of things", but voluntary, loving cooperation that will bring us through the present crises and into an abundant world bright with hope and filled with wonder. This is the practical significance of the demise of dualism and the ascendancy of the "Law of One" in human affairs. The forces of co-operation, of unity, power the Universe; we have only to align ourselves with these forces, rather than constantly struggling to maintain an ego-driven, artificial, illusionary and ultimately destructive order. This book deals with how that alignment may happen -- and how it can happen to us in spite of ourselves!

Sounds pretty idealistic, eh? Well, in my work as an intuitive counselor, I see visions of the future. Some I see as only *possible* outcomes; others are *probable*. None are certain. Free will, of course, is the variable. What happens depends on who "votes" for what course of events. Life is truly a democratic experience! But to work properly, any democracy must be peopled by awake, aware and alert citizens. It's my hope that this book will help to empower its readers to become exactly that, and to give to our future leaders the best possible learning and growing environment, so that the future we co-create will truly be one worth living.

Part I

Tales of
My "Shift"

Tales Of My Youth

As early in my life as I can recall, I felt "watched": Was it God? At that time I knew of no other possibility, so I thought about "God" a lot. And just to be on the safe side, I was an especially -- even obsessively -- good girl. I loved going to church, which was convenient because my family went to church a lot -- or more accurately, my family went to a lot of churches. My parents, believing a religious background was important, took my six siblings and me (I'm the third of seven children), to the Methodist church, then to the Baptist, Presbyterian, Seventh Day Adventist, Jehovah's Witnesses and, finally, to the World Wide Church of God, from which we were excommunicated because my mother "asked too many questions". My mother was always searching for the "truth" to teach her flock of kids. She questioned everything -- almost.

I always felt -- well, different somehow. My mother told me she spelled my name CarYl rather than CarOl because she knew when I was born that I was special. (I bought the story and sure enough, I always felt special!) My father, all seven of his children and one nephew were born with "V" shaped birthmarks on our foreheads. My Grandmother said it was because she looked at a fire when she was pregnant with Dad. (I don't know the source of that belief, but it certainly "fired" my imagination!) I have no idea what the birthmark means, but I always felt that it had some sort of significance. Any insights on this from readers would be most welcome.

My father's mother was quite a character, I understand. She died when I was ten, but I've heard several stories about her psychic ability. One day when my father was away on military duty during World War II, she announced to my mother that "Clarence is coming home today on the four o'clock train. We

13

have to go meet him." He wasn't expected, and there was no reason to believe he would be coming home, but my mother told me she got herself all dolled up and went down to the train station anyway. Sure enough, he was on that four o'clock train.

My mother tells another story about being called to my father's parents' home in the middle of the night. When they arrived, my grandmother told my parents that she knew she was going to die, because she had seen herself up in the corner of the room looking down on her body. She had been ill and apparently had an out-of-body experience; to her, it meant she was going to die. She was fine by the time her family all arrived to hear the story, and went on to bounce back from her illness rather quickly.

My mother vividly recalls awakening one bright moonlit night at the age of four to the sound of tinkling bells and exquisitely beautiful music ("like a music box"). She saw "about ten" colorfully dressed, perfectly formed "little people holding hands and dancing in a circle on my comforter -- right on top of me!" They were "laughing and. . .having a wonderful time." Once they finished dancing, "they put their hands together in a position of prayer and bowed their little heads. I didn't hear voices but they were obviously saying a prayer. When the prayer was finished, one of the little men went to the edge of the bed, hopped off, and just sort of floated to the floor. He then made a fold in the blanket and all the rest of them slid down, laughing and giggling all the while. I watched with great wonder as they marched in single file right into my closet." At no time, she said, did they take any notice of her. For her part, my mother was so "dumbstruck" that she never moved or spoke throughout the experience.

A voracious reader throughout her life, my mother already knew how to read when she started school (also at four years old); she had learned by observing as her mother taught her older brother to read. (She in fact fits much of the profile of the "intuitive child".) Put succinctly, my mother is a Biblical scholar with strong fundamentalist beliefs, who also believes in reincarnation and UFO's. She believes the Rapture is imminent; the Chosen Ones will be evacuated before Armageddon -- probably in ET craft. She is a practicing astrologer was well. As you can see, I came by my "paranormality" honestly!

My father, on the other hand, is a gentle, funny, quiet soul -- very quiet now. I remember my mother, who is quite outgoing and excitable, yelling at Dad, "Talk to me! I can't read your mind. Tell me what you want!" In 1977, he developed throat cancer and had a complete laryngectomy. He never really liked to talk anyway; now he has an excuse not to speak -- what perfect manifestation! He does, however, have a Servox talking device and when he gets it out, you'd better be listening. He was a hard-working auto mechanic throughout his working career, which -- so he was told -- contributed to his cancer. He usually worked two jobs, and was always wheeling and dealing something -- usually cars -- to feed his ever-growing family. I have never in my life seen my father drunk or even tipsy, and he never "went out with the guys"; he is devoted to his family.

I was born in Lansing, Michigan, but we moved to Clearwater, Florida when I was two. My mother was very ill and her doctor told her if she didn't get to the sunshine soon she would leave her three children without a mother. His prescription was to go to the beach every day and soak in the salt water and sun; she did and it worked! We went to the beach almost every day for the first four years we lived in Clearwater. It was a wonderful place to grow up. We usually had a boat of some sort and we all loved the water.

My sister Marcia was born after we moved to Florida, and Mom had fraternal twins, Terri and Tim, when I was ten; fourteen months later, my youngest brother Ted arrived. I suddenly found myself changing diapers almost constantly (or so it seemed to an overwhelmed eleven-year-old); it often fell to me to shepherd Marcia, the twins and Ted while Mom was working or busy elsewhere in the house. I spent so much time with a baby on my hip that, at the age of fifteen, I wound up with scoliosis (curvature of the spine) -- obviously, there were other factors that contributed to the scoliosis (like falling down the stairs when I was twelve), but no doubt carrying those kids around helped! All that early experience with infants formed a big part of the decision that I made in my twenties not to have children of my own. I had a very clear picture of the responsibility involved.

Because our family kept growing, it seemed we were always looking for a bigger house. One of our family hobbies was taking long drives in the country looking for interesting places to live. (Besides, young children often sleep during rides, and you can keep track of them more easily in a car!) We found some doozies, too: An old abandoned school building; a round, three-story silo house; a ski resort in Michigan; a mansion on Madeira Beach and various other huge old houses.

My mother is really responsible for teaching me about creative visualization. On our outings we would go through some run-down old house and she would ask us, "Which room would you want? How would you decorate it? Where would you put your bed?" We would all get excited and start planning, talking and thinking about creating our dream home. It was very good exercise.

When the twins were babies, and before Ted was born, we finally found my mother's dream home -- a beautiful old two-story colonial with five fireplaces, four porches and even maid's quarters in the back, where my newly-married oldest sister Linda and her husband could live. It was humongous! There was one little detail the previous owners forgot to tell us, though -- it also was haunted! At the time, my parents didn't believe in ghosts or haunted houses, so when we kids talked about seeing people walking around at night, they dismissed it as imagination. But when my mother saw lights going on and off and heard mysterious footsteps in the hall, she had to admit something unusual was happening. My father, on the other hand wasn't convinced; he quickly lost patience with being awakened during the night.

My brother Tim was about three when he started talking about the ghost he was seeing around the house. My mother was quite startled when he announced one morning, "That man was back again last night." She inquired, "What man?!" He explained, "The man that comes and sits on the end of my bed and just watches me. I can feel the end of the bed go down." When asked what he did about it, Tim said, "I just cover up my head and he goes away."

One afternoon the four youngest children were all playing in my older brother Steve's bedroom. For no apparent reason, the closet door began to slowly creak open. They all ran screaming from the room -- except, that is, for Terri, who was trapped in a sleeping bag they had been playing with. She was nearly hysterical by the time Mom got to her. There was definitely something strange about that closet. The plumbing access for the bathroom between my brother's room and mine was in that closet. Every time I went into that bathroom I could hear strange scratching noises. Assuming it was mice, bugs or my brother being a brat, I repeatedly had my parents inspect the closet, but of course they never found anything. I learned some years later that the people who moved into the house after us nailed the bathroom doors closed!

Something startled my mother awake one night, and she got up to find the hall lights on. She knew they had been off when she went to bed. After checking to find everyone else asleep in their beds, she woke us all up so we could go downstairs to check it out. We were very surprised to find almost all the lights on downstairs, although the windows and doors were locked. No one could explain it.

The haunted house episodes are my earliest conscious recall of paranormal activity -- except, perhaps, for the vivid, recurring dream I had when I was six, seven and eight of what I described to my mother as "pirates" dragging me, kicking and screaming, out of my bed and into the living room. It was quite terrifying, and after reading the UFO literature, I now wonder if my recall of pirates is what is known as a "screen memory". That particular can of worms I have never opened -- but there would be others!

As if puberty isn't traumatic enough, I spent mine watching ghosts (or something) walking around my bedroom, while hearing from my parents that I wasn't seeing anything. My folks soon became rather intolerant of my frantic screams in the middle of the night, so, as I got older, I tried to contain myself -- unless "they" got too close to me. I had insomnia for my entire fifteenth year. Instead of sleeping, I watched the dark figures walk around my bedroom and down the hall. My little brother Ted, at that time about two years old, would sneak into my bed late at night because he saw "things" too, and was terrified! Not everyone in my family saw "them", however, which lack of validation only added to my confusion, but no one could tell me I wasn't seeing tall, dark, shadowy figures.

We lived in that place for almost seven years, finally selling it when I was sixteen, in order to move back to Michigan. I went back to visit the house when I was thirty-five, just to see what I could psychically sense. The owner told me she was a professional psychic herself, and had done a great deal of investigation and clearing in the house. She discovered that almost everyone who had lived there had seen the ghosts, even describing them in the same way (one ghost, for example always wore a fedora hat). During a seance, that ghost revealed himself as the first owner of the house. He had died there, and because he loved the house so much, didn't want to leave. She felt that she had finally convinced him to go on, because the nightly activity in the house had stopped.

Lansing, Michigan in the middle of January, 1967 was predictably cold and snow- covered. You can imagine how six beach bunnies handled that. We were there about a week and told my father to quit fooling around and take us home. Instead, he found us a quaint old farmhouse out in the country south of Lansing. We tried all the winter sports in an attempt to enjoy the snow. I, for one, was never convinced. The beach has always been my main power source! I did enjoy going to the small local high school; it was primarily a vocational school and had an excellent business department. I was able to get a job as secretary to the vice president of a big advertising specialty company right after I graduated. But I was overjoyed when Dad took us home to Clearwater two and a half years later.

We joined the World Wide Church of God when I was fifteen. As members of that congregation, we adhered to a very strict, fundamentalist belief system, celebrating only the "holy days" in the Bible. When I was about fifteen, Mom announced to us, "This will be the last Christmas we celebrate. Christmas, and all the other usual holidays, are pagan. We won't celebrate them any more either." The younger children had a hard time with this drastic life change -- no more Easter eggs, Halloween trick-or-treating, no Christmas presents! But that was only the beginning. The church required that women's skirts had to extend below the knees; makeup was not allowed, and the Sabbath was kept from Friday sunset to Saturday sunset (no more Friday night dances). Drinking ("a little wine for the sake of the stomach"), eating steak and dancing were OK, though. Re-marriage after divorce, however, was completely out. I recall a particularly heart-wrenching example of this rule: The father of a sweet little family with two children had been married (for six months) years before, when he was a teenager. The church found out about it and demanded he and his current wife divorce, if they wanted to stay in the church. Despite the fact that their marriage was a perfectly happy one, the couple acceded to the church's demands rather than be cast out of "the flock". I will never forget the look of abject misery on that man's face as, some time later at a church function, he gazed with tears in his eyes at his former family, now headed by another man (because her first marriage was considered "fraudulent", the church allowed the wife to remarry). Then there was the ugly business in which Herbert Armstrong, the head of the church, excommunicated his son and heir-apparent, Garner Ted, for adultery. Perhaps taking a cue from my mother, I began to question some of the things I saw going on around me. And then my high school sweetheart, whom I'd known before we joined the church, wrote me a "Dear John" letter from Viet Nam, because he just couldn't deal with my religious practices. I was heartbroken, but stayed in the church; I still had confidence my mother knew what she was doing, because she spent so much time studying the Bible.

Because our belief system was so strange to most people, we only socialized with people in the church; when we were excommunicated in 1969, we not only lost our church, but all of our friends as well. It was especially devastating to my mother, but the day we left the church we were all in shock -- except, possibly, my father. Ever resourceful, he rallied his weeping brood with the announcement that he had found an ad in the paper that would set all aright: We were going to get a houseboat! My father, bargain-hunter and wheeler-dealer supreme, still combs the newspaper daily for ads of interest (he often presented his kids with "help-wanted" ads he'd cut out). The houseboat ad certainly turned out to be a winner -- we bought her the next week and named her "Peace". We created our own church! For the next two years, we went out on "Peace" almost every weekend and Mother read aloud from her metaphysical and spiritual books.

My first "real life" adventure occurred when I was twenty. I quit my job and went to Germany to visit my sister, Linda, whose husband was stationed there. It was quite an adventure for a naive young woman like myself. I had the opportunity to take a side trip to Paris, where I experienced my first impression of past lives (other than ghosts!). I loved touring the centuries-old buildings and the museums. Our guide really put life into her stories of Parisian history. Some places we visited seemed strangely familiar to me -- inexplicable rushes of emotion coursed through me as I walked around. At one point, in an old courtyard, I could actually psychically "see" a battle the guide was describing. I do that sort of thing frequently now, but at the time it was quite confusing and rather unsettling.

At the age of twenty-one, I moved in with my first true love and the paranormal again entered my life. He was tall, dark and handsome, as well as a very gifted psychic and a wise, old

21

metaphysical sage -- all at the age of twenty-one and with no formal training whatever. He had been left alone a great deal as a very young child and had learned to communicate with his "guides and angels" for protection and comfort. He taught me about psychic ability, the Laws of Manifestation, and the Laws of the Universe in general. He could "read my mind" (telepathy), as well as move things with his mind (telemetry). His guides came to visit frequently, signaling their presence by turning the water on in the sink, turning appliances cn or off, or other mischief. During the first week we dated, we were lying on the couch watching TV. Suddenly, Marty said, "Watch, something's going to happen." I looked around the room wondering what he was talking about, and noticed the floor fan was slowly coming to a stop. I said, "What's going on?" He replied, "That's not all; go look in the bathroom." I found the water running in the sink. He calmly told me that whenever he was afraid or had a question, he would ask for help and this was how the answers came. "They were telling me you're okay," he said.

In the course of my job, I had to run errands at various times of the day. Marty drove a delivery truck on a route that took him all over the county, yet every single day he would pass me on the road as I ran my errands. Somehow, he always knew where I would be. I could actually feel him "walking in my mind", as I called it. Sometimes I would silently sing "Camptown Races" until he said, "Okay, I'll stop." If I ever wanted to talk to him during the day, I would think, "Marty, call me." Within fifteen minutes he would call and say, "What do you want?"

We had a great time using the Laws of Manifestation to create all sorts of fun places to live, to do and to have. We spent hours at a time planning, drawing pictures of and meditating on whatever we wanted in our lives. Once, we decided we wanted to live on the waterfront, in a cabin, on at least five acres, with animals, and we didn't want to pay more than $100 a month. We went to work on the project and two weeks later manifested exactly that -- only we paid $75 a month! (He taught me to always add the phrase, "this or something better" to my requests.)

When I was twenty-two, I saw a film, *Soylent Green*, that had a tremendous impact upon me. The father of the character played by Charlton Heston had chosen to die. He was lying in a special room in which he was surrounded by vivid and very realistic images of Earth in its natural state -- green forests, unpolluted oceans, babbling brooks, wild animals, mountains and flower-filled meadows. Because of the planetary devastation brought about by war and overpopulation, Heston's character had never seen such things in "real life". Never had a movie affected me so deeply -- I cried for two weeks! I also vowed that I would see as many of planet Earth's unspoiled areas as I could before they disappeared forever under humanity's onslaught. I "knew" it would happen in my lifetime.

A few months later, we decided to do the "hippie, around-the-country-in-a-van" thing that was so popular at the time. Of course, we had no van or money with which to buy one, but Marty assured me that didn't matter; we just needed to focus on what we wanted. We went van shopping, decided what model we wanted and designed our own modifications. We got maps, talked about what we each wanted to see and watched travel movies. Out of the blue, about two weeks later, I received a call from my attorney, who was working on a lawsuit related to an automobile accident I'd been in two years earlier. To my great surprise and delight, he told me the other party was willing to settle for an amount five times larger than we had hoped to get! Needless to say, the next week we found the perfect van, fixed it up, quit our jobs and set off to see the country. For the first time, I visited the great American West; the sheer volume of -- space! -- and the majesty of the Colorado Rockies, the Grand Canyon and other mind-boggling manifestations of Mother Earth's power and creativity seriously altered my reality -- and anchored even more firmly in my dreams the determination to experience as much of her wonder as I could.

During the six and a half years we were together, Marty helped me to understand my childhood visions and to put them in perspective. He taught me that many people saw ghosts and experienced other paranormal activity. I wasn't crazy! It was during this period I decided to embark seriously upon my spiritual search, and I have read (despite my reading disability) many books and taken classes on spirituality, metaphysics and the paranormal since that time.

Through my twenties I "did the corporate thing", mostly in the hotel and resort industry. I was about fourteen when my folks nearly bought that ski resort in Michigan (they decided against it after seeing the condition it was in!); all of us kids loved the idea and, over the years, spent hours sitting around the kitchen table talking about what it would be like to own a resort. As we got older, the resort concept changed to a metaphysical retreat center. I wanted to acquire the skills necessary to operate such a place, should I or my siblings (or anyone else, for that matter) succeed in bringing it into my life.

I continued to take classes and read spiritual books, attempting to define my own "truth". I became fascinated with Atlantis and struggled through every book I could find on the subject. I really "resonated" with those tales -- they felt very real to me, and I frequently saw visions pertaining to the stories, just as though I were reliving what I was reading.

Past lives and the near-death experience also became major interests during that time.

I had by this time found Florence Shinn's book, *The Game of Life and How To Play It*. I had gotten very good at manifesting, particularly places to live. Not long after Marty and I split up, at the age of twenty-seven, I decided I wanted to buy a house. Of course, I didn't have the money, but I knew that wasn't the issue. I knew exactly what I wanted. It had to be near my job, have a bathroom adjacent to the master bedroom, a laundry room in the house and a view of the water. I told a realtor friend of mine what I was looking for and a week later she called to say she'd found my house. It was perfect (okay, I had to look out my bedroom window and WAY down the street to see the water). I did some creative financing and -- POOF-- I bought my house with no money!

I got married when I was thirty to a man I recognized immediately (from a past life, I was sure). We had only known each other a short time, but I felt that strange familiarity and knew we had business to finish. A rocky four-and-a-half years passed before we finally called it quits and divorced. He didn't understand any of my spiritual beliefs, nor was he the least bit interested; I certainly didn't understand why anyone would be so interested in watching or playing football and baseball all the time. I never discovered the nature of our unfinished business, but I did learn a great deal from the relationship. It was the last one I had with someone whom I didn't at least *think* was on a conscious spiritual path.

During our marriage, my husband offered to put me through the school of my choice if I would quit my high-paying (I was making more than he was), high-stress job as director of sales for a big Holiday Inn. I had been cutting hair for years "on the natch" -- something else Marty taught me -- and thought it would be great fun to go to cosmetology school. I worked very hard and finished in record time. While I was going to school, I decided I wanted to work in the salon that was going into the new Holiday Inn then under construction on Clearwater Beach. I knew many of the future employees from working on the beach for years and had a ready-made clientele. Almost every Saturday I parked my car in front of the salon as it was being built and imagined myself working there. I even went so far as to pick my station. As soon as I finished school, I marched into the newly completed salon and told the owner I wanted to work there. She said, "Yeah, you and every other hairdresser in town." But after some persuasion, to the great surprise of all the other hairdressers in the salon (and probably the owner), she hired me. And yes, I got the station I had picked out.

Six months later I opened my own salon and boutique. Color analysis was really hot in the early eighties and I centered my salon, cosmetic company and clothing completely around the color analysis theme; coordinating and organizing clothing, accessories and make-up along the lines of warm and cool colors. The salon was successful from my first month in business, because I had used my prior experience to carefully identify my target market -- businesswomen. I joined the local businesswomen's organizations, but I had such "stage fright" that I would almost vomit while waiting for my turn to introduce myself and tell what I did. I knew I had to overcome my debilitating fear of public speaking. In order to do this I accepted the presidency of a networking group, and was instrumental in developing it into the largest, most influential women's organization in the county. It did wonders for my salon and boutique, as well as forcing me to overcome my stage fright.

The divorce in 1985 played havoc on my nerves, which manifested as an extreme allergic reaction on my hands to the chemicals I used to do hair. Over the next couple of months I closed the salon, did some free-lance haircutting, consulting, publishing and a variety of other things, marking time while attempting to decide what I wanted to do next. Right after the divorce, I manifested the first of several great apartments I've found on Clearwater Beach over the years. This one was located over an ice cream parlor.

A woman I met at that time invited me to attend her church. I hadn't been in a church since 1969 and frankly, after my experience with the World Wide Church of God, the idea repelled me. She told me the members of her church held the same metaphysical beliefs I did. I really didn't buy that, but she kept after me until I agreed to go see what it was all about. I'll never forget the first Sunday I walked into that Unity Church. I couldn't believe all those hundreds of people could be into the same "far-out" things I was. I loved it! I took lots of classes and never missed church for about six months -- until I found out the minister's adoring husband was having an affair with the church secretary. I was totally disillusioned -- again -- and quit going to the church. I realized at that point that "church" was not the answer for me -- my truth was unique and it was within me.

Before I parted ways with the Unity church, I met some people interested in establishing a metaphysical retreat center. One man had a relative who owned a hotel on Vieques, an island off the coast of Puerto Rico; he suggested it as a potential site. Always ready for an adventure -- and always on the lookout for that retreat center -- I gathered up a good friend and a video camera and set out to investigate the situation. We found a beautiful tropical island -- but one not quite suited to our purposes. About five miles long and two

27

miles wide, Vieques had a nuclear waste dump at one end, and a practice bombing range for the military at the other! The people (and the hotel) were in the middle. We were not encouraged; however, during our stay on the island, we learned that one could go swimming at night in an area of phosphorescent ("glow-in-the-dark") water off the island's coast. We hired a boat to take us out there. Our guides, who had grown up on the island (their fathers had been in the military), told us an interesting tale: when, as children, they went fishing at night, they frequently saw large, anomalous underwater lights "zooming all over". Sometimes they even saw the lights enter or leave the ocean. When they reported this strangeness to their parents, the response was that the boys had seen nothing and should stop making up stories. "We know what we saw," they told us. "We still see them." They believed the lights to be some sort of craft. They said, "Lots of other people see things here, too." That tale would come back to me some years later.

After I returned from Vieques, I decided to finalize, by undergoing a tubal ligation, the decision I had made in my twenties not to bear children. I better understand now why I made that decision so early in life. Helping to raise my three youngest siblings (and changing a jillion diapers by the time I was twelve) was certainly part of it, but it was more than that. Had I borne children, I wouldn't feel free now to travel as I do, nor would I have felt free to do or say some of the more controversial things I've done and said in the past ten years. Did I "know" something in my twenties about what I'd be up to in my forties? Not consciously perhaps, but I find it interesting that I have met many other women on a spiritual journey who made the same decision.

In 1986, while participating in a meditation class, I finally found relief from a bothersome physical problem I'd had all my life. I can remember from very early childhood asking my mother repeatedly to look at my left shoulder because it itched. She would inspect the area and assure me there was nothing there. But the itch continued on and off, bothering me almost daily throughout my life. Well, during this meditation class, the instructor told us to ask any question on our minds; at the time my shoulder happened to be itching, so I asked about that. I clearly heard a voice say, "It is so that you will remember who you really are!" No other explanation was offered. I have no idea what it meant; however, my shoulder stopped itching at that moment and hasn't itched since. Life is full of mysteries! I could only file that one away and hope for illumination at some later date.

1986 was also the year that my relationship "issues" jumped up and punched me in the nose. I met a man who, because of all the apparently "cosmic coincidences" involved in our coming together, I felt had to be "the one". I experienced wealth (or at least its appearance) for the first time. I have to admit, I was dazzled by the limousines, the fancy restaurants, the expensive jewelry, the travel, and the big house complete with a maid. It was all so overwhelming, I didn't see what was going on under my nose. Without going into all the gory details, when I escaped (literally) early one morning, I was in big trouble and believed my life was in danger. I was devastated financially, morally, mentally, emotionally and spiritually, and REALLY angry at myself -- not to mention VERY embarrassed. I had ignored all my intuitive signals, and even though this man was a master pathological liar, I had continually dismissed my feelings that something was wrong -- until it was no longer deniable.

The day I returned to Florida, my best friend handed me the book *Women Who Love Too Much*. Desperate to "fix" whatever it was that had allowed me to get into the mess in which I now found myself, I read it as fast as my reading difficulties allowed, plowing through it on sheer adrenaline! When I finished that book I read every other one of its kind I could find: *The Cinderella Complex, Love Is Letting Go of Fear* and *Your Inner Child of the Past,* to name a few of my favorites. I joined two (not one) W*omen Who Love Too Much* support groups, began private therapy, discovered and nurtured my "inner child", did many forgiveness processes and developed a new attitude about life and love. One of the most important relationship lessons I learned was that what I had thought was "love", was really past life recall. I realized that my previous relationships had been about cleaning up old karma. I had a dramatic past life recall at a Dick Sutphen workshop right after I returned to Clearwater that helped me to clearly see why I had gotten into the previous relationship and the karmic meaning of the ensuing mess.

While I worked on untangling my inner self (and tried to figure out what I wanted to be when I grew up), I was unemployed. I was living (on credit cards) in a beachfront apartment, from the eighth-floor balcony of which I could see a non-stop vista of the sparkling Gulf of Mexico, the ever-changing sky, breath-taking sunsets and white sand -- my primary power sources! It was a perfect environment for healing. I walked on the beach as much as five hours a day, meditated, went to metaphysical classes and lectures, did Yoga and became a vegetarian. I also underwent a special form of bodywork called "Multidimensional Bonding" which basically was massage performed by a man who saw visions, usually of past lives, as he worked on his clients. When he described his visions, often the clients, given awareness and understanding of these past-life experiences, could release the blocked energy in the related area of the body. Pain relief naturally resulted. I found it to be very effective. The therapist was just beginning to develop this skill and was "experimenting" with four of my friends, as well as with me. All of us, including the therapist, experienced some rather dramatic consciousness shifts during the four months we worked together: we all developed some form of "channeling", as well as gaining a deeper understanding of our "missions".

At the same time, I was working with Barbara Walter, a psychic healer, to correct my scoliosis. I would lie on the floor of her healing room, relax, and calm my conscious mind; she would then pull my etheric body out of my physical body. I could actually feel this process; it felt like being sucked out of a hole. Due partly, I think, to my visualization skills, we were able to straighten the top curve two to three inches and the bottom about one inch.

All in all, I was in an altered state of consciousness for about three months, so I can't tell you exactly what triggered the next series of events. All I know is that in 1987, the year of the Great Harmonic Convergence, and a year of transformational changes for many people I know, my life began to resemble an episode of the TV program *Outer Limits!*

Tales of Other Voices

One pleasant day in February of 1987, while walking on the beach, I heard a voice. It may have been the same voice that "explained" my itching shoulder the year before; I could not tell then and do not know to this day. At any rate, my impression at the time was of a male voice, situated about a foot from my right ear. At first, it spoke only a few words or phrases, such as "electromagnetic spectrum", "frequency", "pineal gland", "spirals of life", "endocrine glands", and even more puzzling, "rainbow healing" and "science of color." As a person with no science background, who had joined the working world right after graduating from high school, I had no familiarity with or basis for understanding such concepts -- only a working knowledge of color analysis from my days as a cosmetologist. What, I wondered, is an "electromagnetic spectrum"? To my surprise, the voice answered me, saying I should go to the library and look it up.

Which presented another problem -- I had never used a library before! Because of my never-diagnosed "condition", I usually couldn't read for more than a few minutes without my eyes filling with tears, after which I often went to sleep. Although -- often by sheer force of will -- I had struggled to read my metaphysical books, to this day I have never read a novel!

But, as the days went by and the "voice" proceeded to download ever-increasing amounts of information, I was forced to plunge head-first into the role of researcher to find out if what the voice was saying was true. My mysterious new invisible friend would feed me paragraphs of information while I walked on the beach; I would then rush back to my apartment to write everything down, then off to the library to search for verification in various scientific texts -- books on quantum physics, physiology, medicine, and so forth. And I found the information I was receiving to be accurate -- in fact, sometimes I found what the voice told me reflected word-for-word in the books. I had plenty of help, too, in my research. Whenever I was blocked on a particular research pathway, a "coincidence" would come along to get me moving again; for instance, someone might give me a book that s/he "just thought" I should have, and of course the book contained exactly what I needed. When attempting to look up some piece of information at the library, I would stand in front of a shelf in the science section and silently ask for what I needed, while running my hands over the books. I'd get kind of a tingling or buzzing feeling in my hand when I touched a particular book, and sure enough, there would be the information I sought.

Needless to say, I was fascinated. Put simply, I was being taught how to use color to heal physical, emotional and spiritual dis-ease. In my search to validate what the voice was telling me, I entered into the amazing world of vibrational healing -- at that time almost completely new to me. Color, I learned, was a simple and inexpensive way to bring order and harmony to the big collection of vibrations that makes up a human being. I began drinking a gallon of violet solarized water per day, "spinning" my chakras, and using color psychologically in a variety of ways. One evening the "voice" downloaded a powerful rainbow meditation. I recorded it and began using it several times a day. (For more information on color, see the chapter on color in the *Millennium Children* section of this book, and/or my book *Colorology*.)

One thing I did not learn from the voice, however, was its identity. All questions along the line of "Who are you?" were answered only with silence. Most of my many metaphysically-inclined friends were eager to offer explanations: It was my higher self, it was a spirit guide, an angel, a dead scientist or a demon. I was tapping into the akashic records. I was an extraterrestrial or a "walk-in". I was possessed. I was crazy and I needed to be locked up. While I appreciated the input -- most of it, anyway -- none of these explanations "felt right". I must admit, the "walk-in" idea at first seemed to me most viable. Ruth Montgomery, in her book *Strangers Among Us*, asserts that first of all, the original energy (spirit) inhabiting a given body must consent to the walk-in process. Certain "souls" are given the right to skip the birth process and babyhood, because of the nature and urgency of their project or task, and to take over the consenting soul's body -- to "walk in". There were many times when I did feel as though someone else was in my body!

I began to feel as if my life was a big puzzle that some unknown force was now piecing together, or that I was being "danced" through life like a puppet. Not that the feeling was unpleasant; I had been earnestly seeking "my true destiny", and now I was getting what I asked for -- although not what I expected!

During all this research, I came across information about a man who was to become one of my heroes -- Nikola Tesla. It was astonishing to me that a man who was one of the great pioneers in radio, submarines, turbines, and many other key technological innovations of the late nineteenth and early twentieth centuries, as well as the man who developed and ultimately *gave* the technology for alternating current to George Westinghouse, would not be as well known as Henry Ford or Thomas Edison! But as I learned his story, my astonishment faded: here was a man who in 1938 claimed to have developed a means of interplanetary communication -- and was receiving signals from outer space! He also swore that, given the capital and the time, he could create a means of generating unlimited FREE energy! Small wonder that the once renowned inventor -- one of the most brilliant minds Western civilization has seen, and far ahead of his time -- died penniless and in relative obscurity. ETs aside, none of the "old boys" of Tesla's time were terribly interested in fostering a form of energy that could not be metered. No financial future there! I only came to understand later why this man and his work were so important to me.

In April of 1987, my brother Tim was in a serious automobile accident. His convalescence promised to be a difficult one, including several operations, confinement to a wheelchair and long hospital stays. One night I was thinking about him and wondering how I could help. I was learning about the power of color, and knew about positive affirmations; I wanted to combine them to give him something to look at in the hospital. I took a pen and piece of paper, quieted my mind and started doodling in the corner of the paper. Three hours later I "woke up". On the paper was a rainbow with a positive affirmation in each color band that related to the properties of that color. My "Body, Mind & Spirit Healing Rainbow" is the result of that night. Over the next three days I was taught how it could be most effectively used and how to explain the "Healing Rainbow" to others. I was told it was a "visual healing tool." The body has an innate ability to balance; when you look at a rainbow, your body absorbs the color energy it needs in order to maintain metabolic balance (more detail on this in *Colorology*). I decided to make Healing Rainbows available to the world. I had the original art work done, wrote a business plan, raised the money and had the finished product in my hand in six weeks. It was exciting to watch the answers to problems or questions appear, as if by magic. The process felt completely "directed"; if there was a decision to make, I would take a walk on the beach and ask questions. By the time I got to the end of the beach I would have the answers. As exciting as it was to manifest the Rainbows, the response to them was even more gratifying. They have been used in both the birthing and dying processes (and nearly everything in between!). My favorite story involving the Rainbow came from a nursing home. A poster was placed on a wall where Alzheimer's patients could see it. They apparently were able to regain their wits while looking at it -- but only, I was told, for as long as they looked at it. I find the implications of that quite compelling.

In June of 1987, I participated in a "Discover Your Purpose In Life" workshop, which incorporated the processes from Arnold Patent's book, *You Can Have It All*. This wonderful book helps you analyze your talents, skills and experience in order to discover ways of using them in activity that will generate income, as well as provide a blissful way to do service. I meet so many people trying to figure out what they really want to do! They realize that living to pay the bills, without spiritual fulfillment, leaves much to be desired. Many also feel a sense of urgency, a feeling that they have a job to do, if they could only find out what it is! To anyone in that situation, I highly recommend Patent's book. I created my wholesale and retail company, Rainbows Unlimited, as a result of that workshop, thereby manifesting a means of support that allowed me to travel around the country (my dream since I was in my twenties) and give lectures, meet spiritually conscious people, do service, and just generally "follow my bliss" (i.e. have fun)!

The long-awaited Harmonic Convergence occurred on August 16, 1987. My friends and I had all been hearing about what an important day it was to be in the transformation of planet Earth and humanity. Celebrations were planned all over the Tampa Bay area. That morning my best friend and I were led to conduct a ceremony at our special place on the northern end of Clearwater Beach. We meditated at sunrise, and talked

36

about the changes in our lives and our dreams for the future. That evening, I took a walk by myself to reflect on the meaning of the day. I was wading in the surf about two miles up the beach from my apartment when I stepped on the point of a huge conch shell. When I lifted my foot from the water, I saw that the shell had penetrated half an inch into my heel and was stuck there. When I pulled it out, blood squirted everywhere. As I hobbled back to my apartment, leaving a stream of blood behind me, I asked, "What is *this* for, and why *today*?" I heard the familiar voice respond, "To show you how powerful you are." By the time I got back to my building the bleeding had stopped. By the time I got to my apartment to pour peroxide in the wound, it was completely healed: not a scratch, mark or scar! Powerful, indeed!

On another occasion, as I was walking on the beach and reflecting on the strangeness in my life, I wondered if I might really be insane. Desperate, I demanded, "If this is all real and I am on the right track, I want a sign -- now!" To my astonishment, a huge ball of orange light instantly streaked across the sky over the Gulf, and burst into little twinkling lights that fell into the water! I had my sign, and no doubt about it.

For the last three months of 1987, I met every Sunday night with a group of seven of the most spiritually conscious women I knew. We were all trying to figure out what to do with our lives, and came together to provide spiritual and manifestation support for one another. We created an opening affirmation, after which each of us in turn shared concerns or needs. The group then focused its attention on each member in turn, putting our love and energy toward the perfect manifestation into reality of each member's desires -- for the highest good of all concerned, naturally! We then practiced our healing skills on each other and did a healing meditation for anyone we knew in need. We closed with a healing meditation for Mother Earth. We all looked forward to our weekly meetings with great anticipation, because we were all very quickly manifesting whatever we requested.

It was at these meetings that I began to recognize my healing abilities. I got very positive feedback when I "practiced" on my Sunday night cohorts. Unfortunately, I also became aware that I was clairsentient -- in other words, whenever I put my hands on someone in an attempt to share energy with them, I felt all their emotional "stuff" and began to cry. Over the next couple of years, I tried everything anybody suggested to channel the energy through me rather than take it on, but I was unable to get the hang of it, and finally quit doing hands-on-healing on anyone I didn't know. I do believe we all have the ability to heal. Because we're alive, our bodies vibrate with energy, and we can share that energy. Little children instinctively know this. (You'll read some wonderful stories concerning this subject later on.)

I highly recommend weekly meetings with like-minded people when you're in any sort of transition. There's something to the quote from the Bible, "...If two of you on the earth agree about anything they ask for, it will come to them from my Father in the skies, because where two or three are assembled in my name, there I am in their midst." (That version comes from *The Unvarnished New Testament,* translated from the original Greek by Andy Gaus.) It's a matter of focusing energy. The more energy that goes into any concept or desire, the faster the manifestation will happen -- IF your desires are aligned with the order of the Universe and IF what you *think* you want is what you *really* want. Manifestation can be tricky business; the Universe sometimes displays a strange sense of humor! Like the old saying goes: "Be careful what you wish for -- you might get it!"

When I learned that color therapy is still illegal in this country, (see *Colorology* for the details) I decided the best way for me to share the color information I had been given was to give lectures and workshops that would empower people to do it by and for themselves, rather than actually setting up a practice. I gave my first color lecture at my friend Carolene's wholistic healing center in October of 1987. During the first half of the lecture I was so nervous that I read from my notes. Carolene came in during the break and said, "Are you *reading* your lecture?" Someone had complained to her. I turned red. She said, "You know this information. Stop reading your notes and listen to that voice that's been talking to you." I did, and have done so ever since!

As I began making the rounds of "New Age" bookstores and such to sell my Rainbows, I heard some unusual stories. One of the strangest tales I've ever heard was told to me in late 1987 by the owner of a metaphysical bookstore in Orlando, Florida. She said, "Oh, you're interested in color? You'll love the story I'm telling these other people." She told of becoming pregnant, without the benefit of sexual relations. As if that wasn't strange enough, she woke up one morning about three months later to find that her water had broken and the baby was gone. When she went to the doctor he exclaimed, "What happened to you? All your internal organs have melted; we'll have to do a complete hysterectomy." He said he had never seen anything like that and had no idea how it could have happened. The operation was performed on Wednesday and the woman went home on Friday, to return on the following Monday for follow-up. She claimed conscious memory of being taken during the weekend into a "ship". She was instructed to stare at a series of panels, illuminated in the seven colors of the rainbow, located around the interior perimeter of the ship. She did so, after which she was returned to her bed at home. On Monday, the doctor was again shocked. "What happened to you?," he asked. "You have three months worth of scar tissue. Your body could not have possibly healed like that over the weekend." She wasn't about to tell him she had been abducted onto a UFO and healed by looking at colored panels! She simply replied that she didn't know.

"Now", she continued, "I'm pregnant again!" Her condition had been confirmed by the same physician who performed the hysterectomy. He was obviously puzzled, since she now lacked the necessary anatomy to get pregnant; however, tests confirmed his diagnosis. She said she knew "they" would take the baby again. She also said that since her experience, three other women had come into her store and told her similar stories about their babies being taken. I found the whole affair fascinating, particularly because of the aspect of healing with color, but simply filed the information away, trying not to judge it. When I went back to visit her three months later, her shop had closed. I heard from another store owner that the store had closed overnight; no one knew what happened to its proprietor.

In January of 1988, Scarlet, one of the women from my Sunday night group, decided to set out in search of a new place to live, and invited me to travel with her. We set up a few lectures at Unity churches around the country, and off we went. I left town with a suitcase full of Rainbows and $100, to be gone for four months. The voice told me to "trust" and I would be provided for -- and I was! Every time my funds got low, I would walk into a metaphysical bookstore and sell a bunch of Rainbow cards and posters. When we first arrived in a town we would search the yellow pages for metaphysical bookstores and other appropriate venues. Usually, visiting a store led not only to income but to some person, gathering or event that would in turn lead to more adventures. We practiced Joseph Campbell's "Follow your bliss" motto, very deliberately manifesting whatever we needed or wanted. I loved being on the road!

Our second day out, we stopped to see Janice, a friend of mine in Louisiana. As soon as we arrived, she starting talking about a male friend of hers she wanted me to meet. I kept telling her I was too busy having fun to get involved in a relationship, but she was relentless. Finally, she secretly arranged for him to meet us at a restaurant. Louis and I hit it off immediately (another past-life connection, I thought). Although he was considerably older than me, he certainly didn't look or act his age. Over dinner, he told us about several of his favorite places to go when traveling, as so many people had before we left. We continued on our journey, but I promised Louis I'd keep in touch.

Eventually, we arrived in Madrid, New Mexico, to visit friends of a friend. Madrid (pronounced Mad-Rid -- a place to get rid of the madness, they explained) is located south of Santa Fe on the old Turquoise Trail, which is the alternate, scenic route between Santa Fe and Albuquerque. Once a coal mining town, it wound up virtually abandoned during the fifties and sixties. Outlaws and, eventually, traveling hippies discovered this scenic but worn-out old town and began moving in. The houses and businesses were made barely livable with "spit and bubble gum", as my father would say. Many had no indoor plumbing, electricity, or telephones. I had never seen people living in such apparent poverty. They were content, however; they had chosen this rugged lifestyle and remote location. Life in Madrid was simple and very slow. Because there was so little electromagnetic pollution in the area at that time, I could clearly sense the special "vibration" of the place, and I resonated strongly with it. I felt right at home (more past-life connections?).

Scarlet and I were warmly welcomed by our new friends; they invited us to stay with them for a while. Fortunately, they had the nicest house in town -- complete with an outdoor Jacuzzi! They had both been in the corporate world, decided to chuck it all, sell everything they owned that wouldn't fit in their van, and go in search of a new place to live (I sure have met a lot of people doing that over the years). They discovered Madrid and fell in love with it. What I had totally forgotten was that Madrid "coincidentally" happened to be one of the places Louis had told me about.

There was no shortage of strangeness in Madrid; I experienced some myself and heard about more from the locals. On several occasions while lying in my friends' Jacuzzi late at night, I saw a very strange glow appear behind a mountain behind their house. There was nothing but miles of desert on the other side of that mountain -- no one could explain that glow. I was told, "Everybody sees it, but they're afraid to climb the mountain to see what's on the other side when it's glowing." An emergency vehicle driver told me that late one night he was called out into the desert, where a woman had been found, confused and disoriented. She reported that she had been driving down the highway, when her truck filled with light. The next thing she knew, it was two hours later and she didn't know where she was. There were many reports of UFOs and tales of abduction in that area.

I greatly enjoyed Madrid, but Sedona, Arizona was number one on my list of places to see. I had heard a great deal about it and was eager to experience the famous "vortexes" for myself. Since creating the Rainbow, I had been practicing automatic writing and was eager to see what would "come through" in the energy vortexes. At the first location we visited, I sat with great anticipation, calmed myself, and soon

42

wrote, "You don't need this place. I am within you always." Nothing else. Disappointed, I rushed to the next vortex. Again, the same message. We pressed on to the third vortex only to get the same message yet again -- this time in letters about three inches high. I finally "got" the message, and just enjoyed the scenery for the rest of our stay.

Scarlet finally decided to settle in Santa Fe. Louis and I had been communicating a great deal by telephone over the past four months and had gotten to know each other quite well. He was retired and bored, and asked if I wanted a new traveling companion. Not having a travel-worthy vehicle, wanting to stay on the road, looking for someone with whom to share expenses and liking him a great deal, I decided "What the heck!" Goodness knows I had done more impetuous things in my life! Besides, Janice had certainly given him rave reviews. Scarlet dropped me off in Louisiana on her way home to pick up her belongings, and Louis and I hit the road. Madrid was our first stop. I visited Madrid a total of nine times that year!

Louis loved the color work and the Rainbows. We made a great team. He was raised Catholic and although some of my beliefs were foreign to him, he was a good sport and really tried to understand me. On our first day out, I was explaining the Laws of Manifestation to him. As a demonstration I said, "For example, right now I would love to manifest Chinese food for dinner." He said, "Caryl, we're in the middle of Texas -- in the country -- you're not going to find a Chinese restaurant out here." The words were barely out of his mouth before we spotted a billboard advertising a Chinese restaurant located a mile ahead. That was his introduction to my strange world!

As it turned out, though, he had some important information for me. A couple of months before we met, Louis had seen a segment on a TV newsmagazine show about colored eyeglasses that could eliminate learning disabilities and dyslexia. I was very interested in this news, because my reading difficulty was a great hindrance in my research. I did some investigating and discovered I could place a colored plastic transparency over the page and read much more easily -- without my eyes tearing up and without falling asleep. It was a miracle! I immediately began packaging and selling these "overlays", as I call them. (You can read all about them in *Colorology*.)

Louis and I began doing a lot of conferences and color lectures, always traveling the back roads to get from place to place. At a conference in Colorado Springs in 1989, I was given a "Positive Energy Purple Plate", a 3" x 5" piece of purple anodized aluminum that, I was told, had been molecularly altered so that it vibrated very fast. If I kept it in my aura it might ease the pain I routinely experienced in my back. I was dubious, to say the least. My first thought was, "Another New Age gimmick, just what we need!" I had a lot of respect, though, for the person who gave it to me, so I decided to experiment with it. After the conference we went to Madrid again. There, for the first time, I slept with a Purple Plate under my pillow. I've had some strange nights before (especially in Madrid), but this one took the cake! I awoke the next morning with the feeling that I had been at school all night. I immediately asked for paper and colored pens and began feverishly charting the information I had received. When I finished, I mounted the chart on the wall next to the outdoor Jacuzzi and spent most of the day in the water staring at it. My voice telepathically explained it to me, adding more information. I had done so much research over the last couple of years, and much of the information I had gathered was so technical, that my brain just couldn't stretch around it all. That chart helped to put it all together into a coherent and graspable whole. From a "cloud" on the left streamed the seven colors of the rainbow (much like the Healing Rainbow); in each band of color I listed the color's mental, physical, emotional, spiritual and esoteric characteristics, corresponding planet, sound, food, gem, animal, chakra and on and on. Along one side I placed an electromagnetic spectrum. In the "cloud", which represented Source, I wrote all the "names of God" that I knew (and some I didn't!) Somehow, the whole collection brought the cosmic picture into clear focus for me.

The next day Louis and I went to Arizona to meet the inventor of the Purple Plate. (We'll call him James.) He's an old scientist (in his eighties) who in his youth had met Nikola Tesla, and had spent his life researching energy -- electromagnetic and otherwise -- and how to apply it to human problems. By the early seventies he had built a device that used frequency to rejuvenate the body on a cellular level, and was achieving some remarkable results with it. Needless to say the medical establishment quickly put him out of business. He developed the Purple Plates because, he said, "No one will understand them and they'll leave me alone." (More details in *Colorology* and Linda Goodman's book, *Star Signs*.) I brought my drawing along to show him, laid it out on his kitchen table and said, "This is what your Purple Plate did. Is this right?" He laughed knowingly and said, "You got it, kid. That's how the Universe works!" It was another pivotal point in my consciousness shift. I began selling Purple Plates right then.

During my visit, I was led to share with James a vivid and moving past life regression I'd undergone in 1987. I didn't know why I wanted to tell the old wizard this particular tale, but out it came. It was in the last days of Atlantis. I was a

45

"Color Priestess" in one of the many beautiful color healing temples. This one had a ground quartz crystal domed ceiling in the center portion; each of the seven circular healing rooms had a colored gem ceiling, so that the sunlight coming through the ceiling was charged to the appropriate color vibration. It was my job to sit at the door and direct the patients to the color room suitable for their particular affliction. During the regression, I exclaimed, "One day the ships came and made a noise and the ceilings and buildings collapsed and people died." I saw myself dead in my chair at the door. I saw people running through the streets holding their ears, then falling over dead. I asked James if he had ever heard anything like that before. He gazed at me for a while and said, "Yes, I was there too. I've met several other people who were also." (Since that conversation, I too have encountered people who recall the space ships and their deadly "noise". Just coincidence? -- or validation for the theory of reincarnation?)

By the end of 1989, after two years of traveling from coast to coast lecturing, I had received many requests for a book; I was told I had a unique way of explaining the science of color -- very simple and practical. I decided it was time to respond to those requests. I had certainly never entertained any notions of becoming an author, but it seemed to be the next logical step.

Louis and I manifested the opportunity to spend the winter in a beautiful home owned by his cousin. It was perched atop an Arkansas mountain and surrounded by a national forest. It was a perfect place to write the book! In spite (or perhaps because) of my lack of experience as a writer, the words came easily, flowing through my fingers into the computer. It wasn't exactly automatic writing, but it was close! My first book, *Colorology: The Study of the Science of Color,* is the compilation of the information I received telepathically and then verified through research in medical and other scientific books.

Speaking of computers -- that was another adventure. I didn't own a computer, nor did I know anything about them, but, obviously, I was going to have to learn, if I was going to write a book. I ordered a laptop computer and printer by mail. When they arrived I had no idea how to even turn them on, let alone hook up the printer and get it all going -- and then there was the question of software! As I sat there looking at all this equipment on the kitchen table, I had a strange flashback. I remembered having to pound on my manual typewriter at my first job. At one point, I told the other secretaries, "One of these days, typewriters will have a TV screen so you can see the letter and make corrections, and then you'll hit a button and the letter will come out of another machine over there." It felt very familiar -- like I had used such a thing before. This happened in 1968. I had never seen such a thing and I don't know where I ever got such an idea (on a ship, perhaps?). At any rate, encouraged by that memory, I somehow (I'm really not sure how) managed to get the computer up and working. Several times during the process I called the help lines mentioned in the manuals. After they assured me I couldn't do what I was trying to do, I worked it out on my own and called them back to explain it to them. They were impressed and I was surprised!

After changing rooms several times in our mountaintop winter home, trying to find the "perfect vibrational room" in which to work, I settled happily into the study, strewing it with books and papers. The study was on the third floor and had a magnificent view in three directions, overlooking the valley and the eagles soaring above the trees. Shortly thereafter, the owner informed us by phone that he preferred I not work in his study. (He didn't know I'd already moved in!). The next morning, before I had cleared out of the study, I heard the door open downstairs, and then distinctly heard the owner engaged in conversation with Louis. Overcome with guilt and panic, I hurriedly gathered my belongings and fled the study for another room. After taking a moment to gather my wits, I went downstairs to say hello. To my astonishment, Louis told me he had neither seen nor talked to anyone all morning! Was I hearing voices from other rooms now, as well as from other dimensions? Rather perplexed, I returned to my writing.

The next day, I was hard at work in my new location when, once again, I heard the owner come in the front door and, once again, engage Louis in the same conversation I had overheard the day before! This time, though, when I went downstairs, the owner was indeed present! I interpreted those events as both a blessing and a warning from the Universe.

ET Tales

In March of 1990, while in Eureka Springs, a unique and charming town not far from our mountaintop retreat, Louis and I learned of a big UFO conference that was to be held there the following week. While my limited exposure to the UFO phenomenon had certainly piqued my interest, it was not an area I had investigated to any significant degree. When I was fourteen or so, my mother and my sister Marcia spotted a light in the sky that behaved very oddly -- moving about erratically, hanging motionless, and so on. That sighting (one of many occurring in Florida during the mid-sixties) inspired my mother and father to join a UFO group for a period of time. Occasionally we would have family sky-watches; but at that time in my life I was far more interested in chasing boys than in chasing UFOs! The whole business made very little impression on me. I was intrigued by this conference, however, and curious to see if there were any more stories like the one I'd heard from the woman in Orlando. An ET angle to color healing might be a good addition to my book. I reserved a table to sell my Rainbows, with the intention of talking to -- or rather, listening to -- as many people as possible.

I was amazed and horrified at what I heard at that conference. I had never heard of cattle mutilations, crop circles or underground ET bases -- not to mention all the conspiracies. It was unbelievable to me that these things were apparently happening on my planet and I knew nothing about it. I had been involved with the paranormal most of my life -- how could I have missed this? At the conference I asked a few of the researchers about the baby-snatching aspect of the phenomenon, and was shocked to discover that it is frequently reported and even has a name -- the "missing fetus syndrome". I was told the fetus is usually removed in the first trimester. What's more, this activity has been reported as far back as the

49

Vedic literature and before. While no one I asked had heard of ETs healing with color, there had been many reports of miraculous cures at their hands -- or claws, or paws, or whatever.

The entire experience left me stunned. I went back up on my quiet, secluded mountain to reflect in horror on what I had heard, and remained in a general state of shock for about two weeks. Finally, I got angry and said, "If this is really happening on my planet, I want to know about it and understand it." But first things first; I had a book to finish!

By April of 1990, I had completed *Colorology* and gone through the trying -- though ultimately gratifying -- process of self-publishing it. (In this matter I had little choice; my "instructions" as to the book's make-up and layout were quite precise, and I despaired of convincing a publisher even to print it on violet paper, let alone leave the text exactly as I produced it!)

At last I returned to doing what I love most -- traveling. On this tour, though, I added UFO conferences to the itinerary of wholistic health, metaphysical, New Age and "new science" conferences at which I spoke and exhibited, and began sharing what I had learned about UFO's along with what I knew about color. (By this time I had been carefully directed by the voice to develop a complete line of color therapy products to fill the need for tools that I was seeing in my travels.) Everywhere we went, I sought out used book stores. I collected all of the books and magazines on UFO's and related subjects that appealed to me, and stuffed them into our already well-stuffed Honda; UFOlogy rapidly became an obsession. And at every conference I encountered more weirdness: amazing tales of close encounters of every imaginable kind -- and, more ominously, tales of cover-up and conspiracy.

I read *Behold a Pale Horse*, written by UFO researcher and "conspiracy buff", William Cooper. In the book, Cooper presents evidence of collusion within and among various groups ("the power elite") and ETs throughout modern history, and shows how that collusion has moved the course of human events into a dark tunnel of betrayal and deception. It was really depressing for "Little Mary Sunshine" or "Pollyanna", as my friends *used* to call me. To make matters worse, I met Bill and had the opportunity to spend time with him. I found him to be an honorable man, who sincerely believed everything he said and wrote. He had, as he said, "done his homework".

During the 1990 tour, Louis and I visited some friends in Durango, Colorado. They told us of the many UFO sightings that occurred near their house. One night, our hostess said she could "feel them around," so we shouldn't be surprised at anything that might happen. Just before I went to bed I happened to look out the window, and saw a huge, bright light very low to the ground. It was too big to be a star and too bright to be a street or house light. I watched it for a few minutes, then called Louis. We watched it together for a few more minutes. Having heard about people telepathically communicating with UFOs, I exclaimed aloud, "Dance for me!" Immediately, the ball of light bounced up and down erratically, five or six times. Louis and I looked at each other in amazement, then watched the UFO for another five minutes, after which I again said, "Dance for me!". Immediately, the ball of light responded in the same manner. Finally, it slowly moved away from us until it faded from view.

We went to bed, and I fell asleep repeating to myself, "I want to have a positive UFO experience," while clutching a Purple Plate in each hand. I had been selling the Plates for some time by then. I'd had several more remarkable experiences with them, as well as hearing many stories from others. I sold one to a young man who was having unpleasant ET contact that he wanted stopped. His negative experiences ceased entirely after he began carrying the plate. I called the inventor to discuss the matter with him, and he said others had reported the same experience; however, he obviously couldn't make any claims in writing about it.

At any rate, when I awoke in the morning, I knew something had happened -- but I couldn't remember what. Louis took one look at me and reacted with shock. "What happened to you?" he cried. When I protested that I didn't know what he was talking about, he told me to go look in a mirror. I did so, and there in the middle of my forehead was a two-inch-wide bright red circle! It didn't fade away until two days later. For reasons I cannot now comprehend, we neither photographed it, nor made any effort to discover how it got there. Being unable to remember anything that may have happened during the night, I simply put the whole business on the back burner and went on with my life.

During the discussion portion of the UFO slide presentations I was now doing, I heard one remarkable story after another of people's encounters with UFOs and extraterrestrials of all descriptions. A few reported positive encounters; however, most were left fearful and confused, feeling that their lives were out of control. They all were delighted to meet someone to whom they could talk openly. I realized just how widespread the phenomenon was and how many seemingly "normal" people had been affected by it. I also discovered more conspiracies everywhere I went. I heard stories like "I took a picture of a UFO and by the time I arrived home, there were men in black suits in a black car, waiting for me demanding the photographs." I talked to military pilots who reported UFOs while in the service, only to be ridiculed and threatened. Someone gave me the book, *The Rockefeller Files*. I was absolutely horrified at the negative impact the "ruling elite" have had on our daily lives, from changing our history books to eliminating natural healing schools. It was astounding to me that the American public could be so complacent. The conspiracies were really beginning to weigh me down!

By the following winter, I had accumulated some 120 books and magazines. Once again we were blessed with the opportunity to house-sit that beautiful retreat atop the Arkansas mountain, so I decided I would spend the winter reading all that material, and try to make some sense out of it. Thanks to the colored reading overlays, I was able to average about twelve to fifteen hours reading per day. However, I soon realized I had to do something to organize and retain all that data. I created a computer database, extracting all the dated events I could find, including the date, subject, book, page number and what happened. I included UFO and medical cover-ups, major sightings, abductions, crop circles, cattle mutilations, weird things that happened in space and a variety of other high strangeness that has transpired on this planet throughout history. I also added what we as a society were doing, like when wars began and ended, when we marched on Washington and when important inventions and discoveries occurred. Finally, I sorted the information by date, then by subject, and the result was very interesting, to say the least. I could see all sorts of correlations, patterns and "coincidences". It was fascinating to see the parallels between what was occurring on Earth and the weird and unexplained things happening in space. I did the project for my own research, but when others saw it they wanted a copy too; so was born *The UFO Reference Book*. After all that research, however, I ended up with many more questions than answers -- and I was determined to keep asking them!

Crop circles astounded me. I learned that the massive "circle" phenomenon began in earnest in 1980; however, there are earlier reports, going back all the way to Medieval times. The circles have increased and become more intricate each year, spreading all over the world. Hundreds are reported each year.

These beautiful, profoundly moving formations are reported to appear within 1-3 seconds. The wheat, rye or other crop is bent (not broken) a few inches from the ground and continues to grow. Magnetic anomalies, such as camera and electrical dysfunctions, occur within the circles, which often appear near ancient, sacred sights like Stonehenge. People have experienced reactions ranging from illness to euphoria inside these formations; most animals refuse to enter them at all.

When viewing aerial video and photographs of these "pictograms", I have experienced intense emotions that brought tears to my eyes. Others have had similar experiences, especially when actually inside the formations. Whatever else they might be, they are awesome, magnificent works of art!

Strange lights, balls of fire, unidentified flying objects, black helicopters and military vehicles have all been seen in and around the area where a crop circle has been formed or is about to be formed. Dowsers (originally, people who used a forked tree branch to locate underground water; but dowsing has expanded to include the use of a variety of tools -- pendulums, L-rods, even muscle testing -- to access a wide variety of information) have found that ley lines (roughly, Earth's equivalent of our bodies' acupuncture meridians, along which courses vital energy) sometimes change location in the area of a formation. L-rods or pendulums may spin wildly, indicating a powerful vortex of some sort.

No, two fellows from England did not create all the crop circles, as the media reported in 1991! "Doug and Dave" (and by now a number of groups in England, and probably elsewhere) did indeed create some of the less spectacular "pictograms", and quite ingeniously; but after even cursory research into the phenomenon, one quickly discovers that the molecular changes that have been shown to occur in the grain as well as the stalks, seem to be caused by intense heat of short duration (perhaps a kind of pulsed microwave, as some researchers have suggested) not something easily done with a board and rope!

In the beginning, some people attempted to explain the circles away as a result of "dust devils" or other weather anomalies. But the persistence, intricacy and precision of these incredible formations render such explanations inadequate, to say the least. Most of the relatively few serious researchers have come up with tentative theories as to the glyphs' origin, but at this point every open-minded observer is compelled to admit that we have only a general idea of how they are created (microwave pulses?) and no solid evidence at all as to exactly who or what is creating them -- or why! Perhaps they are being made as a part of some secret research project conducted by who knows what government or military agencies, but why? And why not tell the public? Perhaps the crop circles are ever-more blatant attempts by some other-worldly entity to get humanity's attention for reasons we have yet to guess. Perhaps it's Mother Earth talking. It does seem obvious to me that no one should continue the absurd behavior of the U.S. mainstream media -- ignoring the circles almost completely!

Cattle mutilations, as they were originally called, or unusual animal deaths, a more accurate term now in use, began occurring with some frequency in 1970. Since then they have increased and continue today, especially in the United States. They are a particularly unpleasant aspect of the UFO phenomenon. Linda Moulton-Howe has written the textbook on the subject, *A Strange Harvest*, and has done the most to research and document this rather repulsive business.

Cattle, usually the best in the herd, are normally the target of the unknown perpetrators of the mutilations; however, other animals such as deer, raccoons and even household cats and dogs have been taken. There were one hundred wild horses found mutilated in Nevada in 1989.

Clean, bloodless incisions are made into the ears, eyes, lips, tongue, udder, sex organs and rectum of the animal, using some sort of high heat, laser-type technology that we here on earth do not possess in a form that can be taken into the field (unless, of course, we are looking at a top secret research project, which of course is always a possibility). The incisions go between the cells, rather than blasting them apart like the laser equipment being used today, which incidentally weighs between 500-600 pounds, is the size of an office desk and requires special electricity. These are truly precise surgical incisions -- not "mutilations".

There is usually no blood found either around or in the animals, yet there is no vascular collapse, such as would occur with the use of known methods of removing blood. There have been incidents reported in which entire joints and bones have been removed from the animal, with no visible signs of entry -- impossible, according to experts who have ventured public comment on this phenomenon. Care must be taken in handling the carcasses, due to the fact that burning or irritation of the skin or other medical problems have been reported as a result of touching the carcasses with ungloved hands. Also, predators usually will not come near the carcasses, which may often lay untouched for days before being discovered.

No footprints or tracks are found around or near the carcasses, which are often left in wet soil or snow. While the animals are usually returned to the area from which they were taken, there have been cases reported in which entire herds of 50-100 animals have completely disappeared. And in August of 1994, 850 cows and 850 of their calves -- 1700 head of cattle in all -- disappeared from a breeding farm in Oklahoma over a period of four days -- no signs, no tracks, no witnesses, no evidence! The rancher's bank and insurance companies were quite perplexed -- and disturbed, as they have to pay off on the missing animals!

Christopher O'Brien, a UFO researcher from the San Luis Valley area of Colorado and author of *The Mysterious Valley*, told me that when a genuine mutilation is found and reported in the media, "sloppily" mutilated cattle are often discovered in the same area. Another attempted "cover-up", perhaps?

Satanic cults and predators have been blamed in the media from the beginning; yet no cult members have ever been arrested and charged with a mutilation. And the precise nature of the "surgery" is, again, beyond the capability of any known techniques or technology.

UFOs are frequently seen where a mutilation is occurring or about to occur; there have even been sightings of non-human beings at the scene of a mutilation. Earthly military vehicles and personnel have also been reported near these sites.

Some researchers theorize that the phenomenon may be part of some sort of planetary genetic experimentation. There is a similarity between cattle blood and human blood; the former can actually be substituted for the latter in an emergency. Some believe the cattle are being "sampled" to discover what effect underground nuclear testing has had upon living organisms, because many mysterious animal deaths occur in the Four Corners area (where Colorado, New Mexico, Utah and Nevada converge). Nuclear weapons tests, as well as a number of other toxic and dangerous experiments, are known or rumored to have taken place in or near that area for many years.

Some kind of "research" is obviously being done, perhaps by some secret faction of our government, or intelligent beings from somewhere else (or both). If some government agency is the culprit, we have to ask, "Why don't they breed their own cattle for experimentation? And why would they leave the remains of their unpleasant work for anyone to find?" Much is still to be learned -- at least by the general public -- about this mysterious and ugly phenomenon.

The possibility that humans are being abducted against their will by aliens can be a terrifying concept, but the evidence from my research -- and that of many others -- shows that something paranormal is definitely happening to a lot of people on planet Earth. The same basic scenario is being reported by normal, honest, well-adjusted individuals of all ages, from all walks of life and all parts of the world. They awaken during the night to find small, large-eyed, grey creatures with long, skinny arms staring at them. (Other sorts of creatures have been and are reported, but the Greys are currently the most "popular" by far, at least in the U.S.) Often the room fills with light and they are paralyzed. Anyone else in the room with them appears to be frozen or oblivious to what is happening. They report being "floated" out a closed window or through a wall to a waiting UFO. They next find themselves on a table in a round room with recessed lighting, and the small grey beings are all around them. Often, a different type of being -- apparently in charge -- reassures them telepathically, and tells them that they will not remember the incident. A medical examination ensues, usually with particular attention to the genital area. The next thing they remember they are back in bed and it is morning.

They often wake up with mysterious scars, healed cuts, scoop marks, or black and blue spots on their bodies. Sometimes they report bloody noses. Women may find themselves pregnant shortly afterward, often with no remembered sexual contact, only to experience the disappearance of the fetus at approximately three-months' gestation.

Occasionally, the abductees expel small B-B-sized objects from their noses or other orifices. It has been reported that MIT has actually been analyzing some of these devices, and in 1996 several have been surgically removed from people and are being analyzed, in a program spearheaded by researcher Darrell Sims from Houston, Texas and Dr. Roger Leir of Ventura, California.

There are all sorts of variations to this basic story. Contrary to the impression fostered by a *Nova* installment entitled "Kidnapped by Aliens?", abductions occur at all hours of the day or night; they are remembered consciously by some abductees, while others only recall under hypnosis what happened to them. Frequently, if a person is hypnotically regressed once, it seems to unlock the memory banks to other abduction experiences that are recalled consciously. It is simply not possible, given the thousands of reports now on record, that this phenomenon is simply some sort of mass hysteria generated by exposure to science fiction and horror movies! People young and old from all over the world who have no apparent cultural context within which to "imagine" these things report episodes of abduction. Some are taken from their cars late at night, after their car engines die; others see a UFO and follow it. In 1993, I heard of an incident in which 150 people working at a large telecommunications company in the south were abducted at one time! The company's "fail-safe" computer system was down for two hours, and electrical cables were found melted and dripping down the wall inside a Faraday cage. This apparent mass abduction took place during a change of work shifts; the incoming workers wandered in, dazed, two hours late for their shift. Most had been sitting in their cars in the parking lot -- perhaps in "suspended animation"? One witness -- a "middle manager" who was in his office -- said he had just returned to his desk after pouring himself a glass of Coke with ice. He sat down at his desk, turned to look at his computer monitor, and turned back to find that two hours had passed and the ice in his glass had melted. He -- and another witness as well -- recalled under hypnosis that he had seen "aliens levitating people out of the building." Five circular burned areas were found in the grass outside the building; repeated attempts to resod those areas were unsuccessful. They were finally paved over.

And that's not all that was buried. According to the eyewitness reports I heard, management immediately began denying that anything had happened. Within a couple of months, that installation had been closed down and its employees transferred all over the country.

And the good news? People are reporting miraculous cures of everything from cancer and heart disease to color blindness after some sort of encounter. Also, while many of these experiencers feel violated, raped and/or traumatized, I know women who have experienced the "missing fetus syndrome" and feel they are part of a great experiment. They feel they are helping to give a special gift to humanity. Some find the abduction experience to be spiritually enlightening. As with all life experience, it appears to be a matter of perspective.

Some of the mainstream medical profession seems to be taking this phenomenon seriously, as evidenced by the creation of the Treatment and Research of Experienced Anomalous Trauma (TREAT) conferences, first held in 1989. This annual conference addresses the UFO abduction phenomenon, as well as other paranormal events, from a clinical perspective for medical, psychological and technical professionals. Continuing education credit has even been given to attendees.

Dr. John Mack, the Pulitzer prize-winning Harvard psychiatrist, in 1994 published a book, *Abduction: Human Encounters with Aliens,* in which he states that according to his research, the abduction phenomenon -- whatever its nature -- is real and is dramatically affecting many people. His courage in standing up for his truth and research in the face of his peers' disapproval is admirable. We need more professionals of his caliber to come forward with what they know, so that the abduction phenomenon can receive the serious and well-funded public investigation it deserves. There are many traumatized people in need of support and assistance.

The physical and medical evidence, as well as the reports of the abductees themselves, seem to indicate that some sort of experimentation -- probably genetic in nature -- is taking place on planet Earth. Most, if not all, of the well-known abduction investigators at least partly subscribe to that scenario. Who's doing it, why they're doing it, and where "they" come from, are questions which have inspired many theories, but no proven answers.

Conspiracy theories abound in this area; one suggests that the abductions are part of a black-budget mind control and genetics project being carried out by a subversive group within our government using technology developed in the sixties -- with the help, some say, of Nazis!

I also read all the old "contactee" books I could find from the fifties -- those written by George Adamski, Howard Menger, and others -- as well as those produced by some of the modern contactees or "channels". Their stories are much more positive in nature, and I found that the information they presented frequently coincided with what I was receiving (the power of conscious manifestation, the function of free will, the power of unconditional love, even the advantages of vegetarianism!). Of course, there are conspiracy theories concerning the contactees, as well. One suggests that some unknown faction of our government is beaming this information out on an electromagnetic frequency that the brain perceives as an "inner voice" -- microwave mind control, if you will. *That* one made me stop and think -- but only for a minute or two. One would hope "they" have better things to do with the taxpayers' money than to teach me about color!

I also found that -- at least according to references in the Bible, various Buddhist sutras, the Vedic literature, and the stone tablets of ancient Sumeria, to name but a few -- there is a long history of interaction between humans and various non-human beings. There are a number of books -- my favorite is William Bramley's *The Gods of Eden* -- that offer a very different view of who we are and how we got this way. Do not explore this area if you don't want your religious paradigms to be seriously undermined!

It became ever more apparent to me that a lot more than Nikola Tesla had been excluded from our history books.

Reports of strange things in the sky can be found in almost all historical periods; but it is clear that such reports increased significantly beginning around 1942 -- the year that humans succeeded in splitting the atom. Perhaps we became a good deal more dangerous to the Universe, as well as to ourselves and our small blue planet.

1947 was the year of the now infamous Roswell, New Mexico incident. It is easy to see why some factions of our government thought it best to begin the "great cover-up". In 1938 Orson Welles broadcast his famous "War of the Worlds" radio show, and some people, believing the radio broadcast to be genuine and Martians were really invading, panicked, resulting in a number of injuries and a good deal of chaos. How could "the powers that be" tell the public only nine years later, in July of 1947, "We have recovered not only a crashed spaceship (maybe two), but alien bodies as well"? Today, over 300 witnesses have come forward to tell what they know of the recovery, examination and transportation of the wreckage and bodies. Something did indeed happen in Roswell and the details are finally coming to light!

Perhaps, in 1947, society was ill-prepared for such a momentous event as open ET contact. Today, however, we see a situation in which the general public is being inundated by the media with images of ET interactions of all kinds -- but mostly negative, if not downright silly. Science "fiction" has become a staple of children's cartoons, particularly of the Saturday morning variety. Watch them for a while; you may be surprised at the messages being delivered to your children.

More UFO Tales:

1. I often hear people ask, "Well, if they're here, why don't they land on the White House lawn and talk to us?" On three

different occasions in 1952, UFOs were tracked on radar as they zoomed over the Capitol in Washington, D.C., and you will find in the literature many accounts of secret alien/government meetings. True or false? The only people who can tell us are either dead (like Presidents Eisenhower and Truman) or are simply not talking -- yet.

2. In July and August of 1965, UFOs were seen by tens of thousands of people and tracked on radar all across the US and Mexico. In a two-week period in 1975, they made a dramatic demonstration of their power as they invaded restricted air space over North American Air Defense bases, disabling warheads and interfering with computers. Were they delivering a message that they could stop Earth's militarists at will?

3. 1965 was also the year of the Great Blackout, which affected eight states, including New York, and one-fifth of the population of the US. Six days later, blackouts which included four major US military bases occurred in New Mexico, Texas, and Mexico. UFOs were seen and tracked on radar during these events. Did they need our power, or were they just demonstrating theirs?

4. In October of 1962, Anna, a communications satellite, was launched into space; two months later it disappeared from the sky. In May of 1963, Telstar 2 was launched; it also disappeared two months after being put into orbit. One month later, both satellites reappeared in their appropriate orbits -- within three days of each other! Was someone checking out our technology?

5. Beginning in 1989, more than 10,000 people in Belgium witnessed -- with photographs and video -- huge triangular craft making slow flyovers at low altitude. If they were secret

military craft, someone decided to go public in a very odd manner. The Belgian military swore ignorance and entered into a co-operative investigation with a civilian UFO organization, creating the first such open alliance in history.

6. Recently, Gulf Breeze, Florida and Groom Lake, Nevada have been the sites of numerous sightings. Groom Lake, of course, is where the infamous, super-mega-extra-top-secret Area 51 is located. It has for years been a wellspring of tales (and guaranteed views) of extraterrestrial craft and the back-engineering of same. (See George Knapp's article in the September/October 1996 issue of UFO magazine [Vol.11, No.5] for a cogent summation of that story.) Gulf Breeze is still the site of frequent "saucer watches" and since the early '90's has produced a whole raft of interesting characters with fascinating stories, often backed up by very good quality visual aids.

7. Sightings and contacts in Puerto Rico are so numerous, the military has gone to the lengths of restricting and fencing off a wide area where many sightings have been reported. UFOs have been seen in the air, on the land, and, as I learned in 1985, under the water. I have seen film footage of two jets apparently disappearing into a UFO over Puerto Rico in 1988. At one UFO conference I attended, a Puerto Rican researcher made a very provocative remark: "There is so much UFO activity and ET contact in Puerto Rico, I wonder if they (ETs or our government) are not using us, because of our isolation, as a testing ground for open contact." Interesting concept. Now, of course, we have the *chupacabras* adding to the mysterious mix -- red-eyed, spiny, blood-sucking, high-jumping, unfriendly critters that have created, in a very short time, their own special niche in the lore of the paranormal.

8. Military aircraft (including the infamous "black helicopters" -- unmarked aircraft of uncertain ownership) chasing UFOs have been videotaped on a number of occasions and in a number of locations, including Mexico City (where sightings are so commonplace as to be nearly routine) and Colorado's San Luis Valley, which continues to experience mysterious animal deaths and other strange phenomena. There, in the Spring of 1994, a ten-acre field of quinoa (a Central American grain well-suited to high-altitude agriculture) was stripped of every blossom overnight -- without so much as a petal left behind!

And yet our government's official policy -- to the extent they'll admit they have one -- is that UFOs do not exist and people who see them are crazy, or at least hallucinating. If people who see UFOs are crazy, we're in big trouble! The following people have publicly reported UFO sightings: Ex-President Jimmy Carter, Ex-Florida Governor Haydon Burns, Prince Charles, Henry Ford II, Arthur Godfrey and Jackie Gleason, as well as Astronauts Neil Armstrong, Frank Borman, James Lovell, Jr., Scott Carpenter, James McDivitt, Edward White, John Young, Michael Collins and Gordon Cooper (he even addressed the UN on the subject). Sightings have also been reported by military and commercial pilots, radar technicians, air traffic controllers and astronomers, to name a few -- all people we depend upon and trust for various reasons.

The question is often asked, "If UFOs exist and our government knows about it, why hasn't it leaked out by now?" Well, the leaks have happened, but researchers' efforts are often muddied by disinformation, ridicule, and the resolute refusal of the mainstream "establishment" media to deal seriously with the subject of "flying saucers." The major wire services apparently have a policy of not picking up local stories pertaining to UFOs. Also, a regulation published as

Joint Army-Navy-Air Force Publication Number 146 (JANAP-146) declares anyone making a public statement about UFOs to be liable for a $10,000 fine and ten years in jail. While there are rumors that this regulation has been rescinded, it is easy to understand why military personnel have largely remained silent on this subject. Then, too, there is the well-known National Security Oath. In short -- "they" have ways of keeping people quiet!

The last public U.S. government UFO investigation was terminated in 1969 with the tainted Condon Report, which determined that the evidence proved UFOs "posed no threat" to the national security of the United States (and not whether they exist). With all the video tape, pictures and evidence available today, don't we deserve a new study? Imagine what would happen if the media joined forces to investigate the question of ET visitation with the passion and diligence -- and air time -- that was lavished on, oh, say, the O.J. Simpson trial?!

To assume we are the only sentient life form in this vast Universe of billions of stars and planets is egotistical, arrogant, uninformed and really quite absurd. Ancient tablets, artifacts and history abound with indications that we have been visited and interacted with by non-human intelligence since the beginning of time. All life goes through cycles of birth, death and rebirth, as evidenced by all of nature, including stars, planets, plants and even Homo Sapiens. The natural instinct to survive would force any dying species on a planet to search for a new home, just as earthlings are doing today. In searching the neighboring stars (or dimensions!) these beings might come upon a beautiful blue planet in a ripe stage of evolution to sustain life, inhabited by beings of a low enough mental and spiritual development to be recklessly destroying the planet's ecology and each other. The visitors might well be tempted to replace such an aberrant species as the dominant life form on the planet, if only to stop the destruction. After all, if you came to this planet from elsewhere in the galaxy and monitored its inhabitants by, for example, watching CNN, what would you think? Perhaps interstellar travelers would perceive Homo Sapiens in much the same light as we perceive the animals that we use in our "scientific" laboratories. This, of course, is but one possible scenario among dozens.

I believe the evidence indicates that we are being interacted with at an ever-increasing rate by a variety of visitors, some apparently with the highest benefit of humanity in mind, some perhaps less benevolent, and some seemingly strictly in their own interest. Yet as a society, we remain strangely indifferent to the world-shaking implications of contact with beings from other worlds, or dimensions, or levels of consciousness, or whatever metaphor one likes. We relegate this story to entertainment media, to be considered only in our "spare time". Most people's focus is on the struggle to survive or to needlessly accumulate greater wealth. Meanwhile, the "visitors" intrude upon our 3-D reality more and more each day. *Why*? Is there a question of more importance to humanity's future than that one?

Many abductees and contactees have been told that the visitors will not allow us to destroy this beautiful planet, either by raping its resources or by nuclear war. Although there is a Universal Law of Free Will, the universal repercussions of our irresponsible and destructive actions may well be galactically unacceptable. The generally respected (no one in this field is universally loved and trusted!) UFO researcher Jacques Vallee ventured this opinion in his book *Messengers of Deception*: "I believe that there is a very *real* UFO problem...[that] is being manipulated for political ends. And the data suggest that the manipulators may be human beings with a plan of social control." In view of such a grave probability and its implications for the freedom of humanity, it would be well for all of us to work to break through the official government denial of the existence of nonhuman "visitors" -- which merely reflects the extent of society's willingness to ignore the UFO phenomenon -- and the policy of ridicule of experiencers. We as a species must open our minds and our hearts to this new reality. We have no other choice. This is no fantasy!

References

Extraterrestrials Among Us - George C. Andrews (Good overview of the UFO phenomenon)

Childhood's End - Arthur C. Clarke (Classic fictional look at a possible end-time scenario)

Clear Intent - Lawrence Fawcett and Barry J. Greenwood (Excellent overview of the UFO coverup)

Alien Impact: A Comprehensive Look at the Evidence of Human/Alien Contact - Michael Craft (Published in the summer of '96)

Above Top Secret: The Worldwide UFO Cover-up and Alien Update - Timothy Good (Lots of good info on what the "powers that be" know that they aren't telling us)

A Strange Harvest - Linda Moulton Howe (THE book on "unusual animal deaths")

The Andreasson Affair, The Andreasson Affair Phase Two,

The Watchers and The Watchers II - Raymond Fowler (Amazing saga of one abductee/contactee over a thirty-year period; good insight into ET identity and agenda)

The Gods of Eden - William Bramley (One of many in-depth studies of the ancient history of ET-human interaction)

The Earth Chronicles - Zechariah Sitchin (Some half-dozen scholarly and meticulously documented volumes dealing with humanity's "ET history" - and possible future)

Forbidden Archeology: The Hidden History of the Human Race - Michael A. Cremo and Richard Thompson (The lowdown on how old we *really* are -- 900 pages worth -- archeological finds that don't fit into accepted history!)

Alien Identities - Richard L. Thompson (A Vedic scholar surveys the UFO phenomenon -- highly informative)

Extraterrestrials in Biblical Prophecy - G. Cope Schellhorn (One of my favorites -- you only think you know what the Bible's about!)

Abduction: Human Encounters with Aliens - John Mack, M.D. (A Harvard psychiatrist weighs in on the abduction phenomenon -- a pivotal work)

Missing Time, Intruders: The Incredible Visitations at Copley Woods, and *Witnessed: The True Story of The Brooklyn Bridge UFO Abductions* - Budd Hopkins (Three classics by the best-known investigator of the abduction phenomenon -- *Intruders* was made into a TV miniseries)

Communion, Transformation, and Breakthrough - Whitley Streiber (One best-selling author's three-volume account of his journey through terrifying abduction experiences to spiritual epiphany)

This list could go on and on -- there are many other researchers who have over the years contributed much of value to the field: Jacques Vallee, Frank Reynolds (one of my heroes!), and Michael Lindemann. There is also a great deal of channeled material on this subject, which of course one must approach with great discernment. I've already mentioned *Preparing For Contact*, by Lyssa Royal and Keith Priest; they have produced other books as well (*The Prism of Lyra: An Exploration of Human Galactic Heritage*, and *Visitors From Within*). Barbara Marciniak is a well-known channeler of "Pleiadians" (*Bringers Of The Dawn, Earth*). Norma Milanovich brought us *We, The Arcturians*. Skeptical, even scornful of channeling in general? Try Jon Klimo's work *Channeling: Investigations on Receiving Information From Paranormal Sources.*

Resources

Greenleaf Books (800) 905-8367. Mark Davenport (author of *Visitors From Time*, an excellent work exploring the time travel aspect of the UFO phenomenon) and Leah Haley (abductee and author of *Lost Was The Key* -- about her experiences -- and *Ceto's New Friends*, a children's book about ET contact) have amassed THE largest collection of books and tapes on this subject. In addition, if you can tell them a title and author, they'll get any book in print and mail it to you.

UFO Magazine, P.O. Box 1053, Sunland, CA 91041 (Subscriptions $25/year -- six issues)

Mutual UFO Network UFO Journal, 103 Oldtowne Rd., Seguin, TX 78155-4099 (Subscriptions $30/year -- 12 issues - The largest civilian UFO investigation organization, with chapters around the world and an annual convention.)

UFO Clipping Service, #2 Caney Valley Drive, Plumerville, AR 72127 (Monthly reports from all over the world)

Websites

If you're already a "Web-surfer", you already know how much information there is "out there". If you're a beginner -- good luck! (Both of the above-mentioned magazines have plenty of information on what's going on in cyberspace and how to get in on it.)

Videotapes:

There are many good videos available on the UFO phenomenon. My favorite is *UFOs: The Best Evidence*, produced by George Knapp, the Las Vegas telejournalist who brought us Area 51 engineer Bob Lazar. It's an excellent overview.

Underground Video, P.O. Box 527, Beverly Hills, CA 90213-0527 (Send $2.00 for a catalog)

UFO Central Home Video, 7538 Woodley Ave., Van Nuys, CA 91406 (Send $2.00 for a catalog)

Greenleaf Books also carries a wide selection of videotapes.

Tales of Transition

By the time I finished *The UFO Reference Book* in April of 1991 Louis was "done". He loved my color work, but he hated the UFO and conspiracy stuff. He was also tired of traveling all the time, so we parted ways, best of friends.

Before Louis took me back to Clearwater, we went to Colorado one more time, to do a show in Colorado Springs. While we were there, someone suggested I call Dean Stonier, the head of a group called the Global Sciences Congress, which held monthly meetings in Denver. What a fateful suggestion that turned out to be! The next meeting, I found out, was to be held the following week and -- surprise! -- the scheduled speaker had just cancelled. Dean said, "I guess the Universe sent me you."

My talk was received sufficiently well that Dean invited me to be a stand-by speaker at the big five-day annual conference in August. So it was that I discovered what has become my absolute favorite of all the events in which I participate; the Global Sciences Congress brings together all the latest and most unusual on every subject: new healing modalities, the supernatural, political conspiracies, new science of all kinds, prophecy, UFOlogy, metaphysics -- I call it the best party in the country, and have not missed one since my first in '91. My co-author, Parker, calls it a "three-ring circus of the strange".

The sheer number and outstanding quality of the speakers and stand-bys that Dean had assembled assured me that there was just about no chance I would be called upon to speak, so I immersed myself in the flood of information and new products, making new friends right and left. Naturally, on Saturday morning Dean asked me to step into a suddenly vacated speaking slot -- on two hours' notice! I was, as they say, petrified! Fortunately, I enter an altered state when I speak (more on that later); that is probably the only thing other than adrenaline that got me through that lecture! The reaction to my talk, though, *really* blew me away -- during the lunch break I was overwhelmed by people throwing money at me for my books and color products. I made more in that hour or so than I had made at any other show I'd done over the previous four years!

When I completed my lecture, I plopped down in the front row of seats, a little weak and still in an altered state. The next speaker was a man named Gordon-Michael Scallion, who told the bizarre tale of his transformation from happy-go-lucky consultant to visionary and Earth changes prophet. He told of light beings who transmitted to him rather dire information about the difficult years ahead, emphasizing that prophecies do not have to come true; they are warnings of probabilities that can be averted by changes in humanity's thought and behavior. He concluded his talk by entering a trance state and taking questions from the audience. Prior to doing so, he invited us to close our eyes and try to answer the questions before he did, explaining that a "synergy" of all present and open minds often occurred when he "channeled" before a group. That sounded like fun to me; I was still in an altered state anyway. To my astonishment, I answered every question before he did -- and our answers were the same! I met him personally that evening and it was the beginning of a great friendship. I didn't find out until much later that during my talk, he had been in the back of the hall, and had told to the person he was with, "I'm going to be working with that woman some day."

At that time Gordon-Michael did individual psychic readings (he no longer does). A few months later, he did one for me. He told me, among other things, that I had only begun to tap into my psychic ability and that when I looked back in a few years, I would be amazed at what I was able to do. I would have to say he was right on the money about that.

Shortly thereafter, a psychic friend gave me a unique pendulum which he said he had made and programmed for a very special purpose, which I had to discover on my own. One evening while taking a shower and contemplating the pendulum, I received the inspiration -- color! I began experimenting with various color-related ways I might use it. One of my "color tools" is a body chart that shows the color (vibrational frequency) of each organ in the body. Using that for reference, I developed a technique of "reading" the body's well-being by holding the pendulum over the chakras and monitoring its movement. I found that I could also determine an individual's "Life Color" by holding the pendulum over his or her right hand, stating my intent, and naming the seven colors. Armed with that information and the principles detailed in *Colorology*, I was able to begin doing readings for people. They have proved over the years to be quite accurate. Although my clients thought I was "being psychic", I was in actuality simply using the science of color I had been taught by my "voice". I added the readings to my repertoire at conventions and shows.

I really got sucked into "Earth changes paranoia" after meeting Gordon-Michael. I asked him to send information packets to all my closest friends and to a couple of relatives in California. I began promoting some of his events and selling his *Earth Changes Map* and *Newsletter*. I even convinced my parents they should sell their house, which was located two blocks from the Gulf, and move to safer ground in north-central Florida. We searched unsuccessfully for property to which the whole family could relocate. Mom and Dad finally got bored with the idea and decided to "stay where we are and wait for the big wave".

I'm embarrassed to tell the following story, but it serves to demonstrate my overall state of mind at the time. I think it was in early '92 when many people started talking about the imminent arrival of the Photon Belt (Gordon-Michael was not one of them). Rumor had it that due to some astronomical event, there would be extreme light for five days, followed by extreme darkness for some length of time I don't remember. Earthlings were advised to buy welding goggles to protect their eyes and tarps to cover their windows; we were cautioned to store water, food and other necessities and to stay close to home until "it" arrived. The story was coming from so many sources, I felt they couldn't all be wrong -- could they? I was convinced, and was able to convince my parents there might be something to the whole business, so we prepared -- just in case. My youngest brother Ted got so upset about it that he broke out in shingles. Needless to say, nothing happened -- at least, nothing has happened yet! I was able to return the welding goggles, but I lost a very old and dear friend over the whole thing. She couldn't stand all the negativity and decided that I had gone off the deep end. She hasn't talked to me since.

I will say in my defense that it is not unusual for people to experience considerable fear, anger or grief (or all three!) when first becoming aware of the dire prospects faced by humanity at this time. Helen Caldicott, founder of Physicians for Social Responsibility and tireless crusader against some of the more toxic aspects of modern technology, often speaks in her lectures of the necessity to "work through" those emotions in order to get to a place from which one can take effective action aimed at correcting our world's problems.

It was my underlying dream of living in community, I think, that led me to buy into the Photon Belt business so strongly. After all, if the Earth hit the fan, so to speak, would not people's options shrink drastically, and force them to overcome petty differences like race, religion and nationality? Wouldn't we have to get together to survive? Isn't that what has already happened in human history more times than we know? Humanity follows Mother Earth's great cycles of destruction and rebirth into wisdom -- we are truly Her children.

Well, the Photon Belt hasn't shown up yet, but there are still comets, meteoroids, the 12th planet, earthquakes, global warming, plagues and God only knows what else out there just waiting to whack us a good one. Why not live in community now and be prepared for the worst *and* the best? Why not come together with like-minded people to manifest a truly decent place to live? Certainly not a dream foreign to the human mind. And I was resolved to have it.

Right about then, as the Laws of Manifestation would have it, I participated in an event in Atlanta that was promoted by my dear friend Mary. Besides promoting metaphysically-oriented events, she had for seven years been publishing Atlanta's only "New Age" newspaper. She informed me that she and her new boyfriend intended to start a community on his farm, which was located about an hour and a half's drive north of Atlanta. This, then, was it! Mary was like a sister to me; the situation looked to be exactly what I was looking for! Once again I had landed in the right place at the right time. I would move to the farm and make it the base of operations for my mail-order business and my travels. At the very least, it was more centrally located in the U.S. than Clearwater, Florida.

The resident "community" consisted at the time of Mary, her boyfriend George, and, once I moved there, me. There were also several other people who were part of the community -- or the idea of the community -- but who didn't live on the farm. One of them was Robyn Andrews-Quail, a close friend I'd met in the late '80's, about whom more later.

The story of that winter on "the Farm" is a tale unto itself. I will only attempt to describe a few events key to our purposes here:

Mary, it turned out, had colo-rectal cancer. Her physician wanted to operate immediately, but Mary, after some reflection, was determined to explore less destructive avenues first. The Universe apparently had ushered me into a "temporary assignment" in service of Mary's healing. And I plunged into it with great zeal.

Among the three of us (Mary, George and me), we pretty well knew of everything going in natural medicine. We went through whatever our limited resources and extensive contacts would permit: ozone, fasting, diets, vitamin IV drips, herbs, bodywork, colonics, visualization -- you name it. Mary's "mainstream" doctor monitored her condition throughout this period -- and both he and her family kept up the pressure on her to undergo surgery.

It all came to a head on New Year's Eve, 1992. The whole community and some friends were scheduled to gather for a big party to usher in 1993. At 6:00 that evening, Mary, having just come off a ten-day grape fast, was lying on the couch in the fetal position, with black-ringed, sunken eyes, fifty pounds lighter than when I came to the farm and sobbing her heart out. I looked at George and said, "My God, I think we've killed her!" He assured me that she was just "detoxing" and would be fine. George's faith in "alternative" medicine (what a silly term!) was unshakable. And, of course, he was right.

When, two weeks into '93, Mary finally consented to surgery, the improvement was sufficiently spectacular that, after the last pre-operative exam, the physician's assistant had a long talk with her concerning just what she'd done to bring about such remarkable reduction in her cancer blood counts and the size of the tumor. The operation itself proved to be minor, relative to what Mary had faced at first; only a small portion of the bowel was removed, and her recovery was quite rapid. "It was truly a miracle," they said -- but *we* knew it was a lot of hard work! And, of course, the employment of modalities frowned upon by the extraordinarily wealthy and powerful guardians of the American healthcare "business". Everywhere, these conspiracies to quash or co-opt ways of seeing and being that don't bring more profits to the greedy! I was weighed down with *way* too many conspiracies.

In the late winter of '93 I was living on the farm during what was called, "The Storm of the Century". We were snowed in for four days. We had lots of time to talk and one evening we got on the subject of storing food (which was one of our plans for dealing with the oncoming tribulation). Who, we wondered, could we not possibly turn away, should they come to us seeking food and/or shelter? The list grew and grew until it was about five hundred people, among the three of us; it finally dawned on me that I wouldn't be able to turn *anyone* away, and I certainly would not shoot someone for being hungry. The "survivalist" lifestyle, I realized, was not for me. Living in the perpetual darkness of "preparing for the worst" -- and believing the worst of my fellow humans -- was the same as "casting my vote" for the worst to happen! At that point I came to the conclusion that I heard Ram Dass express so beautifully some years later: No matter how bleak or beautiful the future appears, there are only three things any well-intentioned person can do -- quiet the mind, open the heart, and do whatever one can to alleviate suffering. My friend Andy said to me, "I want Mary Sunshine Back!" Well, I did too. I resolved to put no more of my precious energy into worrying about conspiracies or the Apocalypse.

Several years earlier in my travels, I had met Robyn Andrews-Quail, a hypnotherapist. She claimed to have regressed (singly or in groups) twenty thousand people during her twenty year practice. She discovered over 600 individuals who told her of UFO-related experiences; however, she didn't believe they were "three-dimensional" occurrences (she theorized that they were some sort of out-of-body experience) -- until a UFO came right down over her house in the middle of Atlanta during a hypnosis session with a man who channeled aliens! Within that group of 600, Robyn found a sub-group whose stories bore great similarity to one another, but differed from the basic UFO abduction scenario. Although a wide range of variations emerged later during in-depth interviews, the similarities were striking enough that Robyn was moved to form a support group to bring all these people together.

One such meeting in late 1992 "happened" to coincide with one of my trips into Atlanta from the farm. Robyn suggested that I attend, because she felt I "had a lot in common with these people". As I listened at the meeting to each participant tell her or his life story, I was indeed impressed by the experiences we had in common (seeing ghosts, feeling watched, hearing voices, having knowledge beyond our education, etc.). A glaring exception was that many of them remembered, often without the aid of hypnosis, having contact with extraterrestrials. I did not. Gordon-Michael Scallion had told me in the reading he did for me that my interest in UFOs was the result of an experience I'd had, and several other psychics as well had at various times assured me that I'd definitely had encounters with ETs. At this point, however, I had no conscious memory of any such thing -- unless you count the events at the haunted house when I was a child. I had certainly considered some sort of ET scenario as a possible answer to the question of the identity of that voice that for the last five years had been helping to guide my actions, but after hearing all those stories that night and seeing the similarities between the group's experience and mine, I began to think that perhaps this was indeed the answer for which I'd been searching. But more important to me at the time was hearing ET tales with a positive point of view -- these people were being given information and technology that could help ease Mother Earth, and the many life forms which depend on her for existence, through the big "shift" -- whatever outward form it might take.

Robyn and I decided to team up and look in detail at the similarities within the group and what sort of lives they had led, with the idea of publishing our findings. In early 1993 I left the farm and moved in with Robyn; we immediately began conducting in-depth interviews with individual group members.

We interviewed the Prodigies about every detail of their lives, including gestation, birth, family history and life experiences. We named the people in Robyn's group "Prodigies", and coined the term "Extraterrestrial Telepathic Intelligence Phenomenon" (ETIP) to describe what had happened to them. The ETIP experience began for many of the Prodigies as follows: Between the ages of two and eight years, usually when they were outside playing (either alone or with others), a "tall man in a jump suit", an "iron man", a "robot" or some such entity approached them. Some of our interviewees recalled being frightened; others were not. The entities did not speak, but the children "knew" what they were thinking. At this point, the children were either given, or touched on the head, with a "wand" or "stick", and suddenly it seemed like the "Discovery Channel" was pouring into their heads! They felt that they suddenly "knew everything about everything." These "big men" were usually described as being more human-looking than the small "greys" so prevalent in current UFO abduction tales. Some Prodigies had no conscious memories of these experiences; recollections did not surface until later in life when something triggered the memories, or they were hypnotically regressed to fill in memory gaps.

The Prodigies did not seem to fit into society from the beginning, having different interests and being smarter than the other kids, and often felt lonely and isolated. They frequently felt as if they weren't "from here" or that their parents weren't their "real" parents. I have actually found many Prodigies who were adopted. They are usually very sensitive, gentle, loving people with compelling, twinkling eyes. Animals and children are drawn to them. Some have unusual physical characteristics and/or health problems, such as unusual blood types, back and vertebrae anomalies, extra fingers or toes, clubfoot, cardiac malformities, esophagus problems or asthma. Often we heard accounts of near-death experiences occurring either in childhood or later in life. They told of awakening with nose bleeds, strange cuts, scoop marks or even scars -- fully healed wounds -- that had not been there the night before. They frequently saw color around people, had "imaginary friends", saw UFOs, fairies, ghosts, devas and angels. They described very vivid "dreams" they felt were somehow not really dreams. They were usually psychic and/or prophetic; some were able to move objects with their minds. Many reported periods of "missing time" from two hours to, in a few cases, days at a time.

School was boring for the Prodigies, because they were usually ahead of the curriculum for kids of their age, knowing things they seemingly could not. Two reported having read every book in their grade school libraries. They often heard voices and felt "tutored", describing the process as "data dumping" or "like being plugged into a computer". They would wake up with ideas for inventions, along with other insights and inspirations. They easily grasped the concepts of time travel, anti-gravity, free-energy, the "new" physics, higher mathematics and/or laser technology; some are able to teach and write in fields in which they have no formal education. As I mentioned earlier, most of the technological innovations they "received" were in the area of what Robyn and I termed "responsible technology", aimed at assisting the planet and society through their healing crises, i.e., free energy motors, magnetics, revolutionary ways to clean the water and air, ways to clean up toxic waste dumps, new healing modalities and so forth. Their boredom, restlessness and inattention in school was occasionally misinterpreted as hyperactivity or some form of learning disability; however, they weren't "stupid", they just learned differently than other children.

Many of the Prodigies lost their connection with the "magic", as one described it, as they went through puberty and early adulthood, until one day a physical, emotional or spiritual trauma jolted their lives. A "shift" of some sort occurred as a result, leaving them feeling "like a different person". Even their names didn't seem to suit them anymore. They often wanted to get divorced, quit their jobs, sell all their belongings or make other major life changes. They focused on spiritual growth, and realized no church, religion or structured belief system was adequate to fulfill all their spiritual needs. Almost all of them described feeling strongly connected to Mother Earth and vitally concerned about her survival.

One of the most consistent threads linking the Prodigies is their deep feeling that they've been "chosen", that they're "here on an urgent mission". They feel driven to do their work. While all of the Prodigies did not report all of the above experiences, there was enough consistency to their stories to indicate at least a pattern, if not an overt agenda.

Most of the Prodigies told of a lack of understanding and support from the people in their lives. They were often branded as oddballs, because of their special gifts, knowledge and talents. Some of them shut down their psychic gifts in an attempt to "fit in". One can only imagine how different their lives and our world would be now if these people had only received moral, let alone financial support for their technological innovations and other insights.

At the beginning of our research, Robyn showed me a book excerpt one of her clients had given her; it was from a medical textbook entitled *Pathology Of The Human Placenta*, by Kurt Kenirschke and Peter Kaufmann. The excerpt was from a section titled "Vanishing Twin Phenomenon". It stated that a high percentage of women who are diagnosed with twins give birth to only one baby. It sounded hauntingly like a variation on the "missing fetus syndrome" of UFO literature; the woman who had given it to Robyn had a very strange and sinister story involving ETs, the military, and a missing baby of her own. However, the information didn't seem to have anything to do with our research, so we set it aside.

But only a few days later, Robyn and I attended a conference being held in Atlanta on the abduction phenomenon. A wealthy businessman had discovered the world of UFOs and abductions, and had decided to devote some of his resources to bringing information to the medical and psychological professions. He financed experts in the field, such as Budd

Hopkins, David Jacobs, John Carpenter and John Mack, to go around the country conducting seminars on the subject. That this conference was being held during the first week of our research was one of many "coincidences" I had been experiencing since 1987, so I had a feeling something significant could come of it. During the question and answer portion of the program, Robyn asked if anyone had ever heard of the Vanishing Twin Phenomenon. No one had. However, a man sitting in the front row turned around with a shocked, almost panicked look on his face and said, "I have to talk to you right away!" We stepped out into the hall with him, and I heard the first of what was to become a long list of "vanishing twin" stories.

It seems he was in the delivery room when his daughter was born, and saw the placenta. There were two umbilical cords: "one freshly cut and one that looked healed over, like an amputee's stump". The doctor had no explanation, except that the baby may have at some point in the pregnancy had a twin. When the daughter was about nine, as she and her father were on their way somewhere in the car, he asked her if she knew she was supposed to be a twin. She exclaimed, "Yes, Daddy, I know. I know where my twin sister is; she's on the spaceship and I talk to her all the time." Fortunately, the father was a therapist, and had also experienced ET contact, so he was able to handle such a remark calmly. She said she wanted to name her twin; they agreed upon the name Corrine. Shortly thereafter, as the father was having a reading done, the psychic paused and said, "Something strange is happening. I usually see dead people on one side of me and aliens on the other, but there's a little girl that keeps going back and forth across in front of my face. Can you explain that?" As the father began explaining that his daughter may have started out as twins, she interrupted him, saying, "Yes, that's it! Twins! Her name is Corrine and she wants you to be sure to get her twin sister the best voice lessons you can afford, because her music will be instrumental in healing people during the coming earth changes." The psychic had no "normal" way of knowing the name they had chosen; nor did she know that at that very time the girl's parents were deciding how to proceed with training the young girl's voice, having already recognized its quality. Thus we received, in the same week, two big "hits" on the subject of twins -- or more specifically, *missing* twins!

A few days later, one of the Prodigies (we'll call her BB) told us during an interview of her work in 1980 with over 100 women who at one time or another had been diagnosed as being pregnant with twins, but only delivered one baby. She was a professional psychic; these women had just started showing up in her life, one after the other. She concluded from her research, intuition and channeling, that these "twins" are conceived by artificial insemination or manipulation of the fetus, not by the typical "greys", but by Pleiadians, Orions, Vegans, Lyrians and many others. Usually between three and four months gestation, the mothers are taken on board a ship and one fetus is removed (although sometimes the procedure is performed right in the mother's bedroom). The twin that is taken is gestated in an incubator aboard a ship, and its development is accelerated in six months to the equivalent of age twenty-one. The twins, by the way, are usually, but not always, the same sex, and may be either fraternal or identical. It is well documented that many twins have a special psychic and telepathic bond. BB told us that the ETs use this bond to "link" the twins so that the one on the spaceship can telepath information of various kinds to the one on Earth. Apparently, she said, reading about Nikola Tesla often triggers the reception of transmissions from the "unearthly" twin. Interestingly enough, BB was living at the time on a piece of property in Cripple Creek, Colorado, where Tesla did some of his work exploring free energy nearly a century before. She said the ETs are engaged in many different experiments involving these twins. As a test of their integrity, the twins on Earth are often told a "secret" of some sort, and warned not to tell anyone. They are observed as they deal with keeping the secret. If they "pass the test," they become geniuses. They may begin inventing all sorts of "space age technology" or dispensing various types of powerful information "to help mankind on Earth". If they are unable to integrate this activation into their lives -- in other words, if they can't deal with "hearing voices" -- the result is often alcoholism, drug addiction or schizophrenia. If they misuse the information or "go over the line" in any way, their memories are erased, because, BB's contact stated, "There will never be another civilization like Atlantis, where this technology was misused."

While she was telling us this story, I looked over at another Prodigy who was present in the room waiting to be interviewed next. He was ghost-white! I asked him what was wrong and he replied, "My mother always told this goofy story about how I was supposed to be twins and when I was born there was only one. This explains it -- that's where my information is coming from." He had produced very technical drawings concerning UFO propulsion systems without the benefit of any earthly education on the subject. We were fascinated; here was the vanishing twin story, yet again -- in the span of a week! We became convinced that all this was indeed an integral part of our research.

I was particularly fascinated because of the presence of twins in my family, and I decided to call my mother to discuss our discoveries. She said, "Well, since you brought it up, I'll tell you something I've never told anyone -- not even your father." She told me that when she was pregnant with the twins, she was so convinced that she was having triplets that when they brought the twins to her, she asked where her other baby was.

87

An X-ray taken rather late in the pregnancy, had shown one too many appendages for twins; Mom had "just had a feeling all along that there were three babies in there". Fourteen months later, she gave birth to Ted; the doctor had told her during the pregnancy that she would probably have twins, due to her size, age and the fact that she had already had one set of twins. After the delivery, she still had labor pains, and remained in bed for three days, until the doctor insisted she get up. A "large mass" fell out of her as the nurse helped her to stand. It was rushed to the lab for analysis, but for some reason she now fails to comprehend (unless it was her concern about surviving, with *three* babies in diapers!), my mother never found out what the "mass" was. When she took Ted to the pediatrician for the first time, he said, "This guy's a twin -- where's his twin?", prompted apparently by the unique cowlick pattern of the hair on Ted's head. Mom also recalled a very strange experience in the middle of the night during the first trimester of the pregnancy. She remembers waking up as she was being "dragged down to the end of the bed"; "something" was then "slurped or sucked inside or out of" her. With all the other strange events in her life (we were living in the haunted house at the time), she just chalked it up as one more piece of strangeness and never told a soul.

Then came the punch line. "Oh, by the way," she said, "it's possible you could have been a twin too, because I bled through your pregnancy." (That's a symptom associated with the Vanishing Twin Phenomenon.) Well, I went numb; if I were a character in a comic strip, a big light bulb would've appeared over my head. Twins! A flood of memories inundated my awareness: my lifelong fascination with twins; how since early childhood I would blame my "twin sister Lulabelle" for anything I'd done for which I wanted to avoid responsibility; how, in the sixth grade, my best friend and I pretended we were twins, at one point making up a skit which

88

we performed to the sound track of my all-time favorite movie, *The Parent Trap* -- a film about twins separated at birth. I remembered attending a twins party with my brother and sister when I was twelve and, feeling an intense sadness I didn't understand, fighting back tears as I looked at all the twins. Could this be the answer? If so, it was a pretty strange one; I would definitely need proof. Over the next few months I feverishly researched the subject of twins, and the Vanishing Twin Phenomenon in particular.

I soon came upon the psychological profile of the "single twin" in the book *Having Twins*, by Elizabeth Noble (herself a single twin). I also found this statement: "I am prepared to suggest that anyone working with multiple pregnancy probably shared the uterus with a twin at some stage." What a remarkable statement! I felt a rush of confirmation. I realized that many of the aspects in the profile fit me. I felt that I was very close to understanding the identity of my "voice", but the idea that I was communicating telepathically with my "vanished" twin was a bit difficult to admit -- to myself or anyone else!

Robyn and I continued to interview the Prodigies, now inquiring more carefully about any possible twin connections. The profile of the Prodigies emerged and we amassed more stories about vanished twins. In fact, we found that many of the Prodigies were twins, were supposed to be twins or had twins in their families. Since sonograms weren't available until the mid-70's and X-rays were only used in emergencies, most of the "single twins" were diagnosed by the presence of two heartbeats or by the simple fact that the mother became unusually large early in the pregnancy -- slim evidence at best. Some only vaguely remembered family stories about doctors saying their mothers were probably going to have twins, but only one baby was born. Many had not realized that their ET contact might have something to do with their possible twinship, but when we told our story, it seemed to make sense to many of them, often answering for them -- as it had for me -- many previously unanswered questions.

What had the greatest impact on me as I took in the Prodigies' life stories, was the emotional pain, the isolation and resulting loneliness they described as a result of always feeling "different". They rarely had anyone with whom to talk about their inventions or insights who would -- or could -- understand them. They were all so excited about meeting one another, that Robyn and I decided to coordinate a Prodigy Conference. We were able to gather thirty-five of the Prodigies together in April of 1993 at Medicine Mountain, a retreat center in north Georgia. It brought tears of joy to my eyes to watch them tell their stories to one another. As one described his invention, another waited, leaning forward in his chair, waiting for an opportunity to jump in and tell how *his* invention would enhance the other's technology. They were all delighted to be among a whole group of people who completely understood what they had gone through; I will never forget the radiant face of one 72 year-old man, as he excitedly told of receiving the plans for 3-D color television in 1938!

As a result of that meeting an attempt was made to form a research group in order to develop some of the Prodigies' leading-edge technology; however, as of this writing it is struggling, for a number of more or less complex reasons.

Robyn and I had by this time finished a preliminary manuscript on our research, and I heard about a job at Medicine Mountain. Mary, who eventually had also left the farm, (so much for that community!) was working and living there. It had been a square dance retreat center for years, until the owners had a "spiritual awakening" and decided to convert it to a center for metaphysical events. Mary was working on the new marketing plan and convinced the owners they needed my expertise. It was located, as the name suggests, on a beautiful secluded mountain with sleeping rooms, an RV park, main lodge with dining room, pool, Jacuzzi, tennis courts, meeting rooms, trails, and even a babbling brook with waterfalls. We worked very long hours, taking turns doing everything from waiting tables, cleaning rooms and washing dishes to office and marketing work. I loved it -- it was my dream come true! It was a ready-made intentional community -- almost. I worked there until they closed for the winter and decided to revert to the square dance retreat idea; the metaphysical theme didn't catch on quickly enough for the owners financially, and there was a certain incompatibility between the square dancers and the "New Age" folks! So I "hit the road" again -- and loved it still.

Through the remainder of 1993, as I lectured on the Prodigy profile Robyn and I had developed, I realized that it also fit many of the "spiritually conscious" people I knew; but whereas the Prodigies were mainly receiving scientific information and high-tech inventions, others were receiving spiritual concepts, visions and prophecy. I met more and more Prodigies and single twins on my travels that year, all of whom had tales to tell! A few people have sheepishly come up to show me ratty old plans they drew years before of various leading-edge technologies; some tell me of their ET interaction or sightings, always happy to meet someone who will understand.

What I find most touching, though, are the women who come up to me after I've spoken -- women who perhaps are single twins, or who at some point had felt they were carrying twins, but gave birth to only one child. Often in tears, they tell me of the emotional connection to the twinning phenomenon they had always felt, and how the information in my lecture had allowed them to articulate and bring into full consciousness the source of that connection: the same "Ah, ha!" that I experienced myself. Those moments more than anything else make the work I do worthwhile.

But as many stories as I heard about older Prodigies, I began hearing even more about children. Parents, therapists or, more often, grandparents would come up and tell me stories about the children in their lives doing the same things the Prodigies were doing, or in some cases, even more outrageous things. Hearing so many of these stories, I wondered if the Extraterrestrial Telepathic Intelligence Phenomenon might be on the increase. I began to record the stories, pay closer attention and ask more questions.

Tales of Initiation

For six years, and periodically throughout my life, I had dreamed of living and travelling in a motorhome. The idea of having my home right there, no matter where I might be, had always held a great appeal for me. My difficulty in manifesting a motorhome into my life (I certainly wanted one) stemmed from my inability to make up my mind just exactly what kind of RV (that's "recreational vehicle", for all you folks stuck in one place) I wanted: Fifth wheel? Or Class C? Or what? How big should it be? And how equipped? These questions and myriads of others had muddied my fantasy for years! Finally, on my way back to Clearwater after another "field test" of my rebuilt mate-picker (I still hadn't quite got the hang of it), the vision crystallized. I had possessions scattered around in three different states, and rarely seemed to be in the right location to have access to something I needed when I needed it. "Enough," I said. "I am now going to manifest my motorhome. I want a Class C, twenty feet, with lots of closet space."

With very little time left before the first engagement in my 1994 tour, things didn't look good. I had no money or credit; the likelihood that I would be able to buy a motorhome, should I find the "right" one, was small. But manifestation, of course, is focusing intent, not thinking about why something can't happen. I kept an image of what I wanted bright in my mind and left the details to the Universe.

One day, while we were on our way in my old Dodge to visit a friend, I was telling my brother Ted of my intention. I was describing the RV I wanted just as we drove by a Class C motorhome parked beside the road. "Just like that one there," I said, pointing at it.

There was a FOR SALE sign stuck in its window.

That night I talked to my older sister Linda on the phone. Her life was none too easy at the time, and she had expressed an interest in "running away from home" for a while.

"Why don't you come on tour with me up to New England next week?"

Short pause. "Okay."

"There's only one problem. I need a motorhome. I found one, but I don't have any money. You got any money?"

"No....I've got credit cards."

"Okay. Let's go buy it."

"Are you gonna pay me back?"

"Yep."

Short pause. "Okay."

Three days later, my sister Linda and I set out for New England in my (our? -- the bank's!) 1978 Georgie Boy twenty-and-one-half-foot Class C motorhome with a 52 inch closet. I named her Magic, and she has been, for almost three years.

Well, somebody forgot to tell the two beach bunnies, who had spent almost all of their lives in Florida, that motorhomes in New England in the winter aren't such a good idea. First, we got only two quick demonstrations of how all the various aspects of the motorhome (hot water heater, furnace, water filling, waste dumping, etc.) functioned; more importantly, nobody told us that pipes freeze in New England, not only in motorhomes, but also in outdoor faucets -- from which, of course, we had to get our water. As you can imagine, it was often like being in a *Three Stooges* movie, but we managed, learning a lot and meeting many helpful new friends.

When we drove through New York City on our way to Connecticut (during rush hour on Friday evening yet! -- this was seriously bad planning), poor Magic hit so many potholes and rough spots that the closet bar collapsed, leaving our clothes in a tangled heap in the bottom of the closet. Linda and I didn't discover that until we opened the closet after stopping for the night. The next day I told Linda that we would simply manifest "a munchkin" to fix it for us. "Like right there," I said, pointing out a small hardware store. Sure enough, a very nice man, after hearing of our problem, came out to the motorhome to fix the closet, and even offered to hang our clothes back up for us! Of course, he, too, had a UFO sighting story and was very tickled with his autographed copy of *The UFO Reference Book*. As my sister will attest, my manifestation skills were very sharp on that trip. We always seemed to find just the right restaurant to feed us whatever type of food we wanted at the time; help was always there when we needed it; and although at times it took some searching, we always managed to find water eventually -- no mean task during March in New England. I also became very handy with duct tape and my trusty screwdriver during that trip (necessary skills with a motorhome, I learned). Sometimes sheer innocence -- not to say ignorance -- got us through when nothing else could!

Our UFO and metaphysical bumper stickers instigated many interesting conversations. One of my favorites was at the fire station in a little town in New Hampshire where we went begging for water. All the firemen came out to see what two women from Florida were doing in New Hampshire in the snow. When we told them, they all had stories to tell. They'd had sightings, a couple of the guys had seen some "strange things" in the military they weren't willing to talk much about, and one fireman's sister thought she'd been abducted. It's amazing; everywhere I go, people have UFO and ET tales they're just dying to share with somebody who will listen. I wonder how large a political party we would make if everyone with a story of UFO or ET contact of some kind were to gather in Washington, D.C.?

On the way back to Florida from a very successful (and educational!) New England "tour", we stopped at Virginia Beach for the Winter '94 edition of the Global Sciences Congress. At that conference I acquired a powerful image to augment my set of manifestation techniques. It came from a man named Mellen-Thomas Benedict, who had died of brain cancer and returned -- completely cured of his cancer, by the way -- to tell of his experiences on the other side. When first informed he had terminal cancer, he decided to study the subject of death as thoroughly as possible, so that he would know what to expect. He devoured books from many cultures and religions. One morning he woke up knowing this was to be the day. He called his hospice worker and friends to say goodbye, then fell asleep. He remembers leaving his body, and he knew that if he went all the way to the Light he would be dead, so on the way he said, "Stop, wait, I have questions!" He said that the entire experience came to a screeching halt and a voice said, "What do you want to know?" He was able to ask all his questions, and the answers make a fascinating and very moving tale. What I found most illuminating was that as he was traveling away from the Earth, he looked back and saw many lights, of various sizes and intensities, emanating from the planet and shooting off into space. He asked what they were, and was told that they were prayers.

The very bright ones were the children's; they were answered first. The rest were answered in descending order of brightness, the brightness being a function of how much emotional energy and intent went into the prayer. That image made clear to me a very important "rule" concerning manifestation; it's not just what you do or say, it's how much energy you put into it!

By the time we got back to Florida, I was much more experienced at RV life. But I was facing a rather disturbing prospect: in only a few short weeks, I would be setting out on a five-month, 15,000-mile tour across the country by myself. Linda's vacation was over. There was no one to go with me. Requirements for a roommate to share a space of twenty by eight feet are pretty restrictive! I did put an ad in the singles section of the local newspaper, but got no responses. And then, all of a sudden, departure day rolled around, and there I was, behind Magic's steering wheel, backing out of my parents' driveway, a woman alone, headed out into the big, dangerous U.S.A.! "Oh, shit," I said, genuinely frightened. My father had tried to persuade me to carry a pistol under the driver's seat (I couldn't even pick it up), and when I refused, absolutely insisted that I take along some Mace and a miniature baseball bat. Everyone was so worried about me that I started worrying too!

Until I'd gone about a block. Then reality set in. My "voice" said in effect, "Quit your whining. This is what you have to do. No one showed up to go with you because you have to do this alone." And that night, at my first speaking engagement (a UFO lecture) I met a woman who believed she was a "walk-in". She told me that I was indeed a twin and that my twin sister would be with me, watching over me. I would never be alone and I would be safe. She said I had to take this journey alone, because what I would be experiencing required solitude. Oddly enough, my RV radio, portable radio and TV did not work for most of the trip (although they were fine when I got home), leaving me with no company or diversions other than myself and the inner voice with which I had become so familiar. In the beginning, that voice had been outside my head, but by now it had "integrated" into my personality and become a "presence" that was with me all the time; I never did really feel alone. I must admit that by the end of that tour, I was actually talking out loud to her! In fact, we had quite an ongoing dialogue.

During that five months, my psychic abilities expanded rapidly; the color readings I had been doing for the past two years developed into something quite different. I began "seeing" past lives. It's as if I have a videotape player in my head. When the client asks about his or her connection with a certain person, for example, the "videotape" goes into rapid reverse search mode, and suddenly I see a picture. I am the person, seeing out of his/her eyes and experiencing his/her emotions. I can then relate what I'm seeing to an issue the client is dealing with at present. I'm usually able to provide at least one detail in each reading that validates for the client that I'm seeing a "real" experience. I've spent many hours analyzing this process in an attempt to understand what is happening. Am I tapping into the akashic records, as some have told me, or am I somehow accessing the DNA (genetic) memories -- the signature frequencies -- of the person's ancestors that are stored in their physical bodies? Since all of us, at one time or another in our soul's journey, experience everything, perhaps we are all at least potentially able to relate to anyone's past experience. I also often wonder if I'm "just making it up", but my clients' confirmations seem to eliminate that option. Whatever is happening, it seems to help and give people greater understanding of their life issues, and for that I am truly grateful. My intent is always to speak from an open heart, offering my visions in the spirit of love and service.

Everyone I met along my journey was wonderful to me, providing me with driveways to stay in, great meals, interesting conversation and long, hot showers (a short hot shower was the best I could do in the motorhome!). I was able to interact with people and yet retain a measure of privacy. I discovered that simultaneously driving and reading maps was extremely difficult, but apparently I had some "help" there, too; I can't tell you how many times I felt sure that I was completely lost, only to discover when I finally asked someone that I was just a few blocks away from my destination!

I was never afraid -- except once. While driving along the Interstate in Colorado, I suddenly heard a terrible racket right above me. Glancing around, I saw something flopping around on the left side of the motorhome. It was a pole from the awning -- somehow it had come loose, flipped over the top of the RV, and was extending dangerously far into the lane of traffic next to me -- the passing lane! I realized I had to get off the road fast, before that pole went through somebody's windshield.

Unfortunately, I was on a bridge, and it was not a short one. There was enough room at the side of the road for me to pull out of the traffic, but just barely. I rolled to a stop and assessed the situation; it was obvious that I had to get up on top of "Magic" and wrestle that pole -- which was still attached to the half-torn awning -- back over to the other side of the motorhome, and then figure out how to reattach it. Bracing myself against the wind, the cold (it was about thirty degrees) and the backdrafts from the big semis zooming by, I crept out of the motorhome and looked over the side of the bridge. Big mistake! Far below me (I guessed 500 feet) was a raging river, just waiting, it seemed, for me to fall off my motorhome (I have a pronounced fear of heights). Gathering courage, I began to climb the ladder to the roof, trying to maintain my balance as the motorhome rocked back and forth in the wind. When I finally reached the top, I was confronted by a great gnarled mass of poles and canvas, all thrashing about in the blasts of cold air. My efforts to bring them under control proved futile -- in fact, I was in short order pinned down in the small space between the air conditioner and the luggage carrier by seventy-five pounds of awning assembly! Do NOT ask how it happened; I could never explain.

So there I was, buried in awning, peeking out pitifully at the oncoming traffic, praying someone would stop and help. No one did; visions of the howling wind grabbing hold of the whole mess and flinging it -- and me -- into the waiting river far, far below began to assault my inner eye. "Abandoned Motorhome Found on Bridge", the headlines would shout; "No Sign of Occupants." I was shaking so hard with fear and cold that logical thought was impossible. Finally, after what seemed hours of struggle, I was able to squirm out from under the awning and wedge the whole mess into my former prison -- that small space between the air conditioner and the luggage carrier. Then all I had to do was get off the motorhome, which was still rocking back and forth like a ship in a storm. Somehow, I managed to ease down that ladder, only to find that the section of the awning pole assembly that had not ripped loose was jutting out about seven feet from the curbside wall of the RV. It was secured at the bottom with six large bolts -- my father had reinforced it. My reaction to this sight was to grab that pole and rip it right out of the side of the motorhome, bolts and all. It was like the stories you hear about mothers who lift cars off their children -- under normal circumstances I could never do what I had just done. For some reason, that realization frightened me even more; I threw the section of pole into the motorhome and scrambled in after it.

I was trembling so badly I could barely grip the steering wheel -- but there was more to come. I had to get off that bridge, but I was on an interstate highway and the next exit was about five miles away. I crept along the side of the road, praying now that the wind would not blow the awning loose again -- or that one of those big trucks wouldn't pass by too close to me!

Five miles at maybe fifteen miles an hour -- well, you get the idea. When I finally reached the exit, I was greeted with -- nothing! No gas station, no people, nothing but one abandoned restaurant. I pulled into the parking lot of that restaurant, got out, and kicked into "resourceful Girl Scout" mode. Obviously, that awning had to come off; it was still held on by, as near as I could tell, only one bolt. If I could get that bolt out, it would release the whole caboodle. Finding a hammer, I hauled off and whacked the bolt with all the strength I could muster (which was more than enough, what with all the adrenaline shooting through me). Sure enough, everything came crashing down -- right on my head! Dazed, I stood there for some time, covered once again in canvas and hollow metal poles. Finally, I extricated myself -- only to find that the damned awning was STILL attached to the RV, up near the roof! Now, frankly, I was getting angry. I took a deep breath, squatted, leapt up as high as I could, grabbed what was left of that awning and yanked it down -- this time for good.

The awning travelled no farther with me. I left it in the dumpster by the restaurant, hoping that someone would be able to recycle the metal, at least. As I drove off, still trembling from the "adrenaline rush", I thought of the Helen Reddy tune "I Am Woman" -- it would have new meaning for me after this experience!

That was not the only test of my "stuff" during that trip -- only the most extreme. There was the time in Nebraska that Magic's universal joint developed a problem; it was Sunday and I was pretty much in the middle of nowhere. But I made it to an exit that just happened to have a repair place and even a mall! And although I was in a hurry (I was racing to get from Vermont to Denver in time for the Global Sciences Congress), I found the respite from driving to be just what I needed -- I was hammered! Some rest and some shopping did me a world of good.

All in all, that 15,000-mile "solo flight" was the most liberating and empowering experience of my life. I grew to love the feeling of freedom, of limitlessness. Although I still had not proved to my satisfaction the identity of that "voice", it nonetheless provided very good company, as well as excellent information and insights when I was doing readings.

And then I found Crestone.

After the Denver Global Sciences Congress, and a lovely stay with some wonderful people in Boulder (lovely except for a nasty case of poison oak), I was headed for New Mexico and a friend advised me, "If you're going south, you *must* stop in Crestone. Go to 'Light Reflections', a little store on the corner of Highway 17 and T road going into Crestone, and you'll know what to do from there." I had a week until my next event and I've learned from past experience that when someone gives me a lead like that I should take it. I wasn't disappointed. Crestone is nestled against the Sangre de Cristo (that means "blood of Christ") Mountains, which mark the eastern edge of the San Luis Valley, a huge, semi-arid, high-altitude (about 7,000 feet) prairie that occupies much of south central Colorado. It is bordered by the San Juan Mountains on the west, and sits atop the largest fresh-water aquifer in the continental United States. About fifteen miles south of Crestone is the Great Sand Dunes National Monument, approximately forty square miles of the tallest (between seven and eight hundred feet!) sand dunes in the continental U.S. The sand contains about 25 percent ground-up quartz crystal; this place has some power, let me tell you!

"Light Reflections" was all my friend promised and more. As soon as I saw the sign in the window, I knew I was in the right place; it said, "UFO PARKING FREE"! I was pleasantly surprised to find, in this small thirty year-old octagonal building sitting by itself pretty much in the middle of nowhere, a shop full of huge amethyst geodes, crystals, assorted gemstones, local art and crafts, jewelry, candles, tapes, UFO and metaphysical books -- just all sorts of interesting things. A life-size poster of Sai Baba adorned one corner. I was greeted by Al Koon, a crusty character who reminded me a bit of my father. When in the course of our conversation I mentioned my work with color, he said, "Well, you'll like my wife Donna's healing room." He led me into a small, windowless room that contained a massage table, surrounded by tables loaded with more huge crystals, geodes and various other rocks. The lighting was minimal and the overall effect was quite peaceful and soothing. I saw, hanging above the massage table, a four-foot long lighting fixture with eight bulbs in it, one each of the seven colors of the rainbow, and one white. "This," I thought, "is going to be a fun place!"

"Light Reflections" became a home away from home for me, and Donna Koon quickly became a "Mom away from Mom." A warm, loving, five-foot-tall "munchkin", Donna is kind of a spiritual Grandmother for the Crestone area; she described her mission to me as being "a healer for the healers." During the time I've spent there, her healing room has usually been occupied with one local resident after another. Crestone and "Light Reflections" are annual stops now -- right after Global Sciences in Denver!

As I mentioned in "ET Tales", the San Luis Valley is a hotbed of anomalous and paranormal activity. I had the good fortune to meet Christopher O'Brien, publisher of *The Mysterious San Luis Valley* newsletter and author of the recently published book, *The Mysterious Valley.* I invite anyone interested in the subject to explore those publications. My experiences in Crestone and the Valley have been quite unusual, and they began during that first visit in 1994.

As I drove the fifteen miles into Crestone from Light Reflections, I could feel an energy, a kind of presence, intensify as I drew nearer to the town. The view of the mountains was so vast and spectacular that I didn't know which way to look -- it was very difficult keeping my eyes on the road! In Crestone, I spotted deer contentedly munching on the vegetation in people's yards, quite oblivious to human presence. Later, when I stopped at a small park for a nap, I awoke to find the motorhome surrounded by about thirty deer, again grazing contentedly and oblivious to my presence. And over all, there was a curious feeling of deja vu, a feeling of being right at home in a place I had never visited in this life.

Over the next few days, as I got to know "the locals," I found that a number of people really had no idea why they were in Crestone, but were somehow "led" to be there. I parked Magic behind "Light Reflections" and spent a lot of time interacting with the people who stopped in. Many of them seemed to be looking for a new home, and many of them were familiar with the Earth Changes maps that hung on a wall in the shop. Only later would I realize the significance of this.

One night, while "camped" behind the store, I looked out the window of the motorhome and psychically "saw" the valley floor covered with tents, as far as I could see. The next day, with that vision still haunting me, I went to the Dunes.

The minute I set foot upon that sand, I felt my vibration began to rise, and by the time I had walked up a couple of mounds, I was beginning to see visions and receive information. I sat in the sand and stilled myself, as I listened to the inner voice: Long ago, in a land located in the Pacific Ocean and known to us as Lemuria, Mu or the "Mother Island", there existed a highly developed, spiritually based society. The word went out that Mother Earth was about to cleanse herself and great changes were imminent. A group of healers, mystics, psychics and teachers heeded this warning and set out in large, sea-worthy ships to find places to build healing outposts, refuges for survivors of the cataclysm. They went where they were divinely (or in some cases "extraterrestrially") guided to go. One group ended up floating over what is now known as the San Luis Valley, where they waited until the waters retreated enough to allow them to build a platform up in the high country of the Sangre De Cristo mountains. As the waters continued to recede, they built their healing center and waited, ready, for the droves of people that would come seeking refuge. These people set up tents and built huts and began new lives in a new land from scratch, without benefit of the technology possessed by their forebears. It was explained to me that many of the people in Crestone and others who are drawn to the Valley are those same healers, psychics and teachers, being drawn back to the valley to, once again, set up healing outposts to serve the refugees from the imminent West

105

Coast earthquakes, floods and other major geographic changes.

All this clarified the vision I had seen the previous night. When I returned to "Light Reflections" and told the people there of my experience at the Dunes, they responded that others had seen similar visions of the future for the San Luis Valley. Some had seen visions of lines of children walking up the highway into the Valley. I did readings for a number of Crestone residents and saw their personal connections to the healing outpost of the past. When I left, I knew I would be back, and at each of my UFO lectures the next year, I talked about the "Mysterious San Luis Valley" and my experience there.

By the time I returned to Clearwater in the late autumn of 1994, I was quite certain that I could handle whatever life might put in front of me -- with or without a partner. I had much more confidence in my psychic abilities; the readings were now quite vivid, detailed, and, according to my clients, accurate. And my greatly increased self-reliance had certainly shown through in my ability to manifest what I needed when I needed it.

And the next thing I wanted to manifest was a monograph on the Vanishing Twin Phenomenon and the ET connection. Over the winter I amassed everything I could find in print on the subject (which really wasn't terribly much) and put together a publication I called *Are Extraterrestrials Really Influencing Human Reality?*

Tales of Karyl

I was about two weeks away from "lift-off" for my 1995 Spring speaking tour, and, once again, facing the necessity of going it alone. Granted, I had learned much and grown a lot touring by myself, but it was exhausting. It was time for me to manifest my perfect mate and partner. I had endured a great deal of therapy and quite enough "practice runs". After all, I had been schlepping around (and perfecting) a 72-point list of my perfect partner's attributes since 1987!

Taking to heart Mellen-Thomas Benedict's observation that the efficacy of prayer is directly related to the amount of emotional energy put into it, I went for a walk on the beach -- *way* up the beach. Then, standing with my feet in the water, I screamed at the Universe, "If you want me to continue this work, you better get me some help! I need help -- NOW!" I then read my entire 72-point list out loud. That was probably as intensely as I had prayed for many, many years -- or at least since I was pinned under that awning on top of my motorhome!

Three days later, on Saturday, January 28, 1995, I presented a lecture at the monthly meeting of the Tampa Bay area chapter of the Mutual UFO Network. Just before I began my lecture a man came up to the podium and said, "I've known about you for two and half years. I heard a tape of a lecture you gave at the Global Sciences Congress on a radio program in Los Angeles and was so impressed, I copied it and sent it to my sister and her husband." He was the brother of the woman who had booked me to speak that day, she and her husband being the MUFON State Section Directors for the Tampa Bay Area. I took one look into his eyes and I knew he was "the one" the Universe had sent. He sat in the first row during my talk, almost directly in front of me. I had to avoid looking at him, knowing that if our eyes met I would forget what I was saying! After the meeting, as I was standing in the back of the room conversing with three or four people, he waved to me and mouthed the words, "I have to talk to you." I coolly waved acknowledgement, thinking, "Yes! Yes you do! Of course you have to talk to me!"

After the meeting, a group of twenty to twenty-five attendees went to a nearby restaurant for food and conversation. I talked with my mother about him all the way to the restaurant. When we arrived, there "coincidentally" happened to be a vacant seat next to him at the table; however, not wanting to seem too anxious, I sat elsewhere. Later, I made my way over to sit next to him and asked, "What do you want to talk to me about?" He told me that he'd met a person claiming to be a walk-in, and he felt that I might be interested in her story. I was interested, all right! Conversation soon ranged over a variety of other subjects; I let it be known I was looking for "a driver". I learned that Parker had relocated to St. Petersburg from Los Angeles four months earlier, and he'd moved into a new apartment in November. "Oh, my God, " I thought, "he's from L.A., he's an actor, and he carries a shoulder bag...Please, please, don't let him be gay!" That would make living together in a twenty-and-a-half-foot motorhome rather difficult to arrange! We said our goodbyes, but I knew it wouldn't be for long.

The next afternoon I was giving my sister Terri a perm and talking about him. He had mentioned a Lunar New Year's party on the following Wednesday and I told Terri, "I hope he calls asking to have a reading on Wednesday afternoon. Then we can go to the party afterward." I didn't realize it, but I had inadvertently unplugged my phone and at the very time I was saying that to my sister, he was leaving me a message with just that request.

I desperately tried to "keep my cool" in the intervening days till Wednesday. My mother kept warning me, "Now, you better be careful doing that reading. Don't you add anything extra you don't see!" I called his sister on Monday with some trumped-up excuse, just to see if I could casually get any more information about him; she wasn't very helpful. Wednesday afternoon finally arrived, as did Parker, right on time. I suggested we drive the motorhome out to the beach to do the reading. Although it was a little difficult for me to focus and enter the altered state in which I do my readings (he was so cute, I just wanted to hug him!), I nevertheless managed to deliver what he said was a good deal of helpful information. I saw first of all that he was a "Violet", an old soul. (A perfect match -- I'm a Violet too!) He had been a powerful healer in many lifetimes and had some issues about using that power; he also was able, or would one day be able, to access intuitive information about special properties of herbs and plants that would be of great benefit to humanity. I saw several lifetimes when we had been together; a couple of times in Atlantis (doing color healing!), one on a great ship leaving Lemuria before that ancient land sank beneath the ocean, and even one where we were both killed -- along with our little daughter -- by marauding barbarians. It was quite a trip.

I soon learned from some of his responses that he wasn't gay; however, I also learned that he was romantically interested in the "walk-in" he had talked to me about. I just knew, though, that the Universe had sent him to me, so I decided to relax and wait until he knew it too.

After the reading, we went for a walk on the beach. It was everything I could do not to touch and/or hug him. We went to the party in his car, returning later in the evening to the motorhome. That was it! It was as if we were old partners, hooking up again after an absence so long that we had slipped each other's mind; we simply said a big cosmic "Howdy", and continued on our way together. I checked my 72-point list the next day to see if the things I knew about him were on it. Sure enough, he qualified -- except he wasn't a mechanic, but he said he had played one on TV! The next evening he came over again. As he stepped through the door, he called out in his best Ward Cleaver voice and with a big Ricky Ricardo grin, "Honey, I'm home!" And indeed he was.

Over the next month and a half (I rearranged my schedule) Parker settled his affairs -- or, as he put it, "I wadded up my current existence into a small ball and tossed it out the window" -- and moved into the motor home. He was delighted to have another opportunity to "get rid of stuff" so soon after the big move from L.A. Lightening the load of material objects is certainly one of the advantages of RV living and a great lesson in letting go of "attachments".

As it turned out, Parker had manifested me as surely as I did him. Rather bored with his career, he had been seeking a way to do service. He just hadn't made a list of requirements -- at least not consciously. So I came as a big surprise to him.

Parker is an old hippie like me, and we both love traveling, living in the motorhome, and attending UFO conferences, various metaphysical events and the like -- not to mention constantly meeting fascinating people. We travel the back roads whenever we can, so that we can "feel" the energy of an area and experience as much of the country and its inhabitants -- human and otherwise -- as possible. It's a different world out there beyond the massive electromagnetic pollution of the urban areas. The "vibes" differ so much from one part of the country to the other that it sometimes feels as though we've changed planets!

Parker provided invaluable support for me as I wrestled with admitting the existence of my twin. It was on April 14, 1995 -- Good Friday -- that a real breakthrough occurred. We were parked in Withrow State Park in Northern Arkansas enjoying a gorgeous Spring day. The park was nearly deserted. We took a long, lovely, meditative walk in the woods. At one point we paused in a clearing; I was feeling somewhat weak, and asked Parker to run some energy for me, using the technique of "chakra spinning" and color visualization that I had learned in 1987. During the process, I became dizzy and somewhat nauseated -- it felt as though all the energy was going to my head! Once I managed to "stabilize" my condition, we went on with our walk. My body still felt rather "buzzed" and decidedly strange. The twin business was much on my mind; I said to Parker, "You know, if I was really going to be honest, I would have to say I'm communicating with my twin." It was the first time I actually admitted it out loud, and I felt something -- well, shift! We soon came upon a manmade waterfall; I was greatly attracted to the rushing water and sat on the bank by myself while Parker wandered off. The "buzzing" feeling grew stronger. I wasn't entirely sure what was happening, but when Parker came back, I told him that it might be a good idea to go back to the motorhome and get out the tape recorder. "I think I'll be able to contact her," I said.

When we were comfortably settled at the picnic table back at our campsite, I centered myself, entered the familiar altered state, and soon began hearing a voice in my head. Parker asked questions, and "she" responded.

She said her name is Karyl (pronounced Ka-*rill*). "We had to work very hard to get you not to change your name when you were trying to; it would have caused too many identity problems for you," she said. (A couple of years earlier I had met a woman whose name was spelled the same as mine. She told me "C-a-r-Y-l" was the French spelling of Carol and the correct pronunciation was Ka-*rill*. We had both agreed to use that pronunciation for a month, but it became such an inconvenience that we both abandoned the idea.) She told me that she is in the fifth dimension, and she "steps her energy down" to communicate with me. Meanwhile, due to all the life changes I made in 1987, particularly using color to balance the energy centers, I became able to "step my energy up", so that we can meet in the fourth dimension. She called this process "meshing", and that's exactly how it feels. I'm still conscious, but there's something "more" present. Karyl said the pineal gland is the "tuner or receiver" used to locate an individual, as well as for de- and re-materialization when transporting him or her to and from a ship. She also stated that a by-product of the stimulation of the pineal gland is increased psychic ability. I could "see" her beaming a white light from her pineal to mine. In responding to Parker's questions, she revealed that she, along with eighteen others, are "on a Pleiadean ship tethered to Earth." Their primary mission is to monitor twins, "to see what the creatures they created will do." I could see through her eyes many "TV screens" on the ship, showing people going about their daily lives. Karyl also revealed that she experiences "3-D" vicariously through me, in order to learn about human beings. (Parker tells me he can tell when Karyl "drops in"!) She said I was to be one of identical twins (they "split" my mother's egg), but "something went wrong" and my identical twin died. Karyl was "put in later" and is a "genetic crossbreed of our mother's genes with those of an ET". My mother told me, incidentally, that she's had numerous dreams of being a "baby factory -- just lying there putting out baby after baby!"

The color information had been "downloaded" to me in order to help bring it back into the conscious awareness of humankind at this critical time. Understanding and using color to balance the energy centers is one of "the secrets to life on planet Earth", she said. What I had done in 1987 was simply to bring body, mind and spirit into balance, using the color "technology" I was given. As that happened, the "voice", which seemed at first to be outside of me, gradually "integrated" into my being until our "communion" was fully accomplished. It was then up to me to simply acknowledge that communion and allow it to exist, without judging or fearing it. That, as it turned out, was the hard part!

Finally, Karyl stated in no uncertain terms that the destruction of planet Earth in the name of greed and power must stop. "If humans don't stop it, we will," she said. She did not elaborate on that point, except to say that the Earth is moving from the indigo frequency into the violet, and that for a number of reasons, it must survive.

As vivid, convincing and real as my first direct communication with Karyl was, I couldn't help asking myself, "Did I make it up?" Could I really be communicating with a twin sister on a 5th-dimensional spaceship? And what does that mean, anyway? It all seemed so farfetched. I needed more validation to give me the courage to step out and actually admit it in public.

A week later, at a psychic fair in St. Louis, a fellow came over to me after I gave a short talk on the Vanishing Twin Phenomenon and said, "As a professional psychic, I can assure you that you are indeed a twin -- I was told to tell you to stop denying it." That night, while drifting off to sleep Karyl showed me a vision of a "community" store in which I would sell used books, recycled clothes and other items. There was also a juice and herbal tea bar where a few health food items were available. And besides all that, I saw a color room which would be available free of charge, along with solarized water to drink. My vision of community had returned with bells on, enhanced and encouraged by my twin -- or so it seemed.

The following week, at a big three-day psychic fair in Kansas city, the "hits" really started coming hot and heavy. I still couldn't admit in public that Karyl existed and was the source of my intuitive information and insight. In my talk I merely discussed my research and told of my experiences. Well, immediately after my presentation, a woman with dark hair and an infectious smile same up to me and said, "You ARE a twin, I've seen you with your twin on a ship at a twin convention. Do you remember the glowing silver balls the twins hold?" Well, she certainly got my attention! She told me that there is a group of five single twins in Kansas City, all communicating with their twins on ships. They "go to school" and interact with their twins at night, and the next morning confirm for each other details of the previous night's events. Later, the woman returned to my exhibit table with another of the single twins, who looked at me and exclaimed, "Look what she's wearing -- sparkling clothes -- it's her!" Once they calmed down, they explained that one night "on board", I told them they would also meet me on Earth. They would know me by my "sparkling clothes". It so happened that due to the chilly weather, I wore sparkly sequined sweaters all weekend. They said they had been looking everywhere for me, and had caused considerable bewilderment for a number of people in sparkling clothes! I was stunned. Not only had I found a whole group of people experiencing the same type of "contact" as I, but we were old friends! Why, then, didn't I remember it?

Prior to my lecture, I had met a young boy (about twelve) and his mother. We had discussed the possibility of the boy being a single twin. His mother had been told before he was born that she would probably have twins. An outstanding poet, and possessed of great psychic ability as well as a high I.Q., he had felt from infancy that he had a twin. This boy (who reminded Parker of a young Lord Byron) came up to me after my lecture and said, "While you were speaking, I felt a pressure in my head -- and they told me to tell you that you're an *inter-breed*." He said nothing like that had ever happened to him before, and that he had no idea what an "inter-breed" might be. Embarrassed, he turned and ran away from my table.

A moment later, an older man dressed in overalls and who had a long, red beard came up to me and said in a gruff voice, "Stop denying it. You are a twin!" and walked away.

But still I wasn't completely convinced. Where was the tangible proof? As a researcher of the paranormal, I am not completely devoid of the "bag and tag one" mentality. If Karyl existed, why hadn't I met her?

We returned to Clearwater after the Kansas City engagement, and I related my experiences to my friend Carolene, a professional psychic who has been tested for her psychic ability since childhood, including examinations by J.B. Rhine and the Monroe Institute. Upon hearing of my experiences, she immediately responded, "I can see her; she has strawberry blonde hair...and she's fraternal, not identical." (I had not told her either of those things -- one I didn't even know!)

The next day, I had a lengthy telephone conversation with another friend, a very famous psychic, who said he had seen Karyl and me together with the "silver balls" on two different occasions. He said that I had told him during one of these meetings that she vicariously experienced 3-D reality through me. I said, "OK, here's the big question. What color hair does she have?" He said, "The first time I saw her I thought, she

115

has hair like the sunset -- sort of reddish blonde." Another home run! Yet -- where was the game taking place, and *why didn't I remember playing?*

A week later, I decided to undergo hypnotic regression in order to explore my 1990 Durango experience. I chose Dr. Robert Koser, a family practitioner who does UFO abduction regression on the side for his personal research. I came prepared with a list of questions. Due to my accelerated psychic ability and my propensity to see visions, it was very easy for me to reach the necessary altered state of consciousness and return in my mind to that night in Durango. I clearly recalled floating, still in a prone position, out of my bed and up through the roof, then into the ship waiting over the house. It was round with colored lights around the bottom, which opened up like an eye, allowing me to enter. After I floated into the ship, whatever force had me under its control deposited me on my feet in front of four very human-looking beings: Karyl, with her strawberry blonde hair, dressed in a white belted dress made of some soft fabric; a tall, sophisticated-looking woman of about fifty named Alenia, who was dressed in a long white shirt and pants (I described her as a "mentor, guide or guardian angel"); a man whom I knew to be a doctor; and another man I did not recognize. We greeted one another warmly; I hugged Karyl and Alenia as if we were family members reunited after a long separation. I experienced no fear at all -- everything felt familiar and very comfortable.

We walked up a ramp and around the ship into a room containing a huge screen that showed a view of planet Earth, slowly receding (presumably as we departed from it) into a blackness ablaze with stars. The screen changed and a lush, very green forest with a babbling brook running through it appeared. I cried out, "It's home!" and I began weeping, both in my memory and in the doctor's office. I felt a great longing and -- well, homesickness; that scene was so very familiar, and I knew it wasn't on Earth. Then there appeared on the screen a panoramic aerial view of a futuristic, white arched city: majestically curving (not domed) buildings of various sizes that reminded me of the great St. Louis arch, multiplied many times. (I told Dr. Koser, "I'm being given a tour of home to make me feel comfortable and jog my memory." I identified the city as being on my home planet in the Pleiades, but could not recall the names of the planet or the city.) The screen then went dark and we all left the room.

The doctor and I entered what I knew to be an examination room, although I could see no equipment of any kind. The doctor said, "We have to do a checkup". I felt no fear or trepidation; it was like I had done it all before. As I lay down on the examining table, the doctor pressed some sort of lever with his foot and a bar of instruments slid smoothly down from the ceiling above me. A two-inch light on an accordion-like device extended toward my head (remember the two-inch red mark?). The moment it touched my forehead, my entire body instantly went numb, and I could no longer see anything in the room. I could feel a slight sensation of pressure as the doctor did something to my stomach, knees and feet, all of which seemed to take just a few minutes. Next, he did something to each fingertip on my right hand, and then repeated the same activity on my left. As he did this, the feeling began to return to my body and I could hear a low humming noise. My entire body began to vibrate. I could feel the vibration from my skin to deep in my internal organs. It felt very good! (I said, "It raises my frequency and helps in the communication process with Karyl.") The vibration increased to a high intensity, then slowly wound down to a stop. The doctor next produced a thin, flexible band about one inch wide which he placed on the top of my head, extending back to front down over my forehead to between my eyes. Again, the procedure was completely painless. When he was finished, he hit the lever and the equipment receded into the ceiling. The doctor told me I was doing well, and that everything was going as planned.

He left the room, returning shortly with Karyl and Alenia. The three of us went into the next room around the passageway. This one appeared to be a recreation area for the ship; it looked like a park, with grass, plants and benches. We sat and talked as fast as we could, catching up on news and life, just like family members who haven't seen each other in a long time. (Unfortunately, I could not recall the specifics of this conversation -- only the "feel" of it.) Finally, Karyl said it was time to leave. We walked back down the ramp, said our goodbyes and hugged one another. I was returned to my bed in the same manner I was taken.

I want to make it clear here that my recall of this entire incident had a feeling of vivid reality, as clear as if I were to recall my wedding day or some other special occasion. The emotion and the sensations were very intense and very "real". I have recounted this tale to others, who have recognized in their contact episodes many aspects of my experience, including the white, arched city, the "park" on the ship, and the examination equipment, as well as the band which was placed on my head. I've been told it's used for the retrieval and implantation of information.

When I finished recounting the Durango experience, Dr. Koser asked if he could talk to Karyl. I said yes and he asked, "What is the nature of the experiment Caryl and you are involved in?" Karyl responded that she is helping to monitor the twin experiments, of which there are many different types, and that Alenia is overseeing the project. She made a big point of saying that all participants had agreed beforehand to take part. When asked if I should write a book about the twins, Karyl said, "Yes, but it is also important that the twins *hear* the information consciously, because that will bring about a sub-conscious awakening." He asked what I could do to enhance the communication between her and I. She replied, "She must learn to be still and listen more. She does not take the time to stop and listen." (I could see a beam of light projecting from Karyl's forehead to mine and was told it was "telepathically bonding us".) He asked about the "glowing silver balls". She said they come in pairs, one for each twin, and are used to "increase the telepathic bond" and "raise the frequency of the twin on Earth."

Dr. Koser asked about the haunted house. Karyl replied that the ghost of the original owner drew lots of other spirits to the house. They served as a cover for the twin experiments that were going on, because "there was a need for the family not to have conscious memory and the ghosts created confusion". He asked for details about the "twin" relationship between Karyl and me. She said, "Our doctors split the egg, but the experiment didn't work right and the identical twin died. In order to save the experiment, I was put in later." He asked about my brother Ted. The answer came: "His identical twin did not develop properly mentally, which created a great deal of confusion for Ted." When asked about the "Greys", she said they are an entirely different group with a different agenda. They have suffered genetic damage and are trying to save themselves. They are renegades, have "less heart" and are creating a great deal of karma as a result of their actions. She stressed that this is an important time on the planet, and there are many different types of experiments happening here. Karyl and her group were here "to see that we didn't destroy the planet."

A few days later, I spent some time with the psychic who'd seen my sister and me together. He claimed that he could see her sitting beside me and declared she wanted to speak to me through him. She asked if I knew when she was "in my energy" -- I do -- and requested permission -- which I gave -- to be in it "more often and to a more intense degree". She said that we are now able to "switch places and experience each other's reality and see through each other's eyes". She then experimented with coming in and out of my body, which I could very distinctly feel and my psychic friend could see. Incidentally, he is not completely convinced that she is actually my "twin", because the first time I introduced them I said, "I want you to meet another aspect of myself." He added that the "silver balls" had been described to him by other experiencers as "communicators with your home planet".

Despite all this "confirmation", I still was not completely convinced. I was well aware of the existent criticism of hypnotic regression as a means of getting at the truth -- there was still no way I could "prove" to anyone else what to me felt quite real. I could just hear the merciless teasing I would get from some of my brothers and sisters if I started acknowledging my "twin" in public!

I should mention that during this period (Spring of '95) Parker and I also experienced a number of what might be called "mundane paranormal events" in the motorhome (and they continue today!) Our first day out on that abbreviated Spring tour, the cruise control ceased operating (I really lost my "Divine Nonchalance", as Parker calls it, when that happened; I need my cruise control for all those long drives around the country!). We were told after extensive diagnosis that it had to be replaced -- to the tune of several hundred dollars. The next day, while I was driving, I heard a loud voice in my head say, "Try the cruise control!" I did, it worked, and it worked for the next fifteen months. One morning a few weeks later I heard, "Check the water in the house battery." It was very low; we would have lost a $150 battery. And one night, just after we went to bed, the voice proclaimed, "The refrigerator door is open." It was, just barely -- we hadn't noticed it. (The "voice" that speaks to me is *not* some sort of feeling or "inner knowing", by the way. It's a distinct voice, speaking distinct words inside my head -- a voice that is not "me", and knows things I don't know.) On another occasion, while en route from one speaking engagement to the next, we had been looking for a propane dealer all day, as our tank was nearly empty. I began driving and said, "If you're really there helping, we need propane NOW!" Less than one block later -- there was a propane dealer! That sort of thing happens pretty regularly.

One of the strangest incidents occurred in May of '95, about a week after my hypnotic regression with Dr. Koser. We took the motorhome to a repair shop for some carburetor work. This was an establishment we knew -- they'd worked on Magic before. When the work was done, we drove over in Parker's car to get her. I started the engine and began backing the RV out of the garage, but found that the power steering didn't respond. I literally couldn't steer. The mechanic looked under the front axle and discovered that the power steering belt had "fallen off" -- it was lying on the floor under the engine. Upon closer inspection, however, that belt turned out to be brand-new -- and three inches too small! Our belt had, apparently, just disappeared. The two mechanics who worked there and the proprietor all swore up and down that they hadn't touched it. They had worked on Magic right where we had parked her -- about halfway through one of the garage's doors. Nor had they even worked on that part of the chassis; the carburetor was accessed by removing the "doghouse" that covered the engine -- inside the motorhome! They said they never so much as raised the external hood.

It was quite puzzling -- why would they lie about such a thing? It wasn't as though we wouldn't notice that our power steering belt was gone! And even if someone at the garage had removed the belt, what possible use would they have for it? Why not get a new one? And why was a new one -- of the wrong size -- lying under the motorhome? Everyone stood around scratching their heads and wondering out loud while the mechanic attempted to put on a new belt. As it turned out, however, they didn't have one of the proper size in stock. (Ah, ha!...A possible motive for theft? But again, why? Why remove a used one, when for a couple of dollars and a few minutes drive, a new one could be had?) Finally, however, they got a new belt, put it on, and got us out of there. They all seemed to be quite "wierded out" by the whole business!

At the beginning of June, Parker and I left Florida once again, this time on a summer-autumn tour extending from Vermont to Arizona. For a month we worked and played, enjoying each other and life on the road. We spent the last weekend in June in Indianapolis at a sonographer's convention. I interviewed everyone who would talk to me about the Vanishing Twin Phenomenon; what I learned is in the VTP section of this book. I made no progress, however, in the search for my celestial sister.

Until the night of Wednesday, July 5th.

We'd had a busy day, making several repairs to the motorhome and otherwise being domestic. In the evening, Parker read aloud from a most informative book by Lyssa Royal and Keith Priest entitled *Preparing For Contact*. (I strongly urge you to read it if you haven't as yet.) Royal channels "Sasha", a Pleiadian expert in interspecies contact; the book is basically a handbook for "phoning ET." We read that the "veils" between the brain wave states (alpha, beta, delta, theta -- more about this later) grow thinner -- i.e., are more easily passed through -- as one's frequency rises. The theta wave state (the so called "hypnogogic" state through which we pass on our way to or from sleep) provides the easiest access to our consciousness for other-dimensional beings. "OK", I thought as I prepared for bed, "let's lift some veils!" As I drifted off to sleep, I said to Karyl, "I want contact and proof you exist -- NOW!" Needless to say, I put lots of mental and emotional energy into it.

Sometime deep in the night, while having what felt like a "normal" dream, I suddenly "popped" through a veil or membrane of some kind into diffused white light -- and there she was. She had long, strawberry blonde hair and was wearing what looked to me like a bathing suit. There were two columns of light on either side of her. (I found out later what -- or rather who they were.) I said, "It's really you, isn't it?" She laughed and said, "Yes, it is." Suddenly, I felt a male presence coming toward us from my left. Not wanting to lose "contact", I waved him off, saying, "No, no, not now!" He went away. Karyl then said she had to leave, because she couldn't "stay in the fourth density frequency" very long. I asked her if I could hug her. She said, "Yes, of course". We embraced, and the feeling is something I will never forget. It was not like a dream. I could feel her body and the intensity of our emotions in a way that I have never before experienced in the dream state -- or awake, for that matter! The scene faded and I woke up.

During the entire episode I had been thinking, "I can't wait to tell Parker." As soon as I woke up I tried to wake him, only to find that he had awakened at the same time. I excitedly told him what had happened. He replied that just before he awoke, he had been having a very odd and disjointed dream, in which everything was suffused in white light. In the course of the dream, he had been approaching (from the right) a "tall woman dressed in a bathing-suit-like outfit, like a showgirl" with the intention of embracing her. Her attention was directed in front of her, however, and Parker received a clear feeling of "not right now, I'm busy; please don't distract me." The scene evaporated, he woke up, and I asked him if he was awake. Parker and I had both seen her! The interweaving of our dreamtime experiences, and the lucid, vivid nature of my experience, were enough to convince me that Karyl does indeed exist -- even if I didn't completely understand how or where.

I now felt that I could say in public, "I am communicating with my fifth-dimensional twin sister, who is on a spaceship tethered to the planet -- and she's the one who downloaded the information for the *Colorology* book." While that scenario might not "mesh" too well with consensus reality, I could no longer deny it and remain mentally and emotionally honest with myself. And the relief, even joy, that I've seen since on the faces of people for whom my story provides validation has convinced me that I'm doing the right thing. I believe it's important that people experiencing "anomalies" know that there are others like them. I know it was helpful to me. And if acknowledging one's "missing twin" can open lines of communication that empower an individual to grow emotionally, spiritually, psychically or whatever, then it's an important part of my "mission" to be of service in making acknowledgement possible.

Now that I've opened to it, Karyl's presence "in my energy" is a very distinct and compelling experience. When I lecture and she "takes over", some people in the audience can sense it; I get feedback like "I've never seen an aura before, but when you were speaking I could see all sorts of color and lights all around you." Others report seeing actual entities around me. It sure makes my job easier to have company up there. It's quite reassuring. When I do readings, I often feel as though I (Caryl) am "in the basement"; the words coming from my mouth have a kind of reverberation, as if they were echoing down a stairwell. Also, when I reach a very "deep" level of awareness in a reading, my eyes sometimes fill with tears. I'm not weeping; I think it has to do with the intensity of the "signal" coming in. There also seems to be a "translation" problem that crops up occasionally. Karyl pauses or stumbles as if searching for a word -- often a very common word, well known to me. One of my psychic friends told me the same thing happens to her.

At the end of August, in (where else?) Crestone, I met someone who provided the most bizarre and yet the most reassuring confirmation of my research and experience of the Vanishing Twin Phenomenon. Parker and I were "hanging out" at Light Reflections (I had arranged to do readings there during our stay); our schedule had, shall we say, rearranged itself to allow us to spend some considerable time in Crestone, and Parker loved the place as much as I do.

On Saturday, August 26th, Parker and I had just settled down to watch a video of a talk by Dr. Norma Milanovich, when two women came into the store. One of them, who was hobbling on a cane, stopped at the door to read a flyer I had posted referring to what I do and my "single twinship". We heard, "Kaley, come read this!" and I knew we were in for another adventure.

Delfina and Kaley introduced themselves and sat down for a chat. Delfina asked about my research and I explained about the VTP. She kept glancing over at Kaley, saying "See, that's what I told you." I finally asked her if she could relate to the information, and she began telling me a tale as strange as any I've heard.

About half an hour or so into our conversation Parker observed, "You know, you two are related somehow." Delfina and I looked at each other and started crying. That was the beginning of a truly unique "remembering" for both of us.

Delfina had dreamed the night before that she would meet someone the next day that would be very important to her. She even saw in her dream that this person would have painted nails, in the somewhat, um, unusual shade that I had just put on my toenails that morning. When they drove past Light Reflections on their way into Crestone, Delfina said, "We have to stop there on the way back; I think there's someone there I have to meet."

She told me that she had always known she was a twin, and often asked her mother where her "twins" were. Finally, when Delfina was a teenager, her mother confessed that she had been taken aboard "a ship" before Delfina was conceived. When she returned, she "knew" that she was pregnant -- with twins. But only Delfina was born. (Her mother now has no recall of telling Delfina this story.)

Delfina's paternal grandmother was a full-blooded Native American; her mother is of Irish descent. Delfina shows no signs of Indian heritage, although she is an initiated medicine woman and pipe carrier, having spent thirty years learning what she describes as "the ancient ways" from her paternal grandmother, also an initiated medicine woman. Delfina said that her Anglo complexion is a result of her ET paternity --

her "legal" father was not part of the process! She also said that she spent a lot of time searching for her "twins" on the beach in southern California, because she could psychically "see" them walking on the beach. I, of course, was on the beach, but on the other side of the country! She often asked her "Nana" (that's the nickname she gave her grandmother and mentor) if her twin was real and if she would ever meet her; Nana assured her that it would indeed come to pass. She longed for her "twins" so intensely that she and a male friend, who was also a single twin, agreed to "adopt" each other as twins until they found the real thing.

When Delfina was in the fourth grade, she wrote a paper for school about her genetics. She said the extraterrestrials took eggs from two different mothers, genetically "spliced" them together, and inseminated them with "alien" sperm; they then "re-split" the ova and implanted them in their respective mothers, one four years later than the other (I'm four years older than Delfina). Once implanted, the fertilized ova were both split again into identical twins. Delfina became quite indignant when the teacher praised her imagination, saying she would make a good science fiction writer. He didn't understand that she was speaking her truth.

Delfina told us that her mother, aunt, and grandmother had all witnessed her vanish into a "blue beam" in a field behind her house. She was around four at the time; this apparently happened repeatedly. When asked where she had been, Delfina replied, "With my friends, going to school." Extremely precocious, she liked to take things apart and put them back together "so they'd work better." Delfina told her mother about MRI's forty years ago! She told us that the first time she saw a Positive Energy Purple Plate, she said, "Oh, somebody down here figured out how to do this!" She'd seen them on the ships.

In 1987, (there's that year again!) eight people witnessed Delfina's death; she was struck by a lightning bolt that descended from a clear blue sky. The witnesses told her later that the lightning completely engulfed her body, "going in and out of all her orifices." No one, including the doctors, understood how or why she survived. While she was "dead", she had a vision of thirteen people that she would meet, all of whom would be very important figures in her life. "You're one of them," she said to me.

I cannot easily describe how I felt during that first meeting; in a way, it was like finding a long-lost sister, but it was more than that. There also seems to be kind of a "soul bond" between us. The two of us somehow add up to more than the sum of our parts, so to speak. She provided confirmation and validation for me in many areas, as did I for her. She knew about the "glowing silver balls". She later checked her journal and found that she had experienced a dreamtime contact with her "twins" on the night of July 5th -- the same night that I had my encounter with Karyl. She believed that she and her twin were the "columns of light" that I had seen during my meeting with Karyl. In addition, she had also had a dreamtime encounter with her twins on Good Friday, when I "channeled" Karyl for the first time.

We soon found that we had many of the same possessions: we wear identical niobium earcuffs (how many people do you know that wear earcuffs at all?); we share a taste for purple clothes and accessories (we both have violet fanny packs); we have identical "space" T-shirts, toy fiber-optic light wands, boji stones, and any number of "rainbow" things. We had both decorated our RV's with identical garlands of silver stars; we even share an unusual musical taste: we both own and love the "Theta Wave Tape", an audio cassette that is sold as a tool to help bring about ET contact. This is not a tape that is generally available.

But most remarkable of all, perhaps, is what happened the next time we met. Parker and I were in Denver over the Labor Day weekend for a big metaphysical fair; Delfina and Kaley came to visit us. I literally felt a pain in my heart when I saw Kaley pushing Delfina in a wheelchair. Delfina was diagnosed early in childhood as suffering from a degenerative bone disease in her hips; she was told that the condition would worsen throughout her life, and that eventually she would be completely unable to stand or walk. That evening as we left the building to go out to dinner, I pushed her along in the chair. "This has got to go," I told her. "This will not do." I felt that she would have to be able to travel to share the knowledge she had inherited from her Nana, and that being in a wheelchair simply was not compatible with her calling.

Well, the next time we saw them, about two weeks later, Delfina was no longer in the wheelchair. Nor was she relying much on the cane. She told me that her condition had begun to improve from the moment I said, "This has got to go." I had come to her in the dreamtime, she said, and had "worked" on her hips. The improvement was remarkable and rapid. I had vague memories of some sort of dreamtime contact with her, but couldn't remember any details. I was glad to be of help, though, whether I remembered it or not!

I will only add that five weeks later, I (and a lot of other people) saw Delfina dancing, prancing and playing with no pain, no cane and certainly no wheelchair.

There is much, much more to Delfina's story; she will perhaps one day tell it herself. I hope to be able to share more about our interaction in another book. For now, I will only say that

129

she stressed to me repeatedly how important it was to her that I "know" that I am indeed one of her three "twins". I do feel that we are related in some way -- sisters of the soul, stardust twins, who knows? Karyl, you will recall, told me that I began as an identical twin, but due to a "glitch" in the "experiment", my twin died and was replaced with Karyl, who wound up in the fifth dimension. Her father was an ET, but was mine? I certainly feel that I am a product of my father here on Earth! It's all very confusing, to say the least. After I met Delfina, Karyl said in a channeling session that we "don't have it exactly right," but that all would be revealed in good time. I, for one, certainly hope so. All I can say for now is that I feel close to Delfina in a way that I have never felt before; I am sure we have some sort of job to do together. Those who saw an impromptu talk we gave at the International Forum of New Science in Fort Collins in September '95 said that something, a synergy of some kind, happened between the two of us; we created something special in that room. People were crying all over the place!

Finally, in November of '95, Parker and I returned to Florida. My intent was to finish the vanishing twin research and get a complete book written. I felt strongly, based on both the number and nature of my encounters with "single twins", that there was a great need for such a book. I had distributed about 125 detailed questionnaires to people I had met over the past two years who expressed an interest in participating in the research.

To my great surprise and disappointment, only six people responded! I couldn't understand it -- was this project not what I was "supposed" to be doing? Was this not the next phase of my "mission"?

Then, in early December, we went to Atlanta to participate in a big "New Age" expo. There, I was barraged with more tales of youthful or baby "Prodigies" -- children with extraordinary and unexplained abilities of various kinds, who may or may not have any relationship to the VTP. And all too often, these kids were under the care of people who -- usually because of a simple lack of information and resources -- were at a loss to deal with the children's unusual talents. I began to get the message that there might well be a bigger story here, one that at least to some degree encompasses the VTP.

During the trip home from the expo, I reflected on the lack of response from my mailing and the desperation of some of the caregivers I had met in Atlanta and elsewhere, and realized that I must take the time to write about the intuitive children. As soon as I told Parker of my decision, it was as if "my body went happy", as I described it to him. Within five minutes I had completed a mind map of the book (see mind map description and instructions in *Colorology*). I knew I was on the right track.

Just as the pieces of the puzzle magically appeared when needed in the co-creation of *Colorology*, the information began appearing for *Millennium Children*. Parker and I spent the winter in Florida writing a preliminary manuscript. (As a bonus -- not even on my 72-point list -- Parker has a degree in English. We work perfectly together; I get it out of my head and into the computer, and he puts it into coherent sentences!)

The holidays slipped by in a haze of books, phone calls, computer screens and rough drafts. By mid-January -- in spite of recurring bouts of the flu and just in time for the Global Sciences Congress in Tampa, at which I was scheduled to speak -- we had put together a monograph titled *The Millennium Children: Secrets of Raising An Intuitive Child.*

I intended to include this information in my Global Sciences talk.

Unfortunately, when the time to talk rolled around, I had a vicious case of laryngitis! My voice was little more than a croak. But this was the Global Sciences Congress, and I had a message to deliver. I ascended the podium on that Friday afternoon determined to tough it out.

But before I got ten minutes into my lecture, it became clear to me that my voice would not survive the hour. A few weeks earlier, my famous psychic friend had told me that he had a conversation with Karyl in which she told him how grateful she was to me for all the help I had given her in understanding the third dimension. He said, "She wants to help you. All you have to do is ask." So, as one part of me was croaking out words, another, silent part was screaming telepathically at Karyl, "You said you wanted to help. Well, now's the time! I can't do this!" Almost instantaneously, my voice cleared, as I felt her come into my body and "take over". In great relief, Caryl retired to "the basement" and let Karyl do it.

After the lecture I was informed by several of my psychic friends in the audience that my aura and voice changed at the same time, about ten minutes into my lecture. Dean Stonier came up to me afterwards and said, "I've heard you speak several times before, but I've never heard anything like that. I want you to speak at the August conference in Denver."

Karyl told me the day after my lecture that it was necessary to weaken me to the point that I would allow her to move into my energy. My need for control had forced my fifth-dimensional friends to take drastic measures! Unfortunately, my body was too weak from those bouts with the flu to bounce back quickly. It took me a week to recover my voice.

Over the next couple of months we put together an expanded version of the *Millennium Children* monograph. In early April we headed for Eureka Springs and the Ozark UFO Conference, which has become a regular stop for me. I had an opportunity to speak and the response to the *Millennium Children* information was most gratifying. As the 1996 tour progressed, people continued to come forward with remarkable stories.

After the Ozark UFO Conference, a group of us decided to investigate a well-known haunted hotel in town. One member of the group had been there before and knew which area of the hotel had "spooks". As soon as I entered the area I got a very strange, tingling feeling. I centered myself and invited the spirit to talk. She said she had been paralyzed and had died in the hotel (it had been a famous cancer clinic at one time). She said she was stuck and couldn't leave the earth plane. One of the women in our group was a hypnotherapist and, having dealt with spirits before, knew how to assist the unquiet ones. She told her to "look for the light". The spirit got very indignant and said she didn't see any "light". The hypnotherapist kept describing the light, telling her she was dead and it was time for her to go on. "Just keep looking for the light," she said. Suddenly I (through this spirit's "eyes") could see a small light above her head and said so. The hypnotherapist told her to take a running start and jump to the light. She did and I felt her energy depart. This was my first experience with what is known in some circles as soul retrieval or rescue.

During a reading a few weeks later, a client asked if together, we could help his girlfriend (who had died a couple of months before) to get to the Light. I told him that I had apparently done it before and was willing to try. Once I made contact, he told her that it was okay for her to go, and assured her that he would be all right. We both focussed our intent on showing her the Light. Soon, I saw a bright light appear to her, and she was gone. During these experiences, I'm able to "tune in" to what the deceased spirit is seeing and feeling, yet retain my identity. It's very similar to what happens when I do past life readings.

Another change occurred in my psychic abilities at this time: I developed the ability to tell the difference between possible and probable realities. I was told that before coming into the physical body we decide according to our "Life Color" what issues we want to work on, what gifts and skills we want to develop, and what karma we want to balance in that lifetime. Life was described as being similar to a maze with many possible pathways. If we pay attention to our intuition, to signs and "coincidences", we will be guided to follow our chosen life path and carry out our "mission". Free Will always exists, however; we have the choice of following the pre-selected path or not. Depending upon our choices, there are possible or probable realities for the future. The "picture" I see of possible realities is shaky and foggy; probable realities are clearer and brighter.

And so I gradually have become comfortable living in a very strange place; it has come to feel like home. My "paranormal" abilities continue to shift and expand, and the adventure continues. I know that there are many other people out there with comparable experience; part of "following my bliss" is having the opportunity to be out on the road meeting them. But whatever the future holds, be it continuing travel from the "home base" of an intentional spiritual community, or some scenario of which I haven't even dreamed, I can only be

134

grateful for the special and wonderful life I have been blessed with so far. I will continue to live in the faith that "the shift", however it manifests, will be one that provides for everyone an unlimited opportunity to do what all of us -- plants, animals, humans, all Life around, on or in Mother Earth -- do best: GROW!!!

Blessings to you on your journey. May the information in this book be of service to you through all your shifts.

Clearwater, Florida
January, 1997

Part II

The Vanishing Twin Phenomenon

Vanishing Twin Phenomenon

I met a fifteen year-old girl in Boston who had become pregnant and had been abandoned by the father. Her parents agreed to help her out, so she resolved to have the baby. Early in the pregnancy, her doctor told her she was carrying twins. She had experienced UFO encounters since childhood, and awoke one morning certain that something had happened during the night. The next time she went to the doctor he informed her she now had only one baby. After her child was born, she was mourning the one that was missing to the extent that she was unable to take care of the baby she had. She was sent to a "post-partum blues" support group. The counselor decided that she was not suffering from that postnatal syndrome, but something was indeed seriously wrong; some sort of treatment was called for. When I met her, she had consented to institutionalization the following week, because she was convinced she was crazy. Weeping with joy and relief and waving one of my books, she said, "Now I know I'm not crazy and I'm not going to let them put me away!" No one ever told this young woman about the Vanishing Twin Phenomenon.

Trudy received a frantic message on her telephone recorder from her granddaughter, Lannie, age three. "Mema, come quick, me and Mommy argue!" A few hours later, when she heard the message, she called her daughter to see what was the matter. Her daughter said, "Oh, Mom, Lannie doesn't know your number and doesn't even know how to use the phone." She was quite shocked when Trudy played back the message for her, and invited Trudy over to discuss the incident. When she arrived Lannie was all excited and said, "Mommy doesn't remember when me and her were in your (Trudy's) tummy." Her mother said, "I have tried to explain to her all day that she was in my tummy and I was in your tummy, but she wouldn't listen." Lannie explained, "No, I was a boy and we were in Mema's tummy, but I didn't want to be a boy this time, I needed to be a girl and Mema couldn't have any more kids." Lannie's mother had been one of twins, and her twin brother had died in utero, a fact Lannie could not have possibly known!

Eric, three, asked his mother one day if she remembered "when he and Granddad were twins."

A woman came up to me after a presentation and said, "Now I know what's happening to my husband; this explains it!" It seems that at times her husband was "different, somehow. He looks the same, but there is something wrong." (She could always tell when they made love.) One day she asked him if he really was her husband. In what she described as "a different, robotic voice", he forcibly responded, "We will not speak of that again!" It scared her so much, they never did! She said, "They're switching him, now I know it for sure." He was supposed to have been twins, according to his mother, and he fit much of the Prodigy profile.

One of the Prodigies is a twin whose mother was never diagnosed with twins, but upon delivery of the first baby the doctor exclaimed, "Here comes somebody else!" and out popped our Prodigy. He has a unique blood type that cures a rare brain disease and does not look like anyone else in his family, including his twin brother. He has come up with a "free energy" motor, as well as many other inventions.

Another single twin I met having learned early in her life about the VTP and the idea that one twin might "absorb" the other, had since been haunted by the conviction that she had "eaten" her twin!

139

Jack and Jim Weiner were part of the "Allagash Abduction" made famous by Raymond Fowler, during which four young men were taken aboard an alien craft while on a camping trip in northern Maine. The abductors were particularly interested in the fact that Jack and Jim are identical twins. The twins also report having visions of ghosts as children. (It's interesting that in a TV interview, they recalled how the end of the bed would "go down" as the ghost sat on it -- just as my brother Tim had described it!)

I interviewed a woman from Louisiana (let's name her "Paula") and her best friend "Jill" who about five years ago discovered by means of a blood test that she was pregnant. Her boyfriend wanted nothing to do with it, so she left him, driving at night to Paula's house to stay with her during the pregnancy. Suddenly her car filled with blue light. The next thing she remembered was being in a roadside park three hours later, covered with a "strange grease" and lying crosswise over her bucket seats with the gear shift sticking her in the back. Having experienced a number of unusual "encounters" and periods of missing time throughout her life, Jill simply collected her wits and went on to Paula's house. Over the next couple of months the pregnancy did not proceed normally -- her stomach didn't grow. She went to the doctor and discovered that she was no longer pregnant. There were not even any physical signs that she ever had been.

A few years later, Jill married and became pregnant again. She went in for a sonogram and the doctors were shocked to find a strange "mass" in her uterus along with the baby. Four different doctors examined her and found this mass was free-floating, not attached to the uterine wall. They were totally baffled, but agreed that it should be removed and made an appointment with a specialist in another town for

140

four days later. When she arrived for the surgery the incredulous doctors found, upon doing another sonogram, nothing except her fetus. When the baby was born, Jill also delivered an empty placenta. She has the sonogram to prove it.

Jill's baby girl has huge blue eyes and thin blonde hair. Jill and Paula both described her to me as "beautiful, but very strange". They also both commented that she has the ugliest temper of any human being they have ever seen. Paula told me that Jill used to run out of the baby's room screaming, because the baby kept doing "strange things" (she wouldn't elaborate) and scared her. At seventeen months the baby would not speak. However, at seven months she had been saying "Mommy", "Daddy" and "I love you". One day the baby's aunt came to visit. The baby said "I love you," and her aunt started to repeat the phrase, but the baby put her fingers on her Aunt's lips to stop her and has not spoken since -- except to jabber incomprehensibly at "thin air", apparently talking to "someone" no one else can see. Jill's story includes numerous encounters with aliens, missing medical records, physical anomalies (she can hear sounds beyond the normal range of hearing), poltergeist activity and missing time. She did not menstruate for a period of five years at one stretch. She has had several "dreams" in which she has given birth to twins.

I learned from Debbie Jordan ("Kathy Davis" in Budd Hopkins' book Intruders) *that one of her sisters is apparently a single twin (another one of those family stories). Debbie tells of being presented by the "intruders" with a number of half-human, half-alien "hybrid" children; she could not recall any twins among them.*

In a very strange book from Wildflower Press entitled Secret Vows, *Bert and Denise Twiggs tell the tale of their intermarriage with a humanoid couple from Andromeda by the name of Beek and Magna. By day an apparently average middle-class American couple with three wonderful children of their own, Bert and Denise (and their children) led a nocturnal existence aboard the Andromedan mother ship, a vast structure that contained a perfect "replica" of a small town on Earth! Even more incredible, Denise and Magna between them bore TWENTY-FIVE more children (including two sets of twins), fathered either by Beek or Bert; Magna delivered twenty-two of them! The four times that Denise carried a child fathered by Beek (one miscarried), the Andromedans used their advanced technology to "mask" the "hybrid" fetus from detection, and removed it before it came to term (these pregnancies occurred when Denise was already pregnant by Bert). The reason for all this complex gynecological activity, according to the Andromes, was that "Andromes...cannot have children within their own society because of severe genetic disturbances that have occurred to their race in recent generations." They had therefore found it necessary to dip into Homo Sapiens' gene pool. All human participation in this activity, contrary to some of the tales of the Greys, is strictly voluntary, but because of the potentially traumatic effects upon the limited psyches of humans, and because of the need to be as unobtrusive as possible in their interactions with humans, Bert and Denise recalled their "other life" only gradually. They also found other couples having a similar experience, with whom they were able to confirm various details of their lives "aboard ship". Of course, their "3-D" children also provided verification that they were indeed experiencing this bizarre double life; the whole family was in it together.*

An obstetrics nurse at a large hospital told me about a patient at the hospital clinic who, in her first trimester, had been diagnosed as pregnant with twins (two heartbeats, abnormally early weight gain). The next month a sonogram was done and two babies were visible. The following month, three babies were visible on the sonogram; this was confirmed by the doctor and sonographer. One month later, to everyone's surprise, only two babies were visible. The following month three babies were visible again. By this time concern on the part of the hospital staff had grown to the point that the woman and the sonograms were carefully checked by several doctors and sonographers. No explanation was forthcoming. Finally, in the seventh month an x-ray was ordered by her doctor. X-rays are rarely if ever done any more due to the risk of radiation damage. Two babies showed up on the X-ray and two babies were actually born.

Ruth, a 58-year-old psychologist, heard a tape of my VTP lecture and called to tell me what a "revelation" the information was to her. She said that her mother had insisted until her death in 1974 that Ruth was a twin. She had been told by her doctor that she was carrying twins, and claimed that she could psychically "see" them. "She delivered under anesthesia, as this was standard practice for her day. When she woke up she found out that she had just one premature baby girl. She became very upset...My father and grandfather had to reassure her that only one baby was born. All her life she was never able to accept this..." Ruth felt for a while that she had a twin but "as I got older I never gave it any more thought." When she heard the tape of my lecture, she said she felt "a deep sense of relief, like some shadow had been lifted from me. It felt right...All my life I have had a missing piece and now it has come to rest."

143

There are predominantly two types of twins: identical (monozygotic) and fraternal (dizygotic). Two thirds of all twins are fraternal, the result of two separately fertilized ova growing in the womb at the same time. Like all siblings, fraternals share roughly fifty percent of their genes. The only real difference between dizygotic twins and single birth siblings is that the former share the womb for nine months. (We'll explore some of the ramifications of that experience in this chapter.) About half of fraternals born are of the same sex; the other fifty percent, obviously, are male-female pairings.

The remaining third of twins born are monozygotic: one fertilized egg divides into two separate (but identical) zygotes (that's what a fetus is called until it's big enough to be called a fetus). Identical twins are essentially "clones"; because their genetic structures are exactly the same, they are always of the same sex, and are nearly if not completely impossible to tell apart; they share similar dental characteristics, handprints and footprints. (Fingerprints, however, remain unique with identicals as with all humans -- another marvelous "mystery of Nature"!) There is a fifty-fifty chance that any set of identical twins will be female.

A variation within the monozygotic group is "mirror" twinning: these pairs have identical characteristics on opposite sides of their bodies -- whorls or cowlicks in the hair, birthmarks, even internal organs.

There are two other types of twinning, both comparatively rare. Two eggs from consecutive ovarian cycles may be separately fertilized and develop as twins; this is known as superfecundation. Or a single egg can divide and each of its halves be fertilized separately. Both of these twin types would be considered fraternals. Triplets, quadruplets, and other

144

multiples may result from either the fraternal or identical twinning process, or as any combination of the two.

In the earliest stages of pregnancy, the zygote lodges in the wall of the uterus and begins a very rapid growth process. It's surrounded by two membranes, or sacs: the inner one is called an amnion, the outer a chorion. Fraternal twins always have separate amnions and chorions, as well as entirely separate placentas. Identicals, however, show a number of variations: about sixty percent have a common chorion and separate amnions (inner sacs); about six percent share both sacs; and about a third have, like fraternals, separate chorions *and* amnions. This last configuration until recent years created some confusion in the birthing world: it was believed that *only* fraternal twins had separate outer and inner sacs. There are probably a number of identical twins walking around today who believe they are "merely" fraternals! See *Having Twins* by Elizabeth Noble, for diagrams and more details on all this, should you be interested.

As we saw earlier, my first glimpse into the Vanishing Twin Phenomenon (hereafter referred to as VTP) came when Robyn Quail showed me the excerpt from the book *Pathology of the Human Placenta*. That excerpt stated in part, "When the diagnosis of twins was made prior to ten weeks, the rate of disappearance was 75 percent. When diagnosis was made between ten and fifteen weeks, the disappearance rate was 62 percent; when twins were first diagnosed after fifteen weeks, none disappeared. The 'vanishing twin' is thus a feature of early pregnancy..."

Research in some other medical textbooks revealed that VTP is a well-documented occurrence, usually explained away by the medical establishment as a process called "resorption", in which a fetus is somehow consumed or absorbed either by its twin or by its mother. This theory holds up only until the end of the first trimester; after that, a fetus is too big to "vanish" without somebody noticing! Several medical professionals I have interviewed, do not believe this is a viable explanation at any stage.

"Teratoma tumors" are sometimes found on or in a surviving twin; they may contain hair, bone, teeth or various types of tissue. Some theorize they might be what's left of a vanished twin consumed by its sibling. There are also a variety of gestation anomalies such as "blighted ovum", "missed abortion", "fetus papyraceous", spontaneous abortion and false pregnancy that could explain a "vanishing" twin (if you want details on these, see *Having Twins*). But I know of two instances in which two heartbeats were detected as late as two hours before delivery, and another in which there were two heartbeats until ten hours before the birth of one child. "Mistakes", say the doctors. "Something's going on here," say the mothers. I tend to agree with the mothers.

In the years before sonograms, diagnosis of twins was usually based on the detection of two heartbeats with a stethoscope, and/or the rate of growth of the mothers abdomen during the pregnancy. Since the mid-seventies and the advent of ultrasound and sonograms, much more precise knowledge of what goes on in the early stages of pregnancy, including twinning, has been possible. Elizabeth Noble writes, "With increasing use of ultrasound, it has been observed that more multiples are lost in the uterus than previously thought -- some studies say as high as 80 percent of twin pregnancies."[15] As near as I can tell from my research, it's about seventy-five percent: three-quarters of the women diagnosed with twins give birth to only one child. Am I alone in finding that quite remarkable?

We have discussed the "missing fetus syndrome" as it has arisen in the UFO literature. The director of ultrasound at a major hospital told me that the vanishing fetus is very common in single conceptions as well; there is simply no surviving twin to expose it. A woman may have a late period accompanied by heavy bleeding and never even know she had been pregnant. He also felt that the resorption explanation applies only during the early stages of pregnancy and certainly not after the first trimester. He had not found any cases of VTP after the first three months; when I told him of the cases related to me of much later disappearance, he said, "They must have been mistakes."

What are the "symptoms", if any of the VTP? The mother may bleed, have cramps, or show decreased hormone levels during the pregnancy. There may well be no indications at all, however. If a woman has already borne twins, she is more likely to do so again. A history of twins in the family increases the likelihood of fraternal twins being conceived, but that does not hold true for identicals -- they appear to occur randomly. Interestingly enough, the "alien abduction" phenomenon also seems to run in families, according to the research conducted so far.

At a sonographers' conference in 1995, I got a look at the difficulties those technicians have with the VTP. After pointing out twins to the mother one month, they find themselves confronted with a situation in which only one baby shows up when the mother returns the following month. "Professional protocol" (only the doctor can discuss bad news with the patient) prevents them from discussing the situation with the understandably confused mother. To make matters worse, the doctor's explanation may be brief and unsatisfactory; his patient load may not permit anything more. While the VTP may be commonplace and easily explained

147

away in the minds of many obstetric professionals, such is not necessarily the case with the woman undergoing the experience! Many women, unable to gain a clear understanding of what has happened to them, are left feeling bereft, with an "emptiness" inside that never goes away. A couple of the sonographers I interviewed shared with me their frustration at being blamed by a physician for incorrectly diagnosing the presence of twins, in the absence of any other viable explanation.

So what's going on here? Is ET making off with human embryos? There is no scarcity of such tales, going back as far as current historical records allow. Fairies, goblins, elves, demons, what have you -- all have at one time or another in human folklore demonstrated a great interest in acquiring our children -- although usually after birth, rather than before! I certainly do not believe that all of these unborn, undeveloped children are being swept up into spaceships of various kinds -- but my research and my personal experience tells me that some are. How we deal with that reality may well have a great bearing on the future of our species.

But regardless of who's doing what to whom, it is widely recognized that the psychological effect of losing a sibling with whom one has shared the womb -- whether before or after birth -- can be devastating. A surviving twin now may be legally compensated for the wrongful death of his/her twin. Many adult "single twins" seek professional counselling in order to find explanations of their apparently causeless psychological problems, only to find that when through one modality or another they become aware of and/or come to terms with their missing twin, the problems often go away, or are at least considerably alleviated. Elizabeth Noble points out in *Having Twins* that "surviving twin" problems are so common that many therapists now specialize in the field.

William J. Baldwin, D.D.S., Ph.D., author of *Spirit Releasement Therapy: A Technique Manual,* has discovered the VTP in his research with "entity attachments". His perspective is that the missing or dead twin astrally "attaches" to the survivor, communicating with him/her and influencing his or her life.

Raymond W. Brandt, Ph.D., publishes *Twins World* magazine for all twins and the *Twinless Twins* newsletter, as well as coordinating an annual summer convention for twins who have lost their twin. His publications are full of stories and poetry by twinless twins (a termed coined by Brandt) attempting to deal with their intense grief. The very special nature of the twin relationship is apparent in the pages of Brandt's magazines. (The movie *Nell,* starring Jodie Foster, vividly dramatizes this bond.) In the September 1996 edition of *Twins World* Brandt writes, "Now couple the 'vanishing' phenomena with what we as medical and scientific practitioners learn more and more about the intensity of early *in utero* bonding of multiples. It may behoove us all to be more broad-minded and open to the awareness that there are far more 'twinless twins' living than were here-to-fore believed. Some estimate that as high as one in ten conceptions begins as twins."

Alice Rose, Ph.D., a Primal Regression therapist and author of *Bonds of Fire,* has also discovered the phenomenon in her practice. She has worked with approximately ten individuals who have spontaneously experienced the pain and trauma of losing their twin in the womb. She described these sessions to me as "gut-wrenching: screaming, begging and crying for their twin not to go, offering them their food, blood and life, if they will only stay." After I described my UFO-related research to her, she mentioned that some of these twins had also described abduction experiences. She suggested that I look at the possibility that the surviving twin is so open and longing for contact with his or her twin, that it leaves him or her open to contact with other entities and dimensions, as well as the missing twin. Dr. Rose is herself a single twin. She does not believe, that missing twins are being taken by ETs.

In *Primal Connections,* Elizabeth Noble -- also a single twin -- shares her work with single twins using primal therapy. She states,

> Loss of a twin at any time is a tragedy; the powerful imprint of this experience in early pregnancy is sometimes more profound than the loss at birth or later. One reason may be the phenomenon of survivor guilt. Survivors of a twin pregnancy...feel that something they did ("took all the nutrients or space") enabled them to live but caused their twin to die. Mothers of a surviving twin have reported various behavior such as the child talking to a make-believe companion, dreaming of a twin, or setting the dinner table for the nonexistent twin." She says about single twins, "...we never give up, to compensate for the twin that did. The conflict over space and survival in the uterus may manifest itself in later life as issues of identity and creativity. Since I understand the impact of twin loss in unknowing survivors, both personally and professionally, I encourage mothers to affirm the twinship of the survivor and acknowledge the death of the twin at anniversaries, discussions of pregnancy or birth, and other family events.[16]

David B. Chamberlain, Ph.D., a San Diego psychologist and author of *Babies Remember Birth,* has also come across the VTP in his clinical psychology and hypnosis practice.

Some of the more common psychological manifestations of the single twin "syndrome" are "always feeling lonely" or feeling like someone or something is missing; being particularly sensitive; having unreasonable feelings of responsibility, guilt and/or haunting feelings of being a parasite or destroyer. Noble says, "...unlike cases of survivor guilt from accidents, the experience of twin loss (*in utero*) is not part of the conscious mind and therefore is unavailable for discussion, rationalization, and integration without assistance...Twins from whom information about a twin's death is hidden or who are not allowed to express their feelings about the loss suffer most."[15]

Relationship issues, such as an inability to make deep commitments for fear of sudden loss or abandonment, difficulty sleeping alone and obsessively seeking a "soulmate" are common for single twins. They often want to be with their mates all the time; they have no desire for time alone. They are usually monogamous, even developing an extreme dependence on their mates. Personal boundaries may be difficult for the single twin to establish.

A fascination with mirrors, silky shimmery material, reflections and facial asymmetry, as well as lefthandedness, stuttering and malformations (such as clubfoot, extra fingers or toes, or heart anomalies) have all been attributed more to twins than to singletons.

Dr. Alice Rose notes the following food and eating issues in *Bonds of Fire:*

> Food and eating are overly important issues for surviving twins. When the womb does not have enough nourishment, the surviving twin can feel that her sister died because she took all the food (which

may or may not be true). So there can be a great deal of guilt associated with food, a lifelong worry about eating too much. Twins can share the placenta and have to develop a system of cooperation with feeding, so all kinds of issues can arise about cooperating or not cooperating around food. Surviving twins may sneak food and eat when no one else can discover them. Or they may be secretly greedy about food. No one, not even their mates, can know how greedy they are. A slow, painful starvation may have preceded the death of one twin, so the surviving twin can feel panicky about getting enough food. They may wolf down food, or be unable to wait to eat. Dieting may feel like an impossibility. It may bring on feelings of dying. On the other hand, I have treated a surviving twin who begged her sister to stay with her. She promised that she would not eat if she would just stay. To this day if she gets upset, she cannot eat.[2]

Dr. Rose also notes that taking food off your mate's plate, but not liking it if they take food off yours, can be symptomatic of a single twin, as can feeling compelled to clean your plate. Bulimia and anorexia can also be an issue.

We see some of the same psychological characteristics in the "intuitive child": unexplainable feelings of loss or of "missing something"; guilt; fascination with mirrors; hearing voices; lefthandedness; the "imaginary friend" and emotional sensitivity.

Christopher Millar is an Australian physical and family therapist who specializes in VTP and is a single twin himself. In *Having Twins,* Elizabeth Noble quotes him on homosexuality:

Millar postulates that confusion about self following the death of a monozygotic twin *in utero* may result in autoimmune diseases. He also believes that the disordered gender identity of homosexuals and transsexuals may be a result of loss of one member of a mixed-sex monozygotic pair. That is, the loss of an identical self of the opposite sex results in sexual confusion. Another suggestion Millar makes is that a lost monozygotic twin may influence the development of schizophrenia, "loss of ego boundaries strongly suggesting some confusion about what is Self and what is not Self."[15]

Graham Farrant is a psychiatrist and a pioneer in the clinical study of prenatal and perinatal psychology. Quoting again from *Having Twins*:

Graham Farrant was approached separately by monozygotic female twins seeking primal therapy. This procedure puts patients in touch with their physical and emotional feelings by causing them to regress to the earliest time at which they experienced those feelings. Both twins suffered from sexual confusion that had affected their marriages and subsequent separations. Extraordinarily, they began to experience similar problems independently and although they were not associating closely with each other, they would relive almost identical experiences. Most striking was their separate yet identical experience of conception. Both recalled two sperm entering one egg at the same time. Both experienced the first sperm pushing the competitor away from the egg, then fertilizing the egg, which split into twins. The brief presence of the second Y sperm, which would have produced a male child, was sufficient to create their sexual confusion. After therapy, one of the women returned to her husband and the other entered a new and meaningful heterosexual relationship.[15]

I received an irate letter from a homosexual twin who had experienced ET contact throughout her life and who took great exception to a reference I made during a lecture to the above material. She was absolutely sure her homosexuality had nothing to do either with her twinship or her ET contact. "Jackie", on the other hand, was stunned when she heard my lecture. Her sexual confusion had tormented her all her life. She said, "I knew I was a single twin, but I never connected that to my sexuality. I wish I had put the two together long ago -- I would have made different choices had I known. I am sure my life would have been much different and a lot less painful." Let me make it clear that I do not mean to judge homosexuality one way or the other here; I am simply presenting the data.

From *Having Twins*: "According to a 1986 article by Elizabeth Bryan, Sudden Infant Death Syndrome (SIDS) is at least twice as common among twins, both monozygotic and dizygotic, as among singletons...Smialek reviewed nine cases of twins dying suddenly and simultaneously but could find no cause."[15] This, of course, brings up all sorts of interesting questions about the physical and emotional bonds between twins.

It has been the case, both for me and for others I have interviewed, that once one acknowledges the possibility of being a single twin, contact with the "missing" twin increases and becomes clearer. Again, I do not insist that someone connecting with a vanished twin is necessarily involved with ETs. For those who believe in a continuation of life beyond our three-dimensional reality, such contact may be understood simply as the dead twin's spirit communicating with the surviving twin. Dr. Rose found that "the dead twin often stays in contact with the surviving twin in a 'guardian angel' type capacity". *Twins World* magazine and the *Twinless Twins* newsletter contain many accounts of single twins who were saved from danger or death by the intervention of their missing twins. Dr. Brandt himself tells a harrowing tale of how his twin, who had died at the age of twenty, saved his life during the Korean War.

The psychic or telepathic bond between twins, particularly identical twins, has been well-documented. Some extreme and fascinating examples of this bond are mentioned in an article in the Australian magazine *Nexus* (Issue No.6). The piece concerns twins separated at birth and brought up totally apart, usually without the knowledge of each other's existence.

> The 'Jim twins' at five weeks were adopted by different families who were each told the other twin died at birth. Raised 130 kms apart they eventually met when they were 39 years old. Both boys were named James, both grew up with adopted brothers called Larry. Both were good at math and hated spelling and both had owned dogs called Troy. Both had married girls called Linda, divorced and then married 'Bettys'. Their first sons were named respectively, James Allan and James Alan. Both families holidayed at the same small beach in St. Petersburg, Florida for years, driving their Chevrolets. Both Jims had worked as petrol pump attendants, deputy sheriffs and at one time in the same hamburger chain. They shared the same nail biting, eating, drinking and sleeping habits and both

shared the same hobbies of carpentry and technical drawing.

Twins have been known to experience simultaneous illness or injury even when separated by great distances. From the same *Nexus* article: "In 1975 Nettie Porter was involved in a car crash. Her identical twin Nita Hurst was at work 700 kms away. Suddenly she felt stabbing pains in her left leg. She rolled up her trousers and was amazed to see bruises appearing up her leg. The matron in the hospital at which she worked bore witness to this phenomenon and the bruises corresponded to Nettie's injuries."

Sometimes pain transference in twins can be fatal; sisters Helen and Peg are a case in point. Again, from *Nexus*: "One night Helen woke screaming and white-faced with a terrible pain in her chest. She managed to reach her father before passing out, but died in the ambulance on the way to the hospital - as did Peg who had been in a car accident at exactly the same time Helen awoke. She died from massive injuries caused by the steering wheel penetrating her chest."

There are a variety of legends and myths about twins including Esau and Jacob, Romulus and Remus, Castor and Pollox, and Leda and the Swan, to name a few. Perhaps the enduring nature of these symbols, as well as society's fascination with twins, arises from the fact that many more people are surviving twins -- although unaware of it consciously -- than anyone ever suspected until recently.

An intriguing legend comes from Nigeria. According to an article by Hillel Schwartz entitled "The Legend of the Vanishing Twin" published in the Summer, 1994 issue of the quarterly *Parabola:*

Among the Yoruba of western Nigeria, whose natural twinning rate is at least twice that of any other people in the world, each individual is thought to be born with a Sky-Double who enacts in the heavens above that which corresponds to the actions of the earthly child below. When twins are born, one is assumed to be a landlocked Sky-Double, but no one can tell which of the two was meant to be born on earth, which in the heavens, so both must be honored equally and welcomed happily into this world as sky-blessings, "majestic and beautiful."

Elvis Presley had a twin who died at birth, and with whom he is said to have communicated throughout his life. In a touching article published in the October issue of *Angel Times* magazine, we find an interesting statement by Mary L. Jones, a childhood friend of Elvis' family:

> I remember Elvis saying so seriously (in 1966)...that he thought he was instilled into his mother's womb along with her natural son (Elvis' twin, Jesse), and that Jesse chose to die, giving Elvis a path to an earth life. He always had visions even as a child and felt that he was somehow different and not of this earth and was held to earth to bring some new understanding and love to its people, to guide them to a higher realm of spiritual awareness through music and that he was doomed because he could not adjust to earth's gravity and pressure, it was burning him up. (Elvis' normal temperature was over 100 degrees.)

According to the article, Elvis is said to have communicated with beings as a child who showed him a vision of "a guy dancing, kind of, on stage under lights dressed in white, with

157

colors all around". Besides meditating and praying, Elvis reportedly read over 1,000 books, mostly on spiritual subjects.

While engaged in the VTP research, I always displayed at my booth at the various events in which I participated a large sign which read:

Vanishing Twin Phenomenon

Current Medical Statistics:

*75% of the women diagnosed with twins only deliver one baby.
*2 in 75 people actually begin life as twins.

Signs of possible "single twin":

*Mother experienced bleeding or cramps during pregnancy
*Clubfoot, excess fingers or toes
*Lefthandedness
*Childhood "imaginary friend"
*Feelings of incompleteness & loneliness
*Fascination with mirrors
*Feelings of responsibility or guilt
*Dreams or paranormal experience of a twin
*High I.Q./exceptional talent

The reactions to the sign of those who resonated with the information for any reason whatever were endlessly fascinating: Some started crying, some trembled or "got goosebumps"; some simply nodded their heads knowingly. Some stood, rooted to the spot, until they had absorbed every word -- then left my booth rapidly, sometimes running! For those who stayed around to seek more information, there were several key questions I always tried to ask:

1. Which of these indications ring a bell for you? 2. Have you ever seen a UFO? 3. Have you ever studied the UFO phenomenon? 4. Are there other twins in your family? 5. Are you psychic?

More often than not, the answer to questions two through five was "Yes". For these people, learning about the VTP seemed to help fit together some previously incongruous parts of their lives.

For some of the mothers of single twins I interviewed (or those who felt they were), learning about the VTP was a great help, particularly to those who had experienced such a pregnancy before the mid-1970's when, as we've already seen, the detection of multiple pregnancies was more "hit or miss". Questions like "Where's my other baby?" were blown off with vague statements about heartbeat echoes and the mysteries of gestation. Granted, there are even now many mysteries of gestation, but such responses offer little comfort to a woman who believes she has just lost a child!

The experiments the Nazis performed on twins at Auschwitz, as monstrous and inhumane as they were, clearly show how ideally suited twins -- especially identicals -- are to medical and genetic experimentation. Are the "Greys", those mysterious entities that are the subject of so much ink and videotape these days -- as well as a number of less well-publicized non-human entities -- using twins, born and unborn, for their research purposes? I came across an Associated Press dispatch that ran in my local paper on October 8, 1993, under the title, "STUDY: MUTATION COULD AFFECT ONE TWIN". It concerned a new study of the VTP and contained the statement, "Two of every 75 people had a twin brother or sister and lost it before birth.". It also contained a direct quote from a Dr. Judith Hall of the University of British Columbia in Vancouver, Canada, that I found extremely interesting: "The recognition of an 'alien' group of cells would lead to a physical separation and the development of another embryo." Numerous attempts to contact Dr. Hall for comment proved fruitless; she was unavailable and never returned my calls. What did she mean by that remark, and why was the word "alien" in quotes? Could she have been trying to tell us something?

Once again, I don't mean to suggest that all missing twins are on spaceships. There are many things that can go wrong between conception and birth; the pollution of our air, food and water, the effects of legal and illegal pharmaceuticals (Remember Thalidomide? It's back as a possible AIDS treatment!), the emotional and physical condition of the mother -- all this and more can create problems in the womb. However, I have as of this writing interviewed some one hundred thirty people who have some relationship to multiple births -- fraternal or identical twins, triplets or quads -- as well as some experience of UFO/ET contact phenomena. Some examples of their stories appear at the beginning of the chapter. Remember also "BB", who worked with about a hundred single twins in 1980. Why did they come to her? How did they know? BB couldn't explain it! Kurt Benirschke, M.D., one of the authors of *Pathology of the Human Placenta*, wrote in another article, "Sometimes, when twins are recognized by sonography, one embryo truly vanishes and cannot be traced, even by skilled examination of the delivered placenta." It does seem we have a mystery here that would bear serious investigation, by medical professionals as well as researchers of the anomalous.

My youngest brother Ted was the perfect example of a single twin who couldn't integrate his experience. As I mentioned earlier, he started out life as a twin. He was never told of his twinship until the night my mother told me that the twins were probably triplets and that something had been either "slurped in or out" of her while she was pregnant with Ted. I called Ted that same night and told him the whole story. My UFO/ET research had always been an uncomfortable subject for him, and he was not very receptive to the concept of a twin somewhere and/or its (or his) possible relationship to ETs. He later told one of our siblings that he didn't want me to ever mention it to him again, so I didn't -- until three weeks before he died of AIDS in August of 1996, five days after his thirty-fifth birthday.

As the twin research unfolded, I couldn't help but reflect on Ted's life, in which I could see all the characteristics of a single twin manifested. Before he was a year old, Ted began screaming hysterically during the night, his little body shaking with terror until my mother came to get him. When she arrived, he would frantically point out the window and under the bed. The only way she could settle him down was to take him to her bed. When he was thirty, my sister and I asked him if he remembered those experiences. His eyes filled with tears as he explained, "The monsters were out there and I knew if I screamed loud enough someone would come to get me so the monsters wouldn't -- and they never got me!" As soon as Ted learned how to crawl out of his crib, he came to sleep in my bed and did so for about two years. He was obviously seeing something and was terrified. He had dreadful nightmares throughout his life from which he awoke screaming, drenched in sweat.

Ted started reading my mother's metaphysical books when he was ten years old. One day, while practicing meditation and

161

spinning his chakras, he had an out-of-body experience. To his shock, he found himself up in the corner of the room looking down on his body! It scared him so badly that he quit all metaphysical pursuits. He was terrified of his considerable psychic ability because, I believe, he related it to his "nightmares". In order to suppress that ability, as well as his awareness of other dimensions (and probably the contact with his twin), he anesthetized himself with either drugs or alcohol, when he wasn't working himself into exhaustion in the restaurant business.

Ted was a very sweet, gentle soul and everybody's friend. In 1986 he moved to New Orleans to "come out of the closet" about his sexuality. That's probably where he contracted AIDS. When I read the information quoted above concerning the relationship between homosexuality and the Vanishing Twin Phenomenon, I immediately thought of Ted.

During his long, painful death journey, Ted and I had lots of time to talk. One day, when we were chatting about his life, I asked him what his favorite job was. He said, "At the Hilton -- except for the stress." He said when the stress got too bad, "Bobby would take over, because Bobby could take the stress." He said his friend Cindy would joke with him about who was there -- Ted or Bobby. This was fascinating to me, because my research into the VTP had revealed just such "identity confusion" as typical of a single twin. Also, I remembered what Karyl had said during that hypnotic regression session in May of 1995: "His identical twin did not develop properly mentally, which created a great deal of confusion for Ted." How might that have contributed to the course his life took? Later that evening I asked Ted if he would like me to give him a reading; he agreed. During the reading he was asked if he wanted to know about his twin. To my great surprise, he said, "Yes". Among other things, he was told his twin would be waiting for him when he got to the other side. After the reading he said he knew what I had said about his twin was correct and that he had always known he existed, but didn't understand. He was even able to psychically see him during the reading. He said it was very comforting to know that someone would be waiting for him on the other side. Later that evening, he thoughtfully said, "So, he's not a lover?" -- again illustrating the sexual confusion sometimes found among single twins. He had probably psychically "seen" his twin throughout his life and like other people I've interviewed, was unable to put the visions into a context that allowed him to understand what he was experiencing.

Ted firmly believed in reincarnation, which of course greatly alleviated his fear of dying. He knew to look for the Light when the time came, and to head for it. He never lost his dry sense of humor, right up to the end. "I'll go first and get it all figured out," he told us. "I'll be waiting for you when it's your turn. I'll even come back and visit you if I can -- and if I'm not too busy."

During that period, Ted was highly sensitive -- to touch, to sounds, to light; he even flinched when I held my hands out toward him and projected healing energy. Over the last couple of days, he repeatedly tried to "pass over". He would slip into a coma, and we would think that the time had come; then he would suddenly jolt awake, look frantically around for me and, upon making eye contact, exclaim, "Oh, shit. I'm still here!"

During the last eight hours of his life, as he drifted in and out of a coma, Ted and I were able to communicate telepathically. (I sat in a chair next to his bed and held his hand for much of that eight hours.) It didn't seem to matter if he was conscious or not; whenever one of us had something to "say", the thoughts were communicated. He told me (I "heard" his voice in my head) how much he loved everyone and how much he appreciated what we all did for him over the last difficult months. He even made jokes and commented on what was going on in the room. On a couple of occasions when I dozed off, I felt him trying to "take me with him". It literally felt as if he was attempting to somehow draw my awareness right out of my body; I clearly "heard" him say, "Come on, come with me." It was very similar to the feeling I experienced when the healer raised me out of my body while working on my scoliosis in 1987. I assured Ted that he didn't need me to go with him because someone would be waiting for him "over there", and he soon ceased his efforts.

At the end, as his breathing slowed to a stop, we saw a little smile cross his face and fade away, and then another. Suddenly, he squeezed my hand, and a huge grin lit up his whole face. His body stiffened for a moment, then relaxed, and we knew he had finally made it. At that last moment, he had apparently seen something or someone that he recognized and that gave him the assurance that allowed him to let go. I hope it was his twin!

I can't help but wonder how the course of Ted's life might have been changed by knowledge and understanding of his missing twin; perhaps much of his fear and suffering would have been alleviated, if not averted. My twin, Karyl, has told me repeatedly that everyone involved in these "twin experiments" has agreed to participate prior to incarnating. That, obviously, is no guarantee of success -- "experiment" is the key concept here, I guess. It's sometimes a little difficult for me to accept that suffering such as Ted's is necessary, but if all is indeed in perfect order, such must be the case! I only hope that Ted's story will be of help to other single twins struggling to cope with their "twinlessness".

Karyl has also told me that each pair of twins involved in her group's experiments, besides agreeing to participate, also vowed prior to incarnating to help "bring in" information on a variety of technology and other topics (color [in my case], free energy, teleportation, prophecy, etc.) that could be of assistance to humanity and Mother Earth at this crucial time in our evolution. Hearing or reading about the VTP helps to open up the conscious mind to information coming from the subconscious, she said, thereby making the connection to "the other" and enabling the contactee to recall his or her particular "mission". "Time is running out and we're pushing to get the connections made and recognized," she informed me.

The following poem by Albert Hufstickler, a twinless twin, was published in the Winter/Spring 1994 issue of *Twinsletter:*

How can you grieve something that never was?
Where do you begin to mend a heart born unwhole, the loss implicit in its structure?
There must be a word for grief never born, for a loss not real but only a flickering of loss -- like light on the surface of water.
And still...all those million shifting specks of light moving inside me, an explosion that continues through my whole life and none of it real,
this happening that never happened in this world yet dominates it.
And where was the body laid? Or was it laid?
Did they bury it like something real?
There's no one to say now.
And even as I write, I begin to doubt.
It was never real.

There was nothing lost.
There is just me here this way --
as though something of total value was lost totally before I
ever was.

Resources

Twinless Twins Support International, 11220 St. Joe Road,
Fort Wayne, IN 46835, (219) 627-5414 (Publishes Twins
World and Twinless Twins Newsletter and coordinates an
annual conference)

Part III

The
Millennium
Children

Prefatory note: The numbered footnotes refer to the list of books in the "Notes" section in the back of this book. Since we feel that all of these books are best read in their entirety, we have not listed page numbers for specific quotes.

Gestation & Birth

Billy, three, asked his mother one day if she remembered the time she and Daddy were on vacation "in that cabin, and saw that UFO". (He never could have heard the story, because his parents had never spoken of the event around Billy.) "That was me, coming to check you out to see if I wanted to come to you!"

At age two, Mark pulled his bottle out of his mouth and announced to his mother, "I came here in a space ship!". Another time he announced, "I used to be a small white man that drove a space ship!" At fifteen, Mark had complete memory of how he came to earth. He was "made of light" and decided to become a human being. He "went down this long white tube" and the next thing he remembers he was a "small white man" piloting a UFO, looking for his mother. He knew just the one he wanted; she had been his mother before and he wanted her again, because "she was a really good one". He found her, "projected" into her and the next thing he knew he was being born. His mother remembers a blue light coming from around her bedroom curtain and "zooming" into her body during the later stage of her pregnancy.

In an attempt to describe to his parents the place one occupies before being born, Roy, four, called it, "the human-maker hotel", explaining that he was trying to "put it in words you might be able to understand."

While listening to his mother and older brother discuss a fire that burned down their trailer while he was in the womb, Jonathan, ten, added, "Yeah, I remember us standing over by the fence watching the fire; we were really scared!" That is in fact where they watched the fire, but that had never been mentioned in his presence.

One day Sammy's mother overheard him, at age three, telling someone else about his Caesarean-section birth. He spoke of "all the blood", and how he was "dizzy and sick to his stomach" because of the medicine and of the "bright lights and people in masks". She had never spoken of any of this in front of him before.

After Mary's mother's exploratory surgery, she was told she could not have children because her fallopian tubes were totally blocked. Years later Mary was born, and two years after Mary, along came her sister. After her sister's birth, the doctors decided a hysterectomy was necessary. Upon examination of the tubes, they were stunned to discover they were still blocked, exactly as they were 13 years earlier. They called it a medical miracle that either of these two children were ever conceived. Mary and her sister were definitely intuitive children. Mary remembers her past lives, is extremely psychic and now works as a counselor helping the next generation of intuitive children.

I have frequently heard mothers of intuitive children say that their children were "medical miracles" for one reason or another. They speak of "difficult pregnancies", with delivery being as much as a month late or three months premature. Why would such gestation and birth anomalies be more prevalent among intuitive children than among "normal" babies? It's my impression that there are "outside forces" at work in some of these cases. Certainly the testimony of both the children and their caregivers indicates strongly that there is some sort of experimentation going on!

At any rate, studies have now proven that children do have memory of their *in utero* experience. Far from being unknowing, unfeeling, "empty slates", newborns are deeply sentient beings, conscious before, during and after birth of their surroundings, and even of their mother's feelings and emotions. Studies have shown that babies even one hour old can respond in kind to researchers making faces, sticking out their tongues or wiggling fingers at them. Studies have further shown that babies who are talked to and read to while still in the womb are considerably brighter, more alert and responsive.[5]

Helen Wambach, in her book *Life Before Life*, reports that in her research with 750 people, 81 percent said under hypnosis that they chose to be born and chose their parents; 86 percent said they became aware of the feelings, emotions and even thoughts of their mothers prior to being born; 89 percent had the feeling that their consciousness was something separate from that of the fetus. They reported "hovering instead of being locked into the fetus before birth, and if one fetus is aborted, apparently it is possible to choose another."[7]

Some intuitive children are apparently able to retain these pre-conception and prenatal memories and are often able to convey their feelings and experiences to their parents at a very young age. Often their *in utero* memories are confirmed by the mother. Thomas Verny, M.D. writes in *The Secret Life of the Unborn Child*, "Birth and prenatal experiences form the foundation of human personality. Everything we become or hope to become, our relationships with ourselves, our parents, our friends -- all are influenced by what happens to us during these two critical periods."[5]

It is obvious from all this that appropriate prenatal care is profoundly important. But what constitutes "appropriate" care? This is a crucial question for any parent-to-be, and not always easy to answer. Some defectors from the ranks of the medical establishment take issue with widely accepted practices -- and history shows it would be well to take heed of such warnings. According, for example, to well-known "medical heretic" Dr. Robert Mendelsohn:

> The babies who are at greatest risk during the first days, weeks or months of life are those born prematurely, before all of their organs are fully developed, and those who lack physical stamina because of abnormally low weight at birth. A balanced nutrient-rich diet obviously can go a long way toward assuring a child's normal development from conception to delivery. Proper diet and exercise will usually prevent abnormal weight gain and many other problems during pregnancy. Your primary concern during pregnancy should not be with how much weight you gain but with how adequately and well you eat. Smoking, alcohol, other mood-altering drugs, prescription drugs, as well as over-the-counter drugs such as aspirin and cold remedies, are best avoided during pregnancy.[12]

There is controversy over the use of prenatal ultrasound. Alice Stewart, a British epidemiologist who heads the Oxford Survey of Childhood Cancers, commented in mid-1983 on "very suspicious hints" that children exposed to ultrasound in the womb may be developing leukemia and other cancers in higher numbers than unexposed children. A World Health Organization report called for extensive research on the hazards of ultrasound and restraint in its use. It stated, "...Because the human fetus is sensitive to other forms of radiation there is considerable concern that it may also be sensitive to ultrasound...Animal studies suggest neurologic (sensory, cognitive and developmental), immunologic and hematologic possibilities for studies in humans."[12]

As we will see often in these pages, informed and empowered parents taking responsibility for their child's well-being before as well as after it is born, and working in enlightened partnership with necessary medical care, are those most likely to have a problem-free pregnancy and a happy baby -- "intuitive" or not!

Studies have shown how the method of birth impacts a child's physical and emotional development. Natural, unmedicated deliveries produce the happiest, healthiest babies. Delivery in the squatting position is the most natural and advantageous for many women. Soft lighting, a warm environment, warm water for the newborn's first bath and/or immediate immersion after delivery, soft music, and loving, calm attendance all contribute to a healthy delivery. (The often super-sensitive intuitive child should particularly appreciate these amenities.) It has also been found that a mother singing or humming the same tune to her baby throughout the pregnancy, and during and after the delivery, can assist in reducing the stress of birth. The sound is recognizable and comforting to the newborn in its strange new environment. Meditation by the mother during pregnancy and delivery can also be helpful in stress reduction for both mother and child.[4]

The infant mortality rate in hospitals is higher than in at-home births, due primarily to aggressive and unnecessary medical intervention in the hospital environment. A troubling trend in this area is the increase of Caesarean births -- too often resorted to by a physician too impatient to wait for the normal birth process. The main reason that home childbirth is less risky than going to the hospital is that much of the most dangerous technology employed in hospitals is not available to doctors or midwives who deliver babies at home. Procedures such as ultrasound diagnosis, internal fetal monitoring, excessive use of sedatives, pain relievers and anesthetics, and Pitocin-induced labor, as well as the temptation to resort to delivery by Caesarean section, are largely avoided during home birth. Home birth practitioners are experienced in identifying mothers who can safely give birth at home and will recommend the proper course for those who cannot. They can also anticipate problems, but with sensible preparations and precautions, and without the interventions that occur in the hospital setting, these problems are few and far between, and home birth practitioners know how to cope with those that do arise.[12]

Shortly before birth, the baby goes into an "extreme stress state" to prepare it for the journey. The hour immediately after birth is crucial for relieving this stress. Verny writes, "As little as an hour spent together after birth can have a lasting effect on both the mother and child. Study after study has shown that women who bond become better mothers and their babies almost always are physically healthier, emotionally more stable and intellectually more acute than infants taken from their mothers right after birth."[5] Bonding occurs through breast feeding, holding, prolonged and steady eye contact, smiling and soothing sounds and massage. All the newborn's senses must be brought into play through physical stimulation, in order to provide the brain the stimuli necessary to coordinate the senses and mind-brain activity. (This is one reason why animals lick their young.) This immediate postnatal contact with the mother also helps her to secrete the necessary hormones to release the placenta, stimulate lactation and the genetically encoded motherly instincts. It could be that this lack of immediate bonding is a cause of the so-called "post-partum blues", as well as a variety of other problems.[3]

Modern high-tech medicine can and does perform miracles in saving the lives of prematurely born babies and in surgically repairing birth defects that only a few years ago meant certain death. Simple "common sense" tells us, however, that for the vast majority of pregnancies and deliveries, the less meddling and medication, the better. What is very important -- and too often overlooked in our high-tech society -- is making a "love connection" with that new life and strengthening it every day!

The routine practice of squirting silver nitrate in babies' eyes upon delivery was first instituted for the purpose of protecting the baby against gonorrhea. According to Mendelsohn, "It causes chemical conjunctivitis in thirty to fifty percent of the babies who receive it. Their eyes fill up with thick pus, making it impossible for them to see during the first week or so of life. Some physicians feel there is also a connection between this practice and other eye problems that occur later in life." The mother can be tested for gonorrhea before delivery and antibiotics are very effective in treating gonorrhea ophthalmia, should it develop, making this an unnecessary and medically risky assault upon the newborn.[12]

Another unnecessary hazard is the practice in many hospitals of using antiseptics in the postnatal bath in an attempt "to avoid the onus of a bacterial epidemic in their germ-laden nurseries".[12] There is no reason to expose a baby to chemicals when plain water will work just as well. An article in the Journal of the American Medical Association (JAMA) in 1972 stated, "There appears to be no need to apply any antibacterial agent to the cutaneous surface of the normal newborn infant."[12]

It is appalling that some hospitals still perform circumcisions on little boys without anesthesia, assuming they cannot feel pain. If performed for other than religious reasons, it is an unnecessary and potentially dangerous procedure. The American Academy of Pediatrics has advised that "there is no absolute medical indication for circumcision of the newborn." A doctor advocating circumcision should be asked why he favors subjecting a baby to the pain, the possibility of infection or hemorrhage, and the risk of death from surgery that has no medical justification.[12]

Mother's milk, time-tested for millions of years, is the best nutrient for babies because it is nature's perfect food. It provides your child with all of the nutrients s/he needs for healthy growth for at least six months -- provided the mother is healthy and eating properly. A breast-fed baby gains from his mother's milk a natural immunity to many allergies and infections that is denied the bottlefed child. In addition, "formula", with its many synthetic ingredients and often high sugar content, is quite costly and can be detrimental to a baby's well-being.

From the article "Message in a Bottle" by Linda Baker, originally published in the August 21, 1995 issue of *In These Times*:

> In the United States, bottle-fed babies are more likely than breastfed babies to contract a variety of illnesses, including ear infections, diarrhea, pneumonia, spinal meningitis and Sudden Infant Death Syndrome. Studies by Dr. Miriam Labbok, director of the breastfeeding division at Georgetown University Medical Center, suggest that if all U.S. newborns were breastfed for at least twelve weeks, the nation would save between $2 billion and $4 billion annually in health care costs.

In addition, breastfeeding provides benefits to the mother: it helps the uterus to contract after birth, it enables the woman to lose weight more easily after the pregnancy, and it reduces the risk of certain types of cancer. Also, while breastfeeding, a woman's fertility is reduced -- a natural aid to achieving a reasonable interval between pregnancies.

Newborns should be fed when they are hungry, not according to an arbitrary schedule. The newborn baby has only three demands: warmth in the arms of its mother, food from her breasts, and security in the knowledge of her presence.

Research has shown that when a recorded heartbeat was played for babies after birth, they ate more, weighed more, slept more, breathed better, cried less and got sick less.[5] *Toys R Us* sells a "Mommy Bear" that contains such a recording. Several mothers have endorsed it to me as a quite effective "stand-in" for their heartbeat!

An interesting discovery I made while researching the birth process is that a hormone called oxytocin, a muscle regulator, controls the rate of labor contractions, but with a powerful "side effect". Verny writes, "Recent research shows that in large quantities, oxytocin produces amnesia in laboratory animals; even thoroughly trained animals lose their ability to perform tasks under its influence. Why this is so is not entirely clear, but we do know a laboring woman's oxytocin floods her child's system. So if few of us are able to remember what happened at birth, it may be partly because like those of the laboratory animals, our birth memories are washed away by the oxytocin we were exposed to during labor and delivery."[5]

This brings up numerous questions and possibilities. Could this be one reason why we don't remember past lives or pre-birth events? Would a child born by Caesarean section before the mother began contractions be more likely to remember these things? How many of the intuitive children are born by Caesarean section? Food for thought and grounds for more research!

References

Natural Pregnancy - Gayle Peterson - 800-238-LINK (Addresses physical, emotional and spiritual development through pregnancy)

Babies Remember Birth - David Chamberlain, Ph.D. (Pre-birth memories)

The Secret Life of the Unborn Child - Thomas Verny, M.D. (Excellent book on fetal development)

Communicating with the Spirit of Your Unborn Child - A how-to manual. Aslan Publishing, 310 Blue Ridge Drive, Boulder Creek, CA 95006, 408-338-7504

Primal Connections - Elizabeth Noble (Birth memories and Vanishing Twin Phenomenon)

The Complete Book of Pregnancy and Childbirth - Sheila Kitzinger

The Passions of Fatherhood - Samuel Osherson

The Holistic Pediatrician - Kathi J. Kemper

Natural Healing for Babies and Children - Aviva Jill Romm

Resources

International Association of Infant Massage, 5660 Clinton St, Suite 2, Elma, NY 14059, (716) 684-3299 (Offers books and instructional videos and trains Infant Massage Instructors)

LaLeche International, 9616 Minneapolis Avenue, Franklin Park, IL 60131 (Breast feeding)

Mother Tongue, P.O. Box 3061, Asheville, NC 28802, (704) 285-8754 (A progressive parenting source of items, ideas and interests)

Parent's Resource Connection, Deanna Sletten, 5102 Deerwood Lane NE, Bemidji, MN 56601 (Directory of over 200 small press and regional parenting publications and local and national support groups. Send three dollars)

Early Childhood

A three-year-old girl told her abusive father, "I'm sorry, but you'll have to leave now -- I can't keep hurting like this." After the father had departed, the child comforted her mother, saying, "It'll be okay. Sometimes these things happen."

Less than twelve hours after her third child was born, a nurse informed Molly, while she was holding her baby, that the routine post-natal blood sample (which necessitates pricking the baby's heel with a needle to draw blood) would have to be redone because the tests had not worked properly. The baby promptly responded with a clear and vehement, "NO!" The mother wasn't too shocked, as her other two children had also begun speaking quite early, but the nurse ran out of the room!

The Book of Enoch, *one of the ancient scriptures not chosen to be included in the Bible, has an interesting description of the birth of Noah: "...a child has been born, who resembles not his father, and whose nature is not like the nature of man. His color is whiter than snow; he is redder than the rose, the hair of his head is whiter than white wool; his eyes are like the rays of the sun; and when he opened them he illuminated the whole house. When also he was taken from the hand of the midwife, he opened his mouth and blessed the Lord of heaven." Apparently, Noah also spoke shortly after he arrived in the world!*

Many parents have told me stories about their children talking -- and walking -- very early. "Molly" said her other two children talked within a couple of weeks after birth.

180

For years, due largely to the behaviorist school of psychology, people labored under the misconception that we are born empty vessels, beginning the learning process at birth only after leaving the womb. Now we know that is inaccurate; however, vestiges of this mindset remain throughout society, as evidenced in our schools and some "how-to" books on child-rearing. The precociousness of the intuitive child is only the most obvious indication that the human mind is far more powerful and mysterious than suspected by those who advance "behavior modification" as a solution to our social problems. The role of love -- of physical and emotional bonding -- in early development is critical.

We know that children who are touched and massaged regularly gain weight faster, grow more quickly and are physically more robust than infants who are not touched. At birth, love is not only an emotional requirement, but a biological necessity for a baby. Without it, and the cuddling and hugging that go with it, it is possible that an infant could literally wilt and die. The name for this condition is *marasmus*, from the Greek word for wasting away.[5]

Today, most women find it necessary to return to work almost immediately after childbirth, disrupting the mother-child bonding process and leaving much early child development and training to complete strangers. Joseph Chilton Pearce points out the devastating impact this has had on the social and moral development of our children.[3] I urge everyone to read what he has to say on this critical subject.

Research also shows that talking to children is extremely important for their proper development -- not always in baby talk, although that has its place, but in concrete, conversational terms.[4] For example, tell the child what is happening or about to happen, repeat his/her name, and name the things that draw his/her attention. This activity greatly aids myelination (creation of neural pathways) and language development.

It's beyond the scope of this book to enter into a detailed discussion of how and why we learn; in *Evolution's End*, Joseph Chilton Pearce explores the subject quite well and offers many references to those who desire more hard data and "deep background". A key point in Pearce's work is that "rote" learning is not the optimal method to impart knowledge to the human mind; indeed, it is all but useless for the child under seven years of age.

From one to three years old, children learn with all their senses and are completely single-minded when processing information about their environment. Mother's little darling isn't exactly ignoring the repeated requests not to touch the new figurine on the coffee table -- she just doesn't hear them! Her entire awareness is engaged in creating a new neurological pattern (the figurine), as she pursues the goal of constructing a fully integrated knowledge of her world by touching, tasting, seeing, smelling, feeling and hearing everything that she possibly can -- one thing at a time.[4]

A young child is so impressionable that a caregiver's unfavorable or frightened response to any out-of-the-ordinary statements or activities can have untold and far-reaching consequences. It's important that parents talk to children quietly, calmly and with an open mind about what they are experiencing.

It's also important that children be treated with respect and dignity. If allowed, as early as possible, to make as many decisions for themselves as reasonably possible, beginning with things as simple as what to wear and eat; if allowed as much freedom of movement and action as possible, they will usually respond by quickly developing their sense of self and responsibility. The intuitive children especially are extremely creative and inventive, and, if encouraged, will surprise their parents with the knowledge and understanding they have -- far beyond what they could have learned in their everyday reality.

Reading to them, telling them stories, asking them to tell stories -- the results of such activities can be gratifying, even amazing! On the other hand, it's obviously not desirable to push a child too hard; one needs to "tune in" to the child intuitively and fit instruction to the child's individual needs, sense with one's heart what the child requires at any given moment. This is the type of special treatment a child cannot receive in a day care center; and for the intuitive child, such treatment may well be crucial.

It is well to remember, when communicating instruction, demands for compliance, or responses to questions to the newborn to four year-old, that unless s/he can touch, taste, feel, see and/or smell as well as hear what is being referred to, no communication takes place. Instruct by example: use his hands on yours when putting on his socks, one step at a time. Use one-word cautions, such as "hot" or "sharp".[4]

By age four, 80 percent of the child's language, world view and ego structure are complete; the other 20 percent should be filled in by about age seven.[4] These first seven years are obviously critical to the child's development. In *You Are Your Child's First Teacher*, early childhood educator Rahima Baldwin Dancy tells us, "The tremendous growth of the first seven years is accompanied by nearly constant movement...During these years the child learns primarily through repetition and movement and by imitating everything around her. Sitting still for long periods is unhealthy if not impossible for the young child, who desires to experience everything through her body."[17]

Most day care providers are not trained to handle the extensive and complex needs of even the "ordinary child" in these formative years, nor are they able in the day care environment to provide the one-on-one attention that is vital to all children, but especially to the intuitive child. The guidance of a bonded, well-informed parent is required. One of the greatest challenges confronting humanity is how to create a society that is "children-friendly", yet still efficient and productive. Intervention by the state has proven marginally helpful at best -- some programs have proven beneficial, others not. A fundamental restructuring of priorities certainly seems called for, but how to bring it about? Most humans seem unwilling to change unless survival is at stake; perhaps the millennial upheavals predicted by many will prove to be the catalyst for change. Let us hope it will come more easily than that.

Reference Books

Evolution's End - Joseph Chilton Pearce

Magical Child - Joseph Chilton Pearce

Magical Child Matures - Joseph Chilton Pearce

Bond of Power - Joseph Chilton Pearce

You Are Your Child's First Teacher - Rahima Baldwin Dancy

Stress Proofing Your Child: Mind-Body Exercises to Enhance Your Child's Health - Sheldon Lewis and Sheila Kay Lewis

Resources

Ann Marie Pineda, Child Development Specialist, Intuitive Therapist, 911 Collyer Street, Longmont, CO 80501   (303) 772-3911

Mothering Magazine - (800) 984-8116

Modern Dad - (312) 465-8088

Parenting Magazine - (303) 682-8878

Parents Magazine - (800) 727-3682

Child Magazine - (800) 777-0222

Child of Colors Magazine - (404) 364-9690

Seasame Street Parents - (800) 289-8979

Physical

At age two, Tommy was run over by a car, which according to his mother, he promptly lifted off his body. Doctors, amazed that he was not injured in any way and was actually able to lift the car by himself, decided to study him. He entertained the hospital investigators by throwing office desks around the room with one hand. (I have heard of other children allegedly possessing "super strength". How much of that ability is actually telekinetic -- the ability to move things with the mind -- remains to be investigated.)

A mother of twins, while visiting a friend who also had twin offspring, heard her friend's twins speaking to each other in their own special language. She noticed, to her surprise, that they seemed to be speaking the same language her twins spoke. The two mothers got their twins together, and found that the four children were indeed able to communicate among themselves in this special language. One set of twins was two years old; the other was three. (The special languages some children speak have been described as "clicky sounds like dolphins", "fluid and melodic", "like birds chirping" or "like a foreign language".)

Dale, four, announced to his mother that he no longer wished to eat steak because he could "hear the meat screaming".

Many parents have reported to me that their intuitive children are hypersensitive to sights, sounds, touch and smells. (You will read about an extreme case of this hypersensitivity later in the chapter entitled "Sounds Like a Miracle".) Loud music or TV, bright sunlight or unpleasant odors are actually painful to some of them. I have talked to parents who have discovered that their children can hear beyond the normal range, even to the extent that they're able to hear their blood rushing through their veins. Some can see color around people, plants and animals, demonstrating their ability to see beyond the normal visible light spectrum. Some children are very light-sensitive, particularly to fluorescent lighting. (Full-spectrum lighting, while always desirable, would seem to be essential for these children.) Some find it necessary to smell everything with which they come in contact, particularly food, and even the silverware. Some children are so sensitive they cannot stand the seams in their socks, labels in their shirts, or the feel of a wash cloth on their faces. Soft, natural fiber clothing and bedding, as well as natural, chemical-free laundry detergents and other products are highly recommended -- along with a great deal of patience.

Because of their hypersensitivity, these children very often overreact to drugs of any kind, prescription or over-the-counter. Many suffer from a variety of allergies. Natural healing modalities (sometimes referred to as "alternative" medicine) such as color therapy, sound therapy, homeopathics, aromatherapy, herbs and nutritional supplementation are less intrusive and violent than allopathic methods and can be very effective for the child with a higher frequency.

In 1995, I met three women who were all born as intuitive children and are now working with the next generation, trying to save them from some of the difficulties they experienced. All three told me independently of being able to see what they call the "energy grid" or "matrix" of the human body. They describe it as similar to a fiber optic system, with lines going "up and down, across and back and forth" through the physical body. When a physical or emotional problem exists, these women are able to see where the lines are "broken or blown" and can psychically repair the breaks, facilitating healings not only of dis-ease, but of learning disabilities and dyslexia, as well. They said that breaks in the lines can be caused by an electrical shock or physical or emotional trauma. They also claimed that the intuitive children are "wired differently"; they vibrate faster or have a higher frequency than most of us, and it's difficult for them to integrate into the 3-D world. Again, all three women have the ability to "see" this grid and described it independently in almost the same way. They have used visualization, color, toning, movement, dance and art to help children integrate "consensus reality" into their high energy frequency.

It's important to understand that the division of the human being into "departments" called "body", "mind", "emotions", and so forth is strictly arbitrary and a product of the culture in which we live. Many other cultures do not make such distinctions. Current thinking in physics tells us that there is no real difference between what we call matter and what we call energy; matter is just energy vibrating at a slower rate. What anything "is", is determined by its vibrational frequency. From this standpoint, it's easy to see how physical symptoms can be eliminated by so-called "vibrational" healing. Many professionals feel that such modalities, previously condemned as quackery and left to the likes of psychics and hysterical fundamentalist sects, are the "wave" of the future. *Vibrational Medicine*, by Richard Gerber, MD, as well as books by medical revisionists Deepak Chopra, Larry Dossey and Bernie Siegel are all excellent sources for information on non-invasive, non-toxic healing methods.

The late Robert Mendelsohn, M.D., offers some marvelously simple answers to everyday medical questions facing every parent in his book, *How To Raise A Healthy Child...In Spite of Your Doctor*. Following are some examples of the many common-sense home remedies put forth in this wonderful book.

Dr. Mendelsohn stresses that most fevers are caused by viral and bacterial infections that the body's own defense mechanisms will usually overcome without medical help. Drugs and even sponging are actually counterproductive. Over-the-counter liquid cold remedies contain a high percentage of alcohol, and in some cases this may be the only ingredient that makes sense...a shot of brandy will do just as well to relax the child and help her sleep, he says. He also recommends a teaspoon of liquor for a sore throat (along with replacement of body fluids and maintaining proper environmental humidity), and ten drops of whisky by mouth for an ear ache, (along with a heating pad and two drops of warm olive oil in the ear). He claims that expensive high-top baby shoes are not essential to proper development of the foot. He is a strong opponent of antibiotics, claiming that they kill "good" germs as well as "bad" ones, thus creating an imbalance that permits drug-resistant infectious organisms to flourish and become dominant. In a double-blind study in the Netherlands, 171 children with ear infections were tested. There was no significant difference in the clinical course of the ear infections between the group that received antibiotics and the placebo group.[12]

Many of the intuitive children have large eyes and fine-boned, fragile bodies -- again, an indication of a "higher" (i.e. less dense) frequency. Many are at risk to develop scoliosis (curvature of the spine), indicating an obvious need for special emphasis on proper diet and exercise. Several times I have heard stories about these children being confined to wheelchairs for various reasons. A benefit arising from such apparent misfortune is that they are often home-schooled, thereby receiving the special attention and education they would probably not get in the public school system. (More on this subject later.)

Not surprisingly, many of the children are left-handed or ambidextrous: The left hand is regulated by the right, intuitive side of the brain. Does their left-handedness contribute to or somehow amplify their intuitive abilities in some kind of closed-loop reinforcement?

Very often these intuitive children choose early in life to become vegetarians. Like "Dale", some claim to be able to "hear the meat scream", or that they can feel the fear or terror the animal felt meeting its death in the slaughterhouse.

Chemists have synthesized hormones to cause livestock and poultry to mature more quickly and grow larger, producing more meat, milk and eggs. The unnatural growth they induce seriously de-stabilizes the metabolic and immune systems in all mammals, including humans. Antibiotics to counter this problem have long been administered to livestock. These antibiotics, as well as the hormones, find their way into meat, eggs and dairy products, creating health problems for some humans, especially children, who consume them. These chemicals were introduced at the same time breastfeeding was being virtually eliminated from most sectors of our society (after World War II). There was an immediate, unprecedented explosion in the growth patterns of an entire generation. Postwar children suddenly towered over their pre-World War II parents. Indisputable evidence exists that these artificial hormones accumulate in the body, inducing premature sexuality, before the child is emotionally and mentally equipped to handle the physical changes.[3]

If you are a vegetarian, you know the "light" feeling this way of eating creates in your body, and with their supersenses, these children can certainly feel it too. It is important to honor their choice, rather than trying to force them to conform to any particular way of eating. Armed with the proper information, parents can assure that their children are well-nourished in any reasonable dietary regimen.

The consumption of refined foods, especially sucrose and white flour, has introduced a number of health problems for all humans, of whatever age. Refer to William Dufty's classic *Sugar Blues* for a hair-raising account of the devastating effect sugar addiction has had on human health and history. First published twenty years ago, it remains an eye-opening indictment of the food-processing industry. Many of our modern ailments can be laid directly at the feet of the gross overconsumption of sugar that is now commonplace nearly everywhere in the world. Any parent truly concerned about her child's health must take control of what that child eats, at least for the first seven years of the child's life. The sometimes delicate faculties of the intuitive child are best spared the destructive effects of an addiction to sweets.

Artificial sweeteners are, if anything, worse. Aspartame (Nutrasweet, Equal, Spoonful) is a molecule composed of three components: aspartic acid, phenylalanine and methanol. Once ingested, the methanol (wood alcohol that has killed or blinded thousands of skid row drunks), converts into formaldehyde, formic acid (ant sting poison) and diketopiperazine (a brain tumor agent). Formaldehyde, a deadly neurotoxin, is common embalming fluid, a Class A carcinogen. Aspartame has been linked to brain tumors and other cancers, chronic fatigue syndrome, mental retardation, seizures, fibromyalgia, multiple sclerosis, Parkinson's, diabetes, Alzheimers, birth defects and many others, less lethal problems. It's well worth the time and energy to read ingredient labels!

One good source of information on diet and its effects is the work of Michio Kushi, currently the world's leading proponent of a much misunderstood (and maligned) way of eating and living known as "macrobiotics". He has written dozens of books, thoroughly covering the subject of nutrition and its relationship to disease and social disorder of all kinds. His teacher, known in the West as George Ohsawa, authored some two hundred books, mostly in Japanese, many of which have been translated into English. No shortage of information here! *The Book of Macrobiotics*, written by Kushi, is a good place as any to start; cooking classes and instruction in the underlying philosophy of Macrobiotics are available in many parts of the U.S. and elsewhere. Look in the book section of your local health food store for more information.

Another phenomenon that touches on the subject of vibrational frequency is the ability of some of these children to interfere with TV or radio reception, switch appliances on or off, and blow out light bulbs or street lights simply by walking past them or looking at them. According to reports I have heard, this often occurs when they are angry or otherwise upset and could be a result of their high frequency. The three therapists just mentioned above are all of this opinion.

I have also heard numerous stories of children recovering "miraculously" from a variety of diseases and ailments after the angels, God or their "little friends" came to get them. And speaking of "little friends", intuitive children sometimes wake with nosebleeds, unexplained scars or marks on their bodies. It's important to watch for these signs, as they could indicate possible extraterrestrial interaction. We will explore this question in more detail in the chapter entitled "Extraterrestrials".

In summary, we may simply say that due to the hypersensitivity of the intuitive child, it's extremely important that parents pay close attention to his or her physical condition and any comments s/he might make concerning it.

Reference Books

Vibrational Medicine - Richard Gerber (Descriptions and methods of using various alternative medicine therapies and modalities)

Love, Medicine & Miracles - Bernie Siegel (Self-healing, healing power of love)

The Consumer's Guide to Homeopathy - Dana Ullman (The definitive resource for understanding homeopathic medicine and making it work for you.)

Therapeutic Touch - Dolores Krieger (Hands-on-healing techniques)

What Your Doctor Won't Tell You - Jane Heimlich (Complete guide to alternative medicine)

Alternative Health & Medicine Encyclopedia - James Marti

Children's Medicine - Ann & James Kepler (Parents guide to prescriptions and over-the-counter drugs, including side effects)

The Book of Macrobiotics - Michio Kushi (Principles and practicalities of a grain and vegetable-based diet)

Health and Light - John Ott (Full spectrum lighting)

Natural Medicine for Children - Julian Scott, Ph.D.

Raising Your Family Naturally - Joy Gross

Sugar Blues - William Dufty

Aspartame, Is It Safe (The Charles Press, P.O. Box 15715, Philadelphia, PA 19103)

The Natural Nursery: The Parent's Guide to Ecologically Sound, Nontoxic, Safe, and Healthy Baby Care - Louis Pottkotter

Resources

Seventh Generation, 49 Hercules Drive, Colchester, VT 05446- 1672, 800-456-1177 (Natural fiber clothing and products)

Real Goods, 555 Leslie St., Ukaih, CA 95482-5507, 800-762-7325 (Natural fiber clothing and products)

Tender Care Diapers, 555 E. 71st St., Suite 8300, Tulsa, OK 74136, 800-344-6379 (Chemical-free diapers)

Jessy Bear, P.O. Box 8940, Warwick, RI 02888, 401-941-1965. (Cotton diapers)

Full Spectrum Lighting, 800-786-6850 (Free catalog)

George Ohsawa Macrobiotics Foundation, 1999 Myers St., Oroville, CA 95966 (Bi-monthly magazine, information, classes)

The Natural Baby Catalog: Alternative Products for Children and Their Parents, 816 Silvia St., 800 B-S, Trenton, NJ 08628 (609)771-9233

Biobottoms: Fresh Air Wear for Kids, P.O. Box 6009, Petaluma, CA 94955 (800) 766-1254

The World Research Foundation, 20501 Ventura Blvd., Suite 100, Woodland Hills, CA 91364 (818) 999-5483 (Information and search services for the public and health professionals on the latest developments in health and the environment; also on healing modalities available outside the U.S.)

Vaccines

The history of vaccines, and the pertussis (whooping cough) vaccine in particular, is a shocking story I uncovered as I researched the general area of the intuitive children's physical sensitivity, and I feel it is important to discuss this issue in some detail. Their sensitive systems would seem to be particularly vulnerable to damage by vaccines, making the issue of childhood vaccination critical for these children; but the sordid history of the so-called "side effects" of infant immunization and how they have been dealt with by the healthcare establishment is a scandal of which everyone should be aware. It is beyond the scope of this work to treat this complex problem in detail; suffice it to say that it lies at the heart of the issues of health freedom and parental vs. governmental responsibility. There are three books that will give the interested reader a clear picture of the history, politics and risks of mass immunization: *DPT - A Shot In The Dark* by Harris Coulter and Barbara Loe Fisher, which began the vaccine safety debate in the US and is a primary source of information on this subject; *Vaccines: Are They Really Safe and Effective?* and *Immunization: Theory vs. Reality* both authored by Neil Z. Miller. It is impossible to overstate the importance to all parents of the information contained in these books, but I also strongly recommend them to anyone who is concerned about the future of our species.

It is (at least apparently) an article of faith in the medical establishment that vaccines are necessary to stave off the legions of lethal microorganisms that await a child upon his/her entry into the world. The most cursory perusal of the history of epidemics that have periodically ravaged human populations, and the apparent success of mass inoculations in eliminating, or at least greatly reducing, these diseases would seem to be quite straightforward and convincing proof of the efficacy, safety and necessity of using serum vaccines in the struggle to protect our health and lengthen our lives. Accordingly, increasingly strict state and federal laws and regulations have been installed which mandate a wide range of "shots" in order for children to be permitted into day care, pre-school or kindergarten. Some doctors even refuse treatment to unvaccinated children. The general public is conditioned to believe that the shots are a routine and vital step in insuring their children's well-being.

But there is a darker side to this story. The authors of the books mentioned above and many other researchers -- a number of doctors among them -- point out limitations in the serum vaccine theory itself, as well as a dreadful (and often suppressed) litany of damage done to untold numbers of children and adults throughout the history of vaccinations, starting with smallpox and pertussis (the "whooping cough") in the 1800's, and continuing to the present day. A large and powerful medical/governmental/pharmaceutical complex now exists which deliberately downplays and conceals the highly questionable methods of vaccine production, and the facts about those vaccines' deleterious effects. Parents of children killed or damaged by vaccines are marginalized and denied access to recompense for their suffering. The legions of statistics marshalled by the anti-vaccination advocates are disturbing, to say the least.

Some illuminating examples:

"As early as 1933, the Journal of the American Medical Association (JAMA), published reports of adverse reactions -- including death -- following pertussis vaccines."[9] In 1947, doctors began reporting the following additional reactions to the pertussis vaccine: failure to develop the power of speech or delayed language development, stuttering, minimal brain damage, neurological symptoms, and two cases involving brain damage that led to death. In 1948, Byers and Moll of the Harvard Medical School published an article describing children whose brains were damaged by pertussis vaccinations. Their findings shocked the medical world and provided the first clear substantiation that the vaccine could cause serious neurological complications in children.[10] In 1950, Lancet published a report describing severe neurological complications -- mental retardation and paralysis -- following a combined pertussis-diphtheria vaccine.[9] Other reports of serious reactions began pouring in during the 1950's from physicians and researchers throughout the world.[10]

Vera Scheibner, Ph.D. writes in the introduction to *Immunization: Theory vs. Reality,* "In 1950 before mass immunizations began, the US had the third lowest infant mortality rate in the world. By 1986, the US dropped to 17th place. In 1995, there were 23 countries ahead of the US, by now world renowned for its appalling infant mortality rate."[9]

In short, the prevailing philosophy (rationalization?) among the "powers that be" is apparently that an epidemic of negative vaccine reactions affecting thousands is a reasonable price to pay to protect the health of millions (and perhaps the profits of a certain multinational pharmaceuticals cartel?). The individual parent, faced with the vaccination requirements that now exist, must fully understand the risk/benefit equation of childhood immunization before acquiescing to the state's demands. Anything less is an abdication of parental responsibility.

Exactly what is being injected into our children that could cause such metabolic mayhem? That is another very unpleasant story. Depending upon the vaccine, the live virus or killed bacteria may be grown on animal tissue cultures such as chick embryos (measles vaccine), monkey kidney tissues (polio vaccine), or use the cell lines from aborted fetuses (rubella vaccine). The viruses or bacteria are weakened by the use of heat and chemicals such as formaldehyde to render them non-toxic and presumably incapable of causing the disease they were designed to prevent. Additives such as aluminum may be added to act as an "adjuvant" to theoretically boost the vaccine's effectiveness. Other toxic substances such as mercury may be added as preservatives. Many of the additives present in vaccines have been shown, in microscopic doses, to cause cancer, neurological damage and death. Yet all of them can be found in childhood vaccines.[10]

From *Immunization: Theory vs. Reality:*

> Congress finally acknowledged the reality of vaccine-caused injuries and death in 1986 by enacting into law *The National Childhood Vaccine Injury Act* (Public Law 99-660). The safety reform portion of this law requires doctors to provide parents with information about benefits and risks of vaccines prior to vaccination and to report vaccine reaction to federal health officials. The Vaccine Adverse Event Reporting System was created and operated by the Center For Disease Control (CDC) and the FDA. This law provides for compensation of up to $250,000 if the child dies or, possibly, millions of dollars to cover the lifelong medical bills, pain and suffering in the case of a living (but brain-damaged) child. The government's estimated future liability for pre-1988 vaccine damage exceeds $1.7 billion.[9]

Originally Congress did not intend for parents to go through an adversarial procedure to claim these funds. The first parents who applied were given the money needed to help with their brain-injured children. Officials had no idea how many parents would apply. Although the law requires doctors to report adverse reactions, according to the FDA only about ten percent actually do. Reactions are blamed on other factors; we therefore have no accurate statistics on how many adverse reactions actually occur.

Unfortunately, according to *The Vaccine Reaction* newsletter published by the National Vaccine Information Center, effective March 10, 1995, the Department of Health and Human Services (HHS) has in essence destroyed the effectiveness of the Vaccine Injury Act by changing the eligibility parameters for compensation. The only adverse events presumed to be associated with DPT vaccinations are anaphylaxis (hypersensitive reaction) within four hours and encephalopathy/encephalitis (brain inflammation) occurring within 72 hours of a DPT vaccination. In order to qualify under HHS's new definition of encephalopathy, a child would have to exhibit a "significantly decreased level of consciousness" (unconsciousness or inability to respond to most stimuli) for more than 24 hours following a DPT shot, and be hospitalized. No longer will a child who suffers classic pertussis vaccine reaction symptoms (such as high pitched screaming, collapse/shock, bulging fontanelle or seizures) within 72 hours of a DPT vaccination, and who sustains permanent neurological damage, including a residual seizure disorder, be presumed to be eligible for compensation in the federal program. This action is being protested by the National Vaccine Information Center and others.

Japan has been using a safer pertussis vaccine since 1981. It has been approved for use in the US only during the last few years and then only for children eighteen months or older. Two, four and six month-old babies are still usually given the old, more dangerous vaccine, even though a new vaccine for this group was approved in 1996. This new vaccine is apparently difficult to obtain, more expensive and not all insurance companies are covering it. There is also the option of requesting a "DT" shot -- which is available now -- thereby eliminating the pertussis vaccine.

At what age a child should begin receiving vaccinations is another highly controversial issue. As mentioned earlier, a baby gains early immunity from its mother's milk. In the natural order of things as a child encounters the usual ailments of childhood, the immune system develops and strengthens by "fighting off" and/or surviving those illnesses. What does not kill us, as Nietzche said, makes us stronger. There is evidence that early immunization can "short-circuit" that process, leaving children more vulnerable to infections against which they have not been immunized. There is also evidence linking infant immunization to serious disorders -- including cancer -- later in life. In 1941, researchers were urging that pertussis vaccinations begin no earlier than the age of seven months: "Most infants did not yet possess the power to develop adequate immunity when they were injected so early in life". In the 1950's, the American Academy of Pediatrics recommended that the series of DPT shots be started at between one and two months of age. According to the authors of a 1962 Parke-Davis Quadrigen vaccine study, "There is also a greater likelihood of completing the recommended series of injections if immunizations can be started early in infancy and coordinated with other reasons for the baby's being brought to the physician's office or clinic. For most practitioners, the age of four to six weeks would be a convenient time to start the series of immunizations against diphtheria, tetanus, pertussis and poliomyelitis..."[10] George Dick, M.D., wrote in 1967 concerning this issue, "It has long been known that increasing the number of B. pertussis per dose of vaccine increased the frequency of reactions. It would be surprising if decreasing the size of the infants receiving a particular vaccine did not also increase the reactions."[10] A two-month-old baby weighing nine pounds gets the same amount of vaccine as a fifty-pound child entering kindergarten.[10] If that isn't bad enough, a new "super-vaccine" is now being developed to be squirted in the mouth of newborn babies before they leave the hospital![9]

Seventy to ninety-eight percent of the cases of whooping cough, polio, measles, etc. now being reported are in children who have been fully or partially vaccinated.[9] The diseases were going away on their own before we began mass inoculations, partially due to better hygiene and nutrition. In countries where mass inoculations did not occur, the diseases disappeared anyway, and the cases reported recently have proven to be much milder and treatable with antibiotics. Yet state and federal governments continue to mandate that our children be given more than thirty potentially toxic vaccines before they enter public school, as well as many day care facilities. Some states do offer an exemption for philosophical or religious reasons, or upon presentation of a signed statement from a doctor. These exemptions will not, however, guarantee a child entry into some public or private schools, or certain day care centers. As mentioned earlier, some physicians and hospitals deny children care if they are not fully immunized; on the other hand, some physicians require that mothers sign a form absolving the doctor of liability if the child is damaged by the shots! Mothers are threatened with the withholding of state aid if they refuse immunization for their children. Some parents are being charged with "medical abuse" or neglect for not having their children immunized, and are even being threatened with imprisonment or removal of the children from the home. This is a very important Constitutional issue and is being contested in many states right now (1996).

It's important that parents know the contraindications of vaccination and that they discuss with their doctor the child's, as well as the family's, medical history before any vaccinations are given. The contraindications (in the child or the immediate family) include a history of: compromised immune system contributing to allergies (particularly to milk and eggs), ear infections or asthma; convulsions, seizure disorders, epilepsy or infantile spasms; difficult pregnancy, low birth weight or premature birth; and neurological problems or previous reaction to DPT shots. It is particularly important not to vaccinate a child when s/he is ill for any reason, particularly with (or just coming down with or recovering from) a cold, the flu or an ear infection. Some scientific literature suggests that if a child has recovered from an illness within ONE MONTH prior to a scheduled DPT shot, it is contraindicated.

It's equally important to be aware of the range of possible adverse reactions to vaccines, including more minor reactions such as pain, redness, soreness or swelling (a purple or blue knot) around the area of the injection, fever, vomiting, diarrhea, cough, runny nose and crying. Subtle and often overlooked reactions (i.e., a slight fever, fussiness, drowsiness) can be, and often are symptomatic of encephalitis, which is capable of causing severe neurological complications months or even years after the vaccination.

More severe reactions include high-pitched screaming and persistent crying, collapse or shock-like episodes, excessive sleepiness, convulsions, projectile vomiting, epilepsy, infantile spasms, loss of muscle control, paralysis, inflammation of the brain, meningitis, encephalitis, encephalomyelitis, bulging fontanelle, blood disorders, diabetes, hypoglycemia, cerebral palsy, blindness and deafness.

Varying degrees of permanent neurological and brain damage have also been attributed to the pertussis vaccine, including mental disorders such as learning disabilities, short attention span (Attention Deficit Disorder), inability to concentrate, poor memory and hyperactivity. We also find clumsiness, sleep disturbances, impulsiveness, emotional disturbances, hearing and speech difficulties, irregularities of mental development and a wide variety of behavioral disturbances.

Also attributed to the pertussis vaccine is the ultimate adverse reaction -- death! In 1979 the Japanese government noted a cause-and-effect relationship between DPT shots and Sudden Infant Death Syndrome (SIDS). In response, that country's health department ordered the postponement of routine DPT shots until children were at least two years old. The result: SIDS has virtually disappeared from Japan. In the US, SIDS still claims about 8,000 babies a year.[9] Wyeth Laboratories, a vaccine manufacturer, stated in their 1984 product information insert, "The occurrence of SIDS has been reported following administration of DPT." SIDS undoubtedly is attributable to a variety of causes, of which the DPT shot is only one, but one wonders how many FULLY INFORMED parents would be willing to take this risk with their children!

I trust this information sheds some light on the dangers and misinformation involved in the vaccination problem, and will inspire the reader to thoroughly investigate this issue. While the intuitive children, with their often acute sensitivities, may be at greater risk than the general population, no one can really be considered completely safe from possible short- or long-term adverse reactions to any given dose of any given vaccine. We must, if our society is to be called "free", reserve the right to make our own decisions concerning healthcare for our children and ourselves. Obviously, most doctors accept what they are taught in medical school, and with the obvious financial benefit the medical establishment derives from the thirty-plus inoculations being mandated by law for each child, not to mention the residual medical care required to alleviate the pain and suffering of the "side" effects of the vaccinations, it would not be in their best interest to request legislative reform on this issue. In addition, the immense political power wielded by big pharmaceutical companies renders unbiased government investigation and reform unlikely. It will require a grass-roots effort by people armed with the facts. Remember, knowledge is power! As the billboards advertising immunization say, *"Your Child Is Depending On You."*

Reference Books

DPT - A Shot In The Dark - Harris Coulter and Barbara Loe Fisher (THE textbook on the dangers of the DPT and other vaccines)

Vaccines: Are They Really Safe and Effective? and *Immunization: Theory vs Reality* - Neil Z. Miller (Evaluates the safety, efficacy, and long-term effects of "mandatory" vaccines)

What Every Parent Should Know About Childhood Immunization - Jamie Murphy

What About Immunizations? Exposing The Vaccine Philosophy - Cynthia Cournoyer

Immunization: The Reality Behind the Myth - Walene James

Resources

National Vaccine Information Center (NVIC), 512 W. Maple Ave., #206, Vienna, VA 22180, 800-909-SHOT. (A non-profit, educational organization founded in 1982. NVIC is the largest and oldest national organization representing consumers and parents of vaccine damaged children. Publishes *The Vaccine Reaction*, a bi-monthly newsletter; parent information packets; books; vaccine laws and exemptions; tapes; vaccine reaction reporting assistance)

New Atlantean Press, P.O. Box 9638-925, Santa Fe, NM 87504, 505-983-1856 (Source for Neil Z. Miller's books. World's largest selection of vaccine information, including laws, books, hard-to-find vaccine resources imported from around the world)

American Natural Hygiene Society, P.O. Box 30630, Tampa, FL 33630, 800-855-6607 (Books, including *How To Raise A Healthy Child* and *Immunization: Theory vs. Reality,* as well as other vaccine-related and natural health books)

Education

A mother received yet another call from her six year-old daughter's teacher, who wanted to know just what night school would be teaching algebra to a six year-old, as her daughter claimed.

While bathing two year-old Rose in the kitchen sink, her mother pointed out the rainbows being created on the kitchen wall by the crystal chandelier, saying, "Oh, look at the pretty rainbows!" Rose proceeded to explain to her mother about the "prismatic effect" of the sunlight being refracted through the prisms of the chandelier. Her mother was so stunned she almost dropped her.

At a parent/teacher conference, Rose, now seven, was complimented for being a very bright student. However, the teacher did not appreciate Rose's interrupting her with corrections. Rose claimed, "That wasn't the way I learned it in my school at night."

In college, Rose was able to write the correct answer to a complex math problem on the board, but she could not show how she got to that answer unless her "twin sister on the ship" was "melded" with her.

Before completing her master's degree, Rose felt compelled to admit to her counselor that she had been cheating and didn't deserve her degree. She explained that she had made straight A's because, when taking a test, she could refer to the text books "in her head", finding the correct page and actually reading the answer from the book. He explained that he didn't care how she did it; she was the most brilliant student he had ever had and definitely deserved the degree.

Rose worked with a supposedly retarded, brain-damaged, "intuitive child". He wanted desperately to go to school with the other children. Rose described how he could create new brain dendrites in an undamaged part of his brain by imagining them as "ink splotches". He knew exactly what she meant and worked very hard on this visualization. The following year he was able to begin regular school with the other children, and quickly rose to the top of his class.

Robert, four, was very excited about his new computer, but commented to his mother, "It sure isn't like the one I used to use. I guess they don't make them as fast or good as they used to."

Danny says he tries "not to be condescending" to his parents and "attempts to speak in terms they will understand". He doesn't think he should have to go to school. "The hardest part of being here is learning to be a kid."

Mark, fifteen, was very eager to show me his drawings. They were drawings of a variety of UFOs, as well as various technical schematics of the propulsion systems that drove each one, which he understood and could describe in detail. He is considered by his teachers to have a "graduate school-level" understanding of physics.

Many intuitive children report "going to school at night with their friends" and acquiring very advanced knowledge, to which their parents know they could not have been exposed in everyday reality. Where and just what this "school" is remains a mystery, although one often hears that it is on a "ship" of some kind, indicating again the possible involvement with the children of some non-human intelligence. Until our understanding of the true nature of this mysterious universe we inhabit is considerably deeper, we can only speculate on the nature of such phenomena.

The education of the intuitive child is one of the greatest challenges for both parent and child. The public school system is simply not equipped to handle the special needs of the intuitive child. Teachers must teach to the level of the average child; these special children are often so advanced that they become easily bored in school and stare out the window, day dream, play or cause some sort of disruption. This may result in their being labelled as learning disabled, or as suffering from Attention Deficit Hyperactive Disorder, if not as just plain trouble makers.

I was absolutely appalled when I began researching the subject of hyperactivity, learning disabilities and attention deficit disorders. Five to ten million children in the US have been diagnosed with Attention Deficit Hyperactive Disorder and/or learning disabilities. In 1988, an article in the *Journal of the American Medical Association* stated that childhood behavior problems, including hyperactivity and learning disorders, may be affecting as many as one in five school children. The learning disability population in the public schools of America has risen from 830,000 in 1958 to 3,234,000 in 1980, according to the National Center for Education Statistics. Public school teachers of "normal" children (not "special ed.") have told me that as many as half of some of their classes have been diagnosed as suffering from one or more of these disabilities.

While the definitions of learning disabilities (LD), dyslexia, hyperactivity, Attention Deficit Hyperactivity Disorder (ADHD) and Attention Deficit Disorder (ADD) seem to overlap to some extent, some of the common symptoms that might lead to a diagnosis of one or another of these conditions are: "excessive" fidgeting or squirming; difficulty remaining seated; being easily distracted; difficulty following instructions; difficulty sustaining attention; frequent shifting from one activity to another; difficulty playing quietly; frequent excessive talking; frequent interrupting; frequent failure to listen; frequently losing things; frequently engaging in "dangerous activities". If this sounds suspiciously like an active six year-old to you, you are not alone; however, I have seen some of these kids and there is definitely something HYPERactive about some of them. Unfortunately, there is no physical test to determine the presence of these alleged "disabilities"; diagnosis is made by personality, psychological and academic tests, along with observation reports from parents, doctors, teachers and counselors.

Wendy Coleman, M.D., in *Attention Deficit Disorders, Hyperactivity & Associated Disorders*, notes a variety of possible causes of these disabilities: "fetal exposure to Dilantin, Fetal Alcohol Syndrome, exposure to heroin, cocaine, amphetamines, prenatal infection, lack of oxygen prenatally or at birth, prematurity, structural abnormalities of the brain, exposure to toxins, lead or heavy metals, severe infection involving the brain (bacterial meningitis or viral encephalitis), brain injury, cranial radiation (i.e. brain tumors), unrecognized seizure disorders, lack of motivation, boredom, gifted, physical or sexual abuse, chronic lack of sleep, inadequate nutrition, family stress and violence, or hyperthyroidism."[14] Note that she points out that GIFTED children may exhibit symptoms of these disorders!

The experts are divided as to whether these "disabilities" even exist. Originally, parents were blamed for bad parenting. Peter Breggin, M.D., says in *Toxic Psychiatry*, "Learning disability is a label of convenience for schoolteachers, educational psychologists and some parents; but it does not correspond to any existing phenomenon within the minds or brains of children." He claims, "Learning disabilities became a financial boondoggle. Behavioral psychology thrived on a whole new subspecialty with unlimited, involuntary clients. The schools also benefited. With little funding for remedial education and no funds for genuine school reform, LD programs could tap state and federal mental health coffers."[11]

Diane McGuinness, in her chapter in Seymour Fisher and Roger Greenberg's book *The Limits of Biological Treatments for Psychological Distress*, states, "Two decades of research have not provided any support for the validity of ADD or hyperactivity."[11] In *When Children Don't Learn*, McGuinness writes "...some 'hyperactive' children misbehave as a consequence of learning difficulties, some because of boredom, some because of the physical constraints of the classroom, and some because they are inherently more active and distractible than other children. Excessive, unremitting hyperactivity is a consequence of brain damage or a biochemical imbalance in less than one percent of the population. Fidgety behavior or the inability to concentrate can be produced by boredom or stress. Children with persistent learning problems begin to worry, then to panic and eventually to give up entirely. For either the gifted or the poor scholar, six hours is a long day. Children will persevere at tasks that are 'suitable', challenging and interesting, but will rapidly lose interest in boring tasks or tasks that are beyond their particular aptitudes."[13]

Seventy-five percent of dyslexics and nearly ninety percent of hyperactive children are male. Boys are acculturated to be more active, aggressive, independent, and defiant; they therefore have more conflicts with harried, inadequate or absentee parents and with boring schools and overworked, underpaid educators. Boys learn their aggressiveness from their male peers, their fathers, from school sports, from the TV and movies -- from everywhere in the culture. Conversely, girls are traditionally taught to be more submissive, to pay more attention to the requirements of other people, and to keep themselves under good control. In school this translates into "paying attention", according to Peter Breggin.[11]

Neil Miller notes some disturbing statistics in *Vaccines: Are They Really Safe and Effective?*:

> Juvenile delinquency, an unprecedented rise in violent crime, drug abuse, and the collapse of the American school system unable to contend with the estimated 20 to 25 percent of students mentally and emotionally deficient, represent other conditions that may be attributed to the vaccines. In some school districts as many as thirteen percent of the children are now enrolled in special education classes...some researchers have indicated that the actual figures for children with this disorder are closer to 15 to 20 percent. Although many children are not diagnosed as learning disabled or minimally brain damaged, teachers complain that nearly all of their students are cognitively inferior and have shorter attention spans when compared to kids they taught in the 1960's. In fact, beginning in 1964 [following the advent of mass immunization campaigns] the average SAT verbal and math scores have continued to steadily decline. In an attempt to appease school administrators, who are often blamed for declining scores, and to safeguard the truth, testmakers have been 'dumbing down' their tests since the 1960's. Our children today are taking tests drastically more simple than those given decades ago."[19]

A recent study reported that 23 million people in the work force cannot read or write well enough to compete in the job market. Another study found that fewer than half of all high school graduates could not compute the change that would be received from $3.00 for two items ordered from a lunch menu. Every day more than 1500 teenagers drop out of school. In 1988, 80 percent of all academic honors and scientific awards in the US went to foreign-born students. Fifty percent of all Ph.D. researchers in the US are foreign born. Armed police officers are required in some schools due to the extreme violence and drug abuse; children are afraid to go to school. As of 1990, every day in the US 135,000 school children were bringing guns to school. Every day ten children die as a result of gunshot wounds, and thirty are wounded.

Again, Neil Miller:

> A disproportionate amount of violent crime is committed by individuals with neurological damage. Dyslexia and other learning disabilities have been found in nearly ninety percent of delinquents. Delinquent children with these disorders are often reclassified as sociopaths upon reaching adulthood. Studies confirm again and again that children with neurologically based disorders often engage in violent criminal behavior as adolescents and adults. In one study, half of the incarcerated delinquents had an I.Q. below 85. In 1988 the *Journal of the American Medical Association* acknowledged that a disproportionate number of felons suffered from hyperactivity during their early years.[19]

In my efforts to research this difficult and complex subject, I attended several local meetings of Children and Adults With

Attention Deficit Disorder (CHADD) -- an organization, incidentally, funded by Ciba-Geigy, the maker of Ritalin. I saw videos and heard heart-breaking stories from the weary parents of these children. Reflecting on my own childhood (I am now 46), I cannot recall children behaving in this disruptive manner in the classroom when I was in school. What happened to create this enormous and growing problem?

Obviously, all the factors noted by Wendy Coleman are viable possibilities, many of which have increased during the last sixty years; however, there was one very obvious omission from the literature. The pertussis vaccine was never mentioned as a contributing factor to LD, ADD, ADHD or hyperactivity in any of the literature I researched. Yet there is extensive medical evidence of a correlation between DPT vaccines and brain damage, learning disabilities and hyperactivity going back to the 1930's.[10] Published in 1985, *DPT - A Shot In the Dark* was the first book to make the scientific connection between brain inflammation induced by the pertussis vaccine and minimal brain damage in children as manifested in LD, ADD and autistic behaviors. I couldn't understand why the education and psychology researchers had failed to acknowledge this connection. What caused the increase in the incidence of LD, ADD, autism and hyperactivity in the past fifteen years? A little digging uncovered some interesting correlations:

Due to the efforts of Senator Dale Bumpers from Arkansas and then-President Jimmy Carter, a nationwide immunization campaign was mounted in the mid-seventies. By 1979, a ninety percent immunization rate throughout the US was achieved.

Also in the late seventies, the types and number of required vaccines increased, and have continued to increase to the present.

An article published in the October 1995 edition of *Townsend Letter for Doctors & Patients* stated that a new nationwide survey of nearly 700 children is showing a disturbing link between children with developmental delays and the amount of antibiotics they have taken:

> The survey, which included youngsters between the ages of one year and twelve years, found that those who had taken more than twenty cycles of antibiotics in their lifetime are over 50 per cent more likely to suffer developmental delays. Children who have had three or fewer rounds of antibiotics are half as likely to become developmentally delayed. The survey's other findings: Nearly 75 per cent of the delayed children had been reported to be developing normally in their first year of life. Developmentally delayed children were 37 per cent more likely to have had three or more ear infections than unaffected children. Affected children were nearly four times as likely to have had negative reactions to immunizations. Affected children were twice as likely to have had ear tubes than unaffected children. According to Patricia Lemer, a National Certified Counselor and co-founder of the Developmental Delay Registry, "The difference in the occurrence of developmental delays between children who take high doses of antibiotics and those who don't is astounding.

An even more disturbing story unfolded as I investigated what was being done to help all these children with LD, ADD and hyperactivity. It seems a therapy of choice is DRUGS and

RITALIN is the primary drug of choice! The current statistics are astounding: at least two million American children were on Ritalin in 1994; three to five percent of all school children are taking Ritalin, a 600% increase in five years; sales of the drug last year alone topped $350 million; twelve per cent of boys between six and fourteen years old are on Ritalin; the rate of Ritalin use in the US is at least five times higher than the rest of the world, according to federal studies; the US keeps kids on Ritalin longer than any other country. In schools throughout the country, at the sound of a bell, children line up in the nurses' offices for the daily "meds".

Ritalin is classified by the FDA as a Schedule II substance, along with cocaine, morphine, opium, methadone, Dexedrine, Desoxyn, Preludin, Percodan, Dilaudid and Demoral. They are all considered to have a "high potential for addiction or abuse, while having some medical value." Ritalin acts as an "upper" for adults and a "downer" for most children before puberty. Doctors and researchers admit they do not know exactly how this drug works.

Some of the known "side" effects of Ritalin are permanent and irreversible damaging of the nerve and muscle system, stunted growth (the literature tells parents not to worry about this because they usually "catch up" later), neurological disorders, Tourette's Syndrome, muscle tics (often mis-diagnosed as Tourette's syndrome), epilepsy, insomnia, nervousness, skin rashes, anorexia, nausea, dizziness, headaches, abdominal pain, blood pressure and pulse changes, psychotic states, depression and schizophrenia. In February, 1996, the FDA released a study involving mice that found Ritalin may have the potential to cause a rare form of liver cancer. The drug's long-term effects are unknown at this time. However, the FDA and the National Institute of Mental Health continue to insist that Ritalin is "safe and effective" and psychiatrists and medical doctors continue to routinely prescribe it at each monthly visit, often without carefully re-examining the child and questioning the parents. A March, 1996 *Newsweek* article stated, "In a recent survey, almost half of the pediatricians said they spent less than an hour evaluating children before prescribing Ritalin." One school psychologist I interviewed said a doctor she works with prescribes Ritalin on her diagnosis alone, without ever seeing the children.

I have interviewed parents whose children on Ritalin wouldn't sleep or eat, thereby experiencing serious weight loss. Some stopped growing; some were so "zombified" they couldn't function at all, or so hyper they were bouncing off the walls. Many children required other medication to counteract their reactions to the Ritalin. On their "drug vacations", as they are called, the "rebound effect" (the return of the children's ADD symptoms after they stop taking the drugs) was far worse than before they began taking medication. Some parents experiment with dosages without consulting their physician, attempting to save money on doctor's bills and to achieve some sort of moderation in their children's behavior. One young mother, describing the severe muscle tic her child developed -- a sign that Ritalin is STRONGLY contraindicated -- said her doctor simply gave her another pill to counteract the tic, never suggesting that the Ritalin should be stopped. She trusted the doctor and didn't know any better. A significant point is that many children do not need the medication at home; for some, these "disorders" seem to be a reaction to school.

I must say here, however, that other parents I interviewed, although they initially resisted putting their children on drugs, claim it has "made all the difference in the world;" "his grades were better;" "he could sit still long enough to hear the assignment;" "we don't get calls from the school every other day;" "we can have a peaceful meal without an argument and the whole family is getting along better -- it's worth whatever risk we're taking." This "risk", however, remains very real and only increases over time.

Most of the parents I met at the CHADD meetings had resisted putting their children on drugs. Shockingly, it was often the teacher that suggested it, and in some cases demanded that a child either be medicated or removed from that teacher's classroom. Parents were driven to desperation as their child disrupted the entire household. Often the parents came into conflict over the proper treatment.

Due to the fact that intuitive children's systems are usually extremely hypersensitive to drugs of any kind, the use of Ritalin or any other narcotic is a high-risk proposition at best.

Although medication seems to be the first solution offered to most of these parents, there is general agreement, even among advocates, that Ritalin never should be given to a child as a primary or sole treatment. Other suggestions offered are: training for parents in effective behavior management and child advocacy; counseling or training ADD children in methods of self-control, attention focusing, learning strategies, organizational skills and/or development of social skills; psychotherapy to help the demoralized and at times depressed ADD child; other interventions at home and at school designed to enhance self-esteem and foster acceptance, approval, and a sense of belonging; setting of achievable goals; and establishing a consistent external reward system.

Positive reinforcement is a unanimously recommended treatment. Encouraging children's strengths, rather than criticizing their perceived shortcomings; expressing confidence in them and recognizing their daily efforts and the improvements they make; showing them respect; giving them as much undivided attention as possible (a minimum of fifteen to thirty minutes each day); concentrating on the contributions they make to the family; establishing house rules, routines and schedules; ascertaining that children understand which behaviors are unacceptable and the consequences for inappropriate behavior; making frequent and prolonged eye contact when talking or listening to them; treating children with tenderness and patience; speaking slowly and clearly to them; praising appropriate behavior; not demanding perfection, just best effort; and avoiding negative labels -- these are all adjustments parents can make to help their children realize their full potential. Nobody ever said it was easy to be a parent! Perhaps incorporating that lesson into the school curriculum would result in fewer unprepared parents down the road.

"Alternative" treatments for LD, ADD and hyperactivity, which are often mocked and discredited in the mainstream literature are: dietary intervention (Macrobiotics, Feingold diet and allergy testing), herbal, vitamin and mineral therapy, anti-motion sickness medication, treatment for candida yeast infection, EEG biofeedback, applied kinesiology, optometric vision training, music therapy and colored reading overlays. These "alternative" treatments have been very effective for many children. An "alternative" treatment considered by some to be "miraculous" will be discussed at length in the next chapter.

It's clear that diagnosis, remediation and treatment must be a group effort among the parents, the teacher, the remedial teacher and therapists, the guidance counselor, the psychologist or psychiatrist, the doctor and most of all the child. The March '96 *Newsweek* article suggested that before Ritalin is prescribed, the first step should be observation by parents, teacher and school counselor of behavioral history and academic achievement. The second step should be a thorough medical exam, including family history. Often other problems exist such as vision, hearing or allergies, for which specialists should be consulted as necessary. The third step should be seeing a psychologist, psychiatrist and/or neurologist to look for emotional disorders such as depression or severe anxiety, or neurological damage. Developmental specialists should be consulted; a speech pathologist or occupational therapist can test for more subtle problems, and search for learning disabilities and perception problems of which inattention may be symptomatic. All of these steps should be taken before medication is considered.

One thing almost all of the experts can agree on, is that children labeled with learning disabilities, ADD, hyperactivity and autism are almost always not stupid. On the contrary, they are usually the brightest, most gifted children. Diane McGuinness suggests, "It is possible that children who refuse to abide by adult admonitions to sit still and conform to rules set by adults for their own convenience are the very children who know what is good for them."[13]

According to child development research, a child develops most of its imaginative and intuitive faculties between the ages of four and seven. At this stage it is obviously not wise to try to introduce systems of abstract symbols (the alphabet, arithmetic) unless it's in an environment of play and movement. That's how children learn at that age. After age seven, children usually have developed the capacity for abstract thinking and can begin to efficiently learn the "three R's".

Of course, there will be exceptions to this development pattern and the intuitive child is likely to one of them. Guiding, encouraging, and supporting are the best strategies for the parent and educator here; let the precocious child set her own pace without being pushed. If there is a situation in which the child is learning material that is far ahead of what's being offered at school, the parent may have to act as a buffer between the child and the educator, who may well be at the mercy of "the system".

Another challenge intuitive children have in beginning school is learning appropriate behavior. If, for example, it has always been acceptable at home to run their toys without batteries, throw balls with their minds, or otherwise demonstrate telekinetic ability, before they begin school they must be taught where and when it is appropriate to do these types of things. I have heard children say that they thought everyone could see color around people and move objects with their minds, until they began school and had some dramatic, embarrassing situation occur that caused them to "shut down" their abilities. It's important that parents instruct the child very carefully, so that s/he does not feel s/he is a freak or strange, but simply has gifts not all children have, and that these are special activities to save for use at home.

What the intuitive children really need is special attention, and they usually can't get it from the public school system. That leaves either home schooling or private schools, such as Waldorf or Montessori schools.

Home schooling is the ideal form of education for the intuitive child, if the parents are willing and able to devote to it the time and energy required, because the curriculum and pace can be tailor-made to the child's needs and interests. Parents also have the flexibility of incorporating psychic or paranormal education and exercises into the curriculum to round out the intuitive child's educational needs. This may seem like an overwhelming task to some parents; however, there are many books to assist you, particularly *Home School: Taking the 1st Step* by Borg Hendrickson, which offers a complete list of providers, resources and hints. Your public library will have a variety of other books and publications to assist you (see resource list below). There is also computer assistance available through the "World Wide Web". Many parents around the country are joining together to create small home schools, thereby sharing the teaching responsibilities, and providing the children the opportunity to interact with each other. Social interaction is also accessible through church affiliations, YWCA's or YMCA's, and specialized classes such as ballet, karate or other martial arts.

The *Waldorf* schools, according to their literature, are "based on Rudolf Steiner's philosophy of education, which seeks to address the full and harmonious development of the child's spiritual, emotional, and physical capacities, so that he may act in life as a self-disciplined and morally responsible human being. Art, music and handicrafts are as important as reading, writing and arithmetic; the curriculum also includes strong moral and spiritual elements. Each day includes activities for the hands, body and heart as well as for the head. The teacher and class remain together for grades one through eight; and the schools are administered by the people most intimately connected with the educational needs of the children -- their teachers. The Free Waldorf School's explicit purpose is to create free, creative, independent, moral and happy human beings. Steiner summarized its task: 'Accept the children with reverence, educate them with love, send them forth in freedom'."

The brochure I received from the International Montessori Society states: "*The Montessori Method*" developed from the work of Dr. Maria Montessori first began in Italy in 1907 --

to scientifically study the child in its free expression within a nurturing supportive environment. Montessori teaching is essentially a way of being with children so that their ordinary expression of general disharmony -- e.g., unstable, lazy, disorderly, dependent, violent, stubborn, disobedient, fanciful, etc. -- disappears to reveal an underlying true 'normal' nature of complete harmony with the environment. Montessori education may be most constructively represented as being a complete commitment to three fundamental principles of nature with the child in the present moment. These three "Montessori" principles are implicated by the following phrases: (1) Observation, (2) Individual liberty, (3) Preparation of the Environment. Such Montessori principles serve as an inner "control of error" to guide one's effective approach and being with the child. This type of 'Montessori teaching' assures and enables the eventual emergence of the child according to its own true "normalized" nature; i.e., loving order and constructive activity, precociously intelligent, independent, joyful and spontaneously self-disciplined."

Margaret Mead once said no education would work unless based on art. The use of music, art, dance and movement has proved to be important in the learning process, as long as such activity is rooted in play, because both the right and left hemispheres of the brain are incorporated into the learning experience. Beginning at age four, children respond well to musical training because it involves "pure body response and action"[3] (they can "feel" it), which is how they learn best at that age.

One of the most exciting uses of color researchers have discovered, particularly in the last ten years, is its employment in education. The right side of the brain is the intuitive, creative, color perception side and the left side is the linear, logical, technical side; when both sides of the brain are used in learning, the information is better integrated and retained. The use of colored pencils, pens, finger paints and reading overlays all help to achieve this "superlearning".[1] Researchers have found that one can read through a colored, plastic overlay placed on a book and relieve eye strain as well as help overcome learning disabilities and dyslexia. Tests show better retention of the material when a child uses finger paints to write out math problems and vocabulary words, and if a vocabulary word is written out with colored pencils or pens (first using different colors for each letter, then the same color for the entire word), it will be integrated more easily and completely into the child's vocabulary.[1]

Intuitive children are often quite inventive and ingenious, showing intense interest and/or special gifts in the sciences and the arts. They should be encouraged as much as possible in whatever area they show an interest. Their ideas and concepts are sometimes very advanced, perhaps even too advanced for the parent or teacher to understand. Patience and support are called for here.

Reference Books

Toxic Psychiatry - Peter Breggin (The truth about drugging your child)

When Children Don't Learn - Diane McGuinness (Learning disabilities)

Children, The Challenge - Rudolf Dreikuris (Learning Disabilities)

Use Both Sides of Your Brain - Tony Buzan (Techniques to help you read efficiently, study effectively, solve problems, remember more and think creatively)

Unicorns Are Real - Barbara Meister Vitale (Creative learning techniques)

Superlearning - Ostrander & Schroeder (Excellent book, particularly mind mapping technique described)

The Brain Revolution - Marilyn Ferguson (Brain research)

Teaching for the Two Sided Mind - Linda Verlee Williams (How to use both sides of the brain)

Home School: Taking The 1st Step - Borg Hendrickson (This book is full of resources and information - EXCELLENT!)

A Survivors Guide to Home Schooling - Luanne Shakelford & Susan White

The Big Books of Home Learning - Mary Pride

Home School Manual: Plans, Pointers Reasons & Resources - Theodore E. Wade, Jr.

The Trust Children - Anna Kealoha (Home school activity guide)

The Home School Source Book - Donn Reed

Good Stuff: Learning Tools for All Ages - Rebecca Rupp

The Passionate Mind - Michael Schulmann (Bringing up an intelligent and creative child)

The Secret of Childhood - Maria Montessori (Insight into Montessori learning method)

Resources

Rainbows Unlimited, 1245 Palm St., Clearwater, FL 34615 (813) 441-2270 (Colorology book, colored reading overlays, other color therapy products)

National Home School Association, P.O. Box 157290, Cincinnati, OH 45215-7290, (513) 772-9580 (Promotes networking of home schoolers)

Home School Legal Defense Association, P.O. Box 159, Paeonian Springs, VA 22129, 703-338-5600 (Provides

information on state laws and a list of state home school organizations)

Association of Waldorf Schools of North America, 3911 Bannister Rd., Fair Oaks, CA 95628 (916) 961-0927 (For school nearest you)

Rudolf Steiner College, 9200 Fair Oaks Blvd., Fair Oaks, CA 95628 (916) 961-8727 (Teacher Training)

Oak Meadow School, P.O. Drawer Q, Blacksburg, VA 24063, (703) 552-3263. (Home school provider, also taped courses on parenting, home schooling and creative teaching. Free catalog.)

Holistic Education Review, P.O. Box 328, Brandon, VT 05733, (800) 639-4122

J.L. Hammett Co., P.O. Box 9057, Braintree, MA 02184-9057, 800-333-4600. (Complete line of learning tools, children's musical instruments, audio tapes, teacher books and aids, games, books, arts and crafts.)

National Academy For Child Development, P.O. Box 1001, Layton, Utah 84041, 801-451-0942. (Innovative techniques for learning disabled)

Brain Gym, Edu-Kinesthetics, Inc., P.O. Box 5002, Glendale, CA 91221. (Exercises for the brain, very effective)

Superlearning, 450 7th Ave., New York, NY 10123 (Tapes and resource material produced by authors of *Superlearning)*

Home Education Magazine, 1814 Hwy 20, Box 1083, Tonasket, WA 98855, (509) 486-1351 (For home schoolers)

Homeschooling Marketplace Newsletter, R R #2, Fontanelle, IA 50846

Montessori News, International Montessori Society, 912 Thayer Ave, Suite 207, Silver Spring, MD 20910, (301) 589-1127 (Programs, services and resources for Montessori education)

Calvert School, Tuscany Rd., Baltimore, MD 21210 (301) 243- 6030 (Home school provider)

Clanlara School, Home Based Ed Program, 1289 Jewett, Ann Arbor, MI 48104 (Home school provider)

Resource Center For Educational Renewal, P.O. Box 298, Brandon, VT 05733-0298, 800-639-4122 (Exceptional resource for alternative, holistic educational books)

Sounds Like A Miracle

As I researched the subjects of DPT and other vaccines and their relation to learning disabilities, Attention Deficit Disorder and hyperactivity, I remembered Susan Calliham, a woman I had once met who had a DPT brain-injured child. Susan and I had talked about her using colored lights with her child, and I knew she had tried a variety of alternative modalities, including something she was very enthusiastic about called Auditory Integration Training (AIT). Now both a practitioner and trainer of AIT, Susan told me when I telephoned her of the seemingly "miraculous" results she had obtained with over two hundred learning disabled and autistic children using this method. She suggested I read *Sound of a Miracle*, by Annabel Stehli and *Hearing Equals Behavior*, by Guy Berard, M.D., as well as interview a woman that worked with her when she had an AIT office in the Tampa Bay area -- which, conveniently, is where I was located.

I learned that AIT was invented by French ear, nose and throat specialist Dr. Guy Berard to treat his own impending deafness. After successfully treating himself, Berard discovered that a majority of learning disabled and dyslexic children have hyper-acute hearing, and that AIT could often reduce or eliminate the learning disability. AIT has been used by doctors and therapists in Europe for thirty-five years, but has only been available in the US since 1992.

Susan explained that AIT is a form of "intensive sensory integration" or music therapy. Sensory integration is the ability to take in, sort out and connect information from the world around us. After a thorough interview and audiogram, to determine which frequencies the client hears too loud or too soft, specially modulated music is played through headphones. The client listens for a period of one half hour,

228

twice a day for ten days. Studies have shown AIT to be of benefit to people with Attention Deficit Disorder, dyslexia, autism and related disorders. An estimated 20 percent of the population suffers from distortions in hearing or sensitivity to certain sounds, which may contribute to inappropriate or anti-social behavior, irritability, lethargy, impulsivity, restlessness and high tension levels. Improvements reported after AIT include more appropriate emotional response, expression and interaction, better articulation and auditory comprehension and an overall increase in academic and social skills.

I spent the next weekend reading (and crying!) through *Sound of a Miracle.* Annabel's touching account of her ultimately successful search for a cure for her daughter Georgie, who was born one month premature and diagnosed autistic, mentally retarded, learning disabled and schizophrenic, described so many symptoms and situations similar to those of the intuitive children I had been researching that I knew AIT was another important piece of the puzzle of how to help these special kids.

Georgia spent almost five years of her life before the age of eleven in residential treatment. At eleven she underwent AIT. Even a few days into the treatment, Georgie seemed less distracted and better able to take instructions. After ten days her audiogram showed her hearing was within the normal range; her I.Q. went from 75 to 97. With some additional tutoring, Georgie went on to graduate from college magna cum laude and received the Charles Salzberg Award in recognition of outstanding achievement. She speaks six languages and she is considered to be one of the most remarkable AIT autism success stories. I saw her on the Sally Jesse Raphael Show, where she demonstrated her photographic memory by drawing a map of Africa and naming all the countries.

What fascinated me most about the book (and is most relevant to our purposes) was Georgie's account, after undergoing AIT, of how acute her senses had been. She had been able to hear street noises three blocks away, toilets flushing at the other end of the building, blood rushing in her veins (the sound of her circulation was a big problem). Certain sounds made her crazy: clanking of dishes in the sink, candles on a birthday cake being blown out, people breathing, the "bink" of a jack-in-the-box, certain people's voices, wind (because she was afraid she would blow away), rain (sounded like a machine gun), rain on an umbrella (sounded like drumming), the ocean (like a tidal wave). If there was peripheral noise like a radio, TV or stereo, she couldn't think straight. The sound of her own breathing bothered her, so she breathed with her mouth open.

She saw colors others couldn't see and they were very intense. She was fascinated by people's hair because she could see every strand. Sunsets made her squint because they were too bright. A merry-go-round "blitzed" her with color and tinny music.

She hated the smell of certain foods and liked others. Certain smells bothered her: people, animals, deodorant, perfume, after-shave. She could smell hand lotion from the next room, but she liked seals because, she said, they didn't smell!

She was insufficiently sensitive in certain areas and too sensitive in others. She didn't feel pain when she deliberately banged her head -- she was trying to feel something to make her "feel alive". Touching was uncomfortable and made her feel "funny". The way people sounded and smelled to her, and how it felt to her when they touched her, left her no choice but to avoid contact with them. When asked why she didn't look at people she said, "There are things that move in people's eyes and the colors bother me, too." Georgie was, in short, a supreme example of hypersensitivity. While this hypersensitivity drove Georgie into autism, we find these same sensitivities in children with learning disabilities, hyperactivity, and Attention Deficit Disorder.

I asked Susan and her colleague if either of them had noticed in their AIT patients some of the other characteristics I had been finding with the intuitive children. They both responded affirmatively. Jennifer ventured a guess that 95 percent of her clients showed intuitive ability. Susan was a little more conservative, but they both agreed that if they asked the right questions in the Pre-Care Questionnaire and interview, they would probably find the psychic and paranormal component more often.

Jennifer, the mother of a son diagnosed with Attention Deficit Hyperactive Disorder and on Ritalin since he was five, was ecstatic with the results of AIT. She exclaimed, "It was truly a miracle!" I asked her if her son had ever demonstrated any psychic abilities. She told me that right after his AIT training they were rearranging his toys in the closet. He stopped and said, "Wait, I know what to do, I saw it in a future dream!" He quickly and efficiently arranged all the boxes in perfect order. When asked what a "future dream" is, he explained that it is "sort of like a snapshot of the future"; he sees it and then it comes true. She asked him when this started and he said he always did it, but didn't mention it because he "didn't think it was important". He also told her of an occasion when he had an out-of-body experience and visited his parents at their workplaces, overhearing a telephone conversation they had about their concern over a bad storm. He accurately described an area of his father's workplace which he had never seen "in the flesh".

Although AIT practitioners are not presently at liberty to boast (see below), I have read and heard some truly "miraculous" stories about the success of AIT, particularly with learning disabilities, dyslexia, Attention Deficit Disorder and hyperactivity. It is often successful with autism; however, that is a more complex disorder and usually requires multiple modalities. No one claims that AIT is the only answer; however, its success rate is truly remarkable.

After interviewing the trainers and parents and reading the above mentioned books (as well as Annabel Stehli's new work, *Dancing In the Rain: Stories of Exceptional Progress by Parents of Children With Exceptional Needs)*, I was truly excited to have a successful modality to suggest to the desperate parents I was meeting. Then came the bad news!

In January, 1994, The Georgiana Organization (formed by the Stehlis to establish AIT in this country by offering training, certification, equipment, information and network support), received a warning letter from the FDA saying that the AudioKinetron (the French AIT machine) had been ruled a Class III medical device and they were no longer allowed to sell or distribute it until it was properly registered with the FDA. In September, 1994, BGC Enterprises (the US AIT manufacturer) in San Diego received a similar warning letter from the FDA.

Since that time, the French manufacturer of the AudioKinetron has taken no action to register the device with the FDA, or to seek approval from the FDA to continue marketing the device in the US. BGC Enterprises has made two applications requesting the FDA to rule that their AIT device is substantially equivalent to an existing hearing aid/auditory training device already approved for marketing.

Both those applications have been denied; the latest denial was received by BGC in February, 1996.

While sale or distribution of any new devices used to administer AIT is prohibited, the use of the devices by practitioners who are certified to use either the AudioKinetron or the BGC device has not been stopped by the FDA ruling. In Florida there is a state law which prohibits use of a medical device not approved by the FDA. Thus, in that state AIT is no longer available. There are, however, about 150 practitioners in the US still offering AIT. It is strongly advised that they claim only that AIT may be of benefit in remediating hearing distortions which may be associated with dyslexia, learning disabilities, Attention Deficit Disorder, Pervasive Developmental Delay, autism and similar disorders.

In order to obtain FDA approval, application for new product approval will have to be made, and clinical studies will have to be submitted to demonstrate the safety and effectiveness of the device. A petition will have to be filed to down-classify the product from Class III to Class II. All efforts will be made to show that AIT is simply a form of non-invasive music therapy. The Georgiana Organization is seeking financing to fund this project; it is hoped that clearance from the FDA to market a new AIT device would be received within about one year from the time the application is actually submitted.

In thirty-five years, no one has ever been injured or damaged by AIT in any way. Here we have a non-invasive, possible solution and, dare I say the word, "cure" for some of the five to ten million children, as well as the many adults, in the US suffering with learning disabilities, dyslexia, Attention Deficit Disorder and hyperactivity -- a means to get some of the two million plus children currently under medication off toxic, damaging drugs like Ritalin safely and simply, in as little time as ten days. Now the FDA has stepped in, hindering and perhaps prohibiting its use, as the agency has so frequently done with safe, alternative medical modalities, and not frequently enough with the toxic chemicals with which the population is assaulted from every quarter. "Outrageous" is not too strong a term for this situation.

This is but one more illustration of the challenges faced by intuitive and other "special" children and their parents. The solution once again lies with an informed, aroused and involved citizenry -- we have no freedoms to lose but our own!

Reference Books

Hearing Equals Behavior - Guy Berard (AIT)

Sound of a Miracle - Annabell Stehli (Autism & AIT)

Dancing In The Rain - Annabel Stehli (Autism, ADD, ADHD, PDD, dyslexia, Fetal Alcohol Syndrome, hyperlexia and AIT - case studies)

Resources

Susan Calliham, (704) 298-2495, Asheville, NC (Certified AIT Practitioner and authorized AIT Trainer)

The Georgiana Foundation, P.O. Box 2607, Westport, CT, 06880, 203-454-1221 (List of Practitioners in other states, books)

Psychic Ability

Kathy knew she should check on her two kids whenever she heard them giggling hysterically. She had caught them on several occasions throwing their toys at each other without even touching them!

Mark, fifteen, can telepathically calm crying babies, and soothe agitated zoo animals. He says babies and animals both "look around for him" when he is doing it, and acknowledge him in some way when they spot him -- the babies, for example, will smile at him.

At her wit's end, a grandmother telephoned me: her five year-old grandson, who when at home routinely ran his battery-operated toy cars without the batteries, had demonstrated his ability for one of his neighborhood friends. The boy told his mother, who promptly banned her son from any further contact with Sammy, who in turn could not understand such a reaction and was deeply hurt.

Her teacher and the other kids at school thought it was "really fun" that Joan could tell them things about themselves she had no way of knowing, until the day she predicted the sudden death of one of the other teachers and it came true.

A psychic friend of mine brought her granddaughter, Lannie, three, over to my house. At the time I was doing some art work with glitter paint and gemstones. I heard Lannie whisper to her grandmother, "See the fairy on her shoulder? She likes the sparkles." My friend could see the fairy too!

One day, when Lannie was about fourteen months old, her mother had a very bad headache. Lannie said, "Mommy, you head hurt, lie down, I fix it." Her grandmother come over shortly thereafter; Lannie's mother was lying on the couch asleep and Lannie had her hands on her mother's head. Lannie exclaimed, "Mommy headache all gone." Her grandmother asked her what she had done. She said, "I put my hands inside her head and made the pain go away." Her mother woke up and said that was exactly what it felt like. Since she was about a year old, Lannie has been able to look at a person, know where it hurts and "fix it".

When Annie was four her grandmother was very sick. That was the first time Annie realized she could "see inside someone's body and touch them and make them feel better." One of her favorite things to do was to sit in the pasture among the cattle, because "the energy beings would come and show me what was wrong with the cows when they were sick and how I could fix them."

Lannie, her mother and grandmother (whom Lannie called "Mema") were riding in the car when Lannie was about two. She suddenly announced, "Mema, I fly with you last night. I came to get you and you had a man and lady sleeping at your house in your big bed in the living room." (She couldn't have known that her grandmother had in fact had overnight guests.) Her grandmother asked her, "What did we do?" The response: "We got Mommy and she didn't have any clothes on and we just went up through the ceiling." As it turned out, Lannie's mother was indeed sleeping in the nude on the night in question!

Randy began displaying his healing ability at eighteen months of age. His father had a headache; Randy touched his head and said, "Ouch, I know that must hurt. If you let it go, it will stop." On another occasion when his father had a sore back, Randy touched it and the pain instantly disappeared.

Jill was three when she told a woman that her baby was "an angel and will go to heaven in two days". The child did indeed pass away two days later.

After meeting and learning to trust his therapist (who was herself telepathic), Danny, age three, announced to his father he would like to invite her over for dinner. When asked why, he responded, "Because I would like some intelligent conversation at the dinner table!" He was so excited to have someone to whom he could relate that he began to visit her astrally (out-of-body) at night. She found it necessary to discuss the concept of boundaries with him.

Sara, at the age of four, began talking to her "friend" that nobody else could see. She would insist that a place be set for her at the dinner table and space be reserved in the car next to her on any family outings. Sara would have long conversations with "Becky", pausing attentively to hear her responses and giggling. When Sara was asked where "Becky" came from, she responded, "From heaven." "Becky" stopped coming to visit when Sara was about nine.

While sitting in church, Patty, age two, suddenly exclaimed to her mother, "Mommy, that big angel sure scared me!" Her mother asked "What angel?" Patty pointed at the stage and said, "That one, can't you see it?" Another day Patty was lying in bed giggling and looking at the ceiling. Her mother asked her what she was looking at and she replied, "All the angels flying around in a circle up there."

Gary, four, says this is his first time on this planet; he "coordinated in on his mother to get here, and has it all mapped out how to get home."

The demonstration of psychic ability can be one of the most disturbing aspects of the intuitive child's development for the uninformed adult and, depending on the reactions of those around him, for the child as well. The intuitive child usually assumes everybody can do and see the things s/he can, until the stark reality hits home, usually when s/he begins school. Intuitive children have reported embarrassing experiences that often contributed to their either curtailing or completely shutting down their special abilities.

According to Joseph Chilton Pearce, "More children display psychic ability than extraordinary overall intelligence, indicating that psychic abilities are so much a part of our genetic fabric that they are even less prone to destruction than other aspects of intelligence. Psychic ability is designed to establish links between self and world and they utilize sound biological procedures in the brain."[4] In other words, in regard to psychic abilities, the intuitive child may be seen as one that has not been deprived of its birthright by the many degenerative influences (poor diet, pollution, drugs, alcohol, stress, radiation, negative acculturation) that act upon it from conception.

The age of four is when the intuitive faculties are supposed to develop -- and they must have "models" in order to develop properly. Remarkably, many of the intuitive children that I have heard about or interviewed have begun demonstrating psychic abilities at a very early age, well before age four. Also, their parents do not or cannot act as models for psychic talents. One might well ask, then, who or what is "modeling" for these children? Who are they imitating? Where are they getting the support and validation to sustain and strengthen their abilities? It may be that the various invisible entities with which these children interact are guides and role models as well as playmates. The intuitive children would seem to have available to them a greater range of mental and psychic resources than "average" children.

Being able to see beyond the visible light spectrum, they are often able to see ghosts, angels, devas, fairies and extraterrestrials. These beings exist at a "higher" frequency than is usually perceptible by most people; however, they are there for those who can "tune them in." Intuitive children will often have a fascination for the woods and nature, because they can see the devas and fairies who live there. Also, "little white energy lights", which they can see dancing and bouncing around, have often been described to me by the children. Many adults see them, too, usually out of the corner of the eye, but they explain them away with comments about needing new glasses.

Clairvoyance is the ability to see beyond the normal range of vision. This includes the ability to see visions of the future (known as precognition), visions of the past, and visions of the present ("remote viewing"). One of the events most likely to shut down a child's psychic ability is the vision of the death of a loved one. This has been frequently reported to me by the intuitive child who sometimes feels in some way responsible for the death. Foreseeing the future has, of course, been a part of our culture since the beginning of recorded history; it is called "prophecy". It is not odd or strange; it is simply a gift some people possess. Nostradamus and the biblical figure Daniel are just two examples.

Clairaudience is the ability to hear "psychically", or what some people refer to as "hearing voices in their heads". I would be willing to wager that many people in mental hospitals are there simply because they are having psychic experiences neither they nor their therapists understand. "Channeling" can be a type of clairaudience; a person hears a voice and then repeats what s/he hears. This does not apply to "full trance" channeling, in which the individual "vacates" the body to provide a channel for some other entity and has no conscious memory of the event. Clairaudience would likely be involved, of course, in communication between the intuitive child and his or her "imaginary friend".

Clairsentience is the ability to psychically feel information or impressions. We often speak of having "a gut reaction" to or "a feeling" about something or someone. Like "Randy", many intuitive children have the ability to actually sense other people's physical and emotional pain without being told about it.

Telekinesis is the ability to move objects with the mind. I have heard many stories of children running toys without batteries, floating objects around a room or closing and opening doors telekinetically. Pearce cites experiments showing this to be a learnable skill.[3]

Telepathy is the ability to communicate directly, mind to mind. I have heard many stories of children communicating with other people and even animals in this manner. This ability can be particularly threatening to some caregivers; how does one control a child that can "read one's mind"?

Additionally, a significant number of children's psychic experiences are related to family members and friends, whose well-being is often the subject matter of the child's experience. A child may, for example, foresee the death or illness of a grandparent. It is easy to imagine the average parent's frightened or perplexed reaction to such a prediction coming true. Here again we see the need for accurate and unbiased information.

The *"imaginary friend"* experienced by many children has exasperated many parents and teachers. The phenomenon has a variety of possible explanations: The child could be communicating with the spirit of an animal or dead child (possibly a twin), or with a fairy, angel, sprite or extraterrestrial. S/he could be having a telepathic or out-of-body experience, or it could simply be the child's vivid imagination. I have, however, read accounts of people other than the child being able to see the "imaginary friend". Sometimes children discover "imaginary friends" when they are lonely or sick -- having someone always around can be very comforting. Some children talk to their "friend" in a language no one else understands. There is no reason for alarm on the part of the parent, unless the "imaginary friend" tells the child to do evil or destructive things. In that case, professional assistance would certainly be desirable. Again, patience is the key word. Ridiculing or denying the existence of the "imaginary friend" or mocking the child in any way can do irreparable damage, causing the child to suppress his or her emotions and feel it is unsafe to confide in the parent. It is not necessary to make a big issue of this; the parent can simply ask about the "friend", accept it as natural, and usually the child will simply grow out of it.

Many of the intuitive children demonstrate a remarkable insight into the character of others. They often have very definite likes and dislikes in people and their insights are usually accurate. I have heard stories from parents about their intuitive children who would not go near a particular neighbor or visitor, and it was subsequently discovered the individual in question had a very dark side.

Doing psychic exercises with intuitive children when they are in the hypnogogic state (about to go to sleep or just upon waking up) can be very helpful in developing their abilities.

Preceding the exercises with meditation, which can include soft music, story-telling, reading and/or breathing exercises, can help to induce the hypnogogic state at any time and enhance the results of the exercises, one of which is to think of a number or an animal and ask the child to guess it. Also, one can make flash cards with shapes the child recognizes, then look at one of them and ask the child to guess what it is. Still another exercise is to have the child close his eyes, hand him fabric of different colors and ask him to guess the color; or one can simply hold something in one's hand and ask the child to guess what it is. By making it a game, the child will develop its abilities much more quickly.

A useful tool in helping a child feel safe is the "White Light of Protection". Guide the child to visualize a small white flame of light in her heart, gradually allowing it to expand to fill her chest, then her whole body, the space around her body, then filling the room, the house and finally the whole neighborhood. The light can be visualized then as a white cloud of protection, keeping one safe from all harm.

It is important for parents to discuss these "psychic" abilities with their children when they are demonstrated, reassuring them that these such talents are natural, but that not every one remembers how to use them. As they get older, children should be given books to read on the subject, so that they can better understand their psychic talents. Most important is encouraging them to talk to you about their experiences. Children have advanced as reasons for not communicating with their parents such remarks as, "These things have always happened, but I didn't think it was important", "I was afraid you would think I was lying", "I thought everybody could do it", "I was afraid you would laugh", "I was afraid you would get mad" or, perhaps most poignant of all, "I didn't think you would understand".

Of course, it's an equally bad idea to thrust an unwilling child into the spotlight, forcing them to display their abilities for others. Such command performances can be as devastating to a sensitive child as the lack of understanding and approval, and lead to the same result -- a shutdown of their talents!

Some parents have found it helpful to keep a journal of their child's progress in this area, until the child is old enough to continue it on his own.

Again, children learn by modeling and imitating. Role models must acknowledge the children's abilities, show them an open mind and a loving heart, and help as best they can in the development of their children's psychic talents. And always be ready to learn, as well as teach!

Reference Books

Develop Your Psychic Skills - Enid Hoffman (Easy to understand descriptions of each type and practical exercises)

You Are Psychic - Peter A. Sanders (Descriptions and psychic exercises)

Future Memory - P.M.H. Atwater (Precognition and the human mind)

Journeys Out Of The Body - Robert Monroe (Out-of-body experiences)

Hands Of Light - Barbara Brennan (Methods of hands-on healing)

Soul Trek - Elisabeth Hallett (Compelling stories of contact before birth and before conception)

Life Before Life - Helen Wambach (Past life research study)

They Travel Outside Their Bodies - Elwood Baumann (Children's book on out-of-body experiences)

Sixth Sense - Larry Kettelkamp (Children's book on psychic abilities)

Mass Dreams of the Future - Chet Snow, Ph.D. and Helen Wambach, Ph.D. (Research based on progressing people into the future)

Near-Death Experience

I recalled under hypnosis an incident that occurred when I was about three years old: During a day at the beach I ducked under the water to avoid hearing an argument between my parents. Apparently I stayed under too long; I left my body and rose into the air. I remember looking down at my family on the beach. Suddenly, my mother jerked me out of the water and I was back in my body, choking. My mother doesn't recall the incident.

Tommy's mother told me he was "never the same" after a near-death experience at age four. He was "smarter and could fix things" and demonstrated most of the intuitive child characteristics.

Lonnie, seven, described her near-death experience as an infant as going back to the "white light where God is and I was before I was born. I wasn't afraid because I remembered it and it was warm there."

In *Future Memory*, P.M.H. Atwater reports on research indicating that Abraham Lincoln, Albert Einstein, Wolfgang Amadeus Mozart, and Edward de Vere, the 17th Earl of Oxford (a man remarkable enough in his own right, but who is also believed by some scholars to be the author of the works of one William Shakespeare!) all suffered near-death experiences as children, which resulted in "a growth spurt in the brain above and beyond what might be expected at their age level."[18]

People who in years past would have died are now surviving accidents and illness; with modern medical technology, it's now possible to literally bring someone back from the dead.

That fact alone accounts for a great deal of the attention lavished upon the near-death experience in recent years. Books by Raymond Moody, Ph.D., Dannion Brinkley, P.M.H. Atwater and many others have shed a good deal of light on what happens when we get to "the other side". We're speaking here, it should be understood, not merely of a brush with "the Grim Reaper"; the true "near-death" experience involves clinical death for a period of time -- on the average, around ten minutes or so -- from which one awakens remembering what happened during that time. And those memories are usually enough to in some way transform one's life. Review the work of the people mentioned above for particulars; the point I want to make here is that many of the "intuitive children" I've heard about have undergone this type of experience.

As with the tales of ET abduction and contact, we see witnesses independently reporting similar experiences. The awareness departs the physical body and perhaps watches resuscitation attempts for a while, then travels through some sort of tunnel toward a warm, inviting white light. The subject is often greeted by deceased relatives and/or pets, and undergoes a life review of some kind. S/he is then presented with a choice of returning to the body or "going on" (obviously, we have no reports from those who have gone on!), or simply told that s/he must return to life to finish a job or mission of some sort. The near-death survivor usually returns with a transformed or at least renewed sense of self and his/her connection to Spirit, as well as greater psychic abilities and the conviction that s/he has a mission of some sort to accomplish.

From *Future Memory*:

With my research of near-death survivors, I found

the spread of impact from the brain shift that occurred as follows (1994 figures): 21 percent claimed no discernible changes afterward, 60 percent reported significant changes, and 19 percent said changes were so radical, they felt as if they had become another person. This range of percentages seems to fit across the board with the universal experience of a brain shift, no matter how caused.[18]

Atwater points out the similarities between the near-death experience and other life-transforming changes including the "ET" abduction phenomenon (see introduction). It is her conclusion that such transformations can have the effect of literally causing the brain to grow (i.e. create new neural pathways), no matter when in life they occur. In other words, any of us might at any time become a "Millennium Child"!

Could these "transformations" be occurring in the womb -- or even earlier, in the so-called "field potential" out of which the three-dimensional universe manifests? Are they being aided and abetted by "Visitors" from elsewhere, or are they an integral part of human evolution? I've heard reports of increasing numbers of children being born with enlarged frontal lobes (the center of "higher", abstract thinking). Is our species being experimented upon, as we experiment upon monkeys, rabbits and mice? If so, who or what is doing the experimenting, and why? Until we know how (and why!) the elements, energy and consciousness interact to create a human being, we'll be groping in the dark for the answers to such questions. Perhaps the intuitive children, drawing upon the powers of their "transformed" brains, will be the ones that find those answers.

Reference Books

Life After Life and *Reflections on Life After Life* - Raymond Moody (Near-death experiences, a classic)

Coming Back to Life: The After-Effects of the Near-Death Experience, Beyond The Light: What Isn't Being Said About The Near-Death Experience, Future Memory - P.M.H. Atwater (Watch for Atwater's new book on children and the near-death experience.)

Saved By The Light and *At Peace In The Light* - Dannion Brinkley

Life At Death - Kenneth Ring, Ph.D.

Return From Death - Margot Grey

The Near-Death Experience: A Medical Perspective - Michael B. Sabom

To Die Is Gain - Johann Christoph Hampe

The Final Choice - Michael Grosso

Return From Tomorrow - George Ritchie

Closer to the Light: Learning From the Near-Death Experiences of Children - Melvin Morse, M.D.

The Door to the Secret City - Kathleen J. Forti, Kids Want Answers Too!, 1544 Bay Point Drive, Virginia Beach, VA 23454 (Child's perspective on the near-death experience)

Resources

International Association for Near-Death Studies, P.O. Box 502, East Windsor Hill, CT 06028   (203) 528-5144 (Nonprofit organization dedicated to educating the public and promoting research on the near-death phenomenon)

Mellen-Thomas Benedict, P.O. Box 1898, Soquel, CA 95073 (For audio tapes about his near-death experience contact Benedict & Associates at (408) 427-5554 -- for information concerning his regeneration technology using light that he received from the other side contact Tru-Light Corporation at (408) 620-1008)

Reincarnation

Dale, five, asked his grandmother, "Why is Johnny down the street so mean?" She responded that she did not know; sometimes kids are angry. He exclaimed, "Well, he better straighten up or he'll just have to come back and do it over again right."

Arthur, three, was looking at a big picture book of the world. He pointed to Africa and said, "I used to live there when I was a little boy." He proceeded to name his mother, three brothers and four sisters and explained how they had to be very careful when they went to get water because there were big animals in the water. He said his skin was brown then.

Melissa spoke of Egypt and the pyramids as soon as she began talking at one year of age. She described to her mother, at length, the beautiful dresses she used to wear and what it was like to live in Egypt as a queen. She continually drew pictures of the pyramids, which she had never seen in this life.

Roy, four, told his therapist, "The hardest thing about being here for the first time is the consciousness. They even believe in death down here. There are more people walking around in their bodies that are like what they think death is, than anything that happens to you when your body shuts away."

No less than eight different women (none of whom knew any of the others) have told me that their children have at one time or another said to them, "I remember when I was big and you were little." They all used the same words!

250

Reincarnation is based on the idea that we are spiritual beings who have repeated physical experiences in order to work out karma (the law of "what goes around comes around" -- cause and effect), and to evolve spiritually, ultimately attaining conscious awareness of our creator source (God) and our unity with it.

This concept, obviously, inspires a great deal of controversy because it does not coincide with traditional Christian dogma. There is some research, however, indicating that references to reincarnation were removed from the Bible during the Council of Nicea in 553 BC. This is a very deep subject and beyond the scope of this book; however, I bring it up because so many of the intuitive children make references to their past lives and to their previous connections with current family members. Mentioning past life connections is often one of the first signs to a caregiver that a child has unusual abilities.

Many well-researched, proven cases exist of very young children having memories of past lives; they give dates, names, places and details of a previous life which are subsequently verified as completely accurate. Many books have been written giving details of these fascinating cases. (See the list of references at the end of this chapter.) Although children can usually access past-life memories consciously or in dreams, many adults have also been able to retrieve them through hypnosis, primal therapy or relaxation techniques. Wambach's research results were that 81 percent of her subjects -- under hypnosis -- said they chose to be born. 87 percent reported that they had known parents, lovers, relatives and friends not just in past lives but "in-between" lives as well. 68 percent, prior to being born, did not relish the prospect of living another lifetime, describing their attitudes as "reluctant", "resigned" or "anxious". Only 26 percent looked forward to the coming lifetime. 90 percent reported previous death experiences as pleasant. 30 percent indicated coming back to resolve "karmic relationships". 24 percent felt they had chosen their sex.[7]

Intuitive children frequently tell past-life stories. They have told me why they chose their parents and other family members: "So that I can work out the mistakes I made before," or "Because they helped me so much before." Sometimes they speak of wanting to experience a specific situation: "I wanted to be rich this time," "I needed to be poor this time," "I needed to learn compassion, so I came back crippled." Usually they express the desire to learn something.

They have also reported "life between life" memories. Mark explained that he was "light and decided he wanted to have a body". The "in-between-lives" state has been described as "floating in a warm, yellow light," being able to "go anywhere and be anything" or as being "a part of everything and everything being a part of me."

Regardless of how one explains or interprets it, the wealth of evidence that we have been here before demands attention. It is vital that the intuitive child's descriptions of past lives not be dismissed out of hand as fantasy or foolishness, much less condemned as heresy; if nothing else, these stories indicate a very healthy ability to imagine the world in special and remarkable ways.

Reference Books

Children Who Remember Previous Lives - Ian Stevenson

Twenty Cases Suggestive of Reincarnation - Ian Stevenson

Reincarnation, A New Horizon in Science, Religion & Society - Sylvia Cranston & Carey Williams

Born Today, Born Yesterday: Reincarnation - Gwen Risendorf (Written for Children)

Have We Lived Before? - Linda Atkinson (Written for Children)

Dreams

Melody, four, woke one morning sobbing that the earth was shaking and people were dying. It was the day of the 1989 San Francisco earthquake -- she lived in Georgia.

Sam, three, woke one morning and announced that "Grandpa came to visit last night. He looked just like he always did, but he didn't have any feet and sort of floated." (Grandpa had died three weeks before.)

Becky, five, insisted she couldn't ride the bus to school one day because she "dreamed it was going to get in a wreck." She was so insistent that her mother drove her to school; the bus was involved in an accident that morning.

Jerry, four, told his mother she should call his grandmother, because he "had been flying again last night and went to visit Gramma, but she wouldn't wake up." "Gramma" had died in her sleep that night.

Rebecca was troubled by her three year-old daughter's nighttime activity. She would awaken to find her daughter walking around the house, apparently sound asleep, talking in fluent French to someone Rebecca could not see! As far as she knew, her daughter had never even heard anyone speak French.

The elusive world of dreams has long been a primary focal point of consciousness research. We have learned that a particular brain-wave frequency is connected to the dream state and to every mode of awareness. The deep sleep state, during which dreams occur, is known as the delta state. Beta is the brain-wave state of waking consciousness, in which one is "locked into" physical reality, and focused on daily activity. Alpha is the brain-wave state one enters when daydreaming, meditating, fantasizing and sometimes even watching TV or driving. Most of us spend a good portion of our day in alpha when we are not actually concentrating on a task. The theta state is the bridge between alpha and delta -- the hypnogogic state, between sleeping or deep meditation and waking. It is the most elusive for humans to attain willfully and maintain, yet it is pivotal for the expansion of consciousness into other realms.

When brain waves shift (for instance, from beta to alpha), the brain literally begins emitting a different frequency, changing to some degree the reality one perceives. As part of the ego's efforts to maintain a coherent experiential structure (in other words, so that we can "know what we're doing"), boundaries are maintained around the "compartments" of consciousness. Normally, we're only awake, functioning and connected with our ego in the beta state, so to our ego-centered awareness, beta is the dominant state. However, the beta reality represents a very small fraction of our total capacity to generate and perceive other realities.

By willfully engaging the theta level, whether through meditation, relaxation or technological devices, one begins to integrate the levels of consciousness by "dissolving the barriers" between them. One can learn, for example, to maintain waking consciousness while in the dream state -- so-called "lucid dreaming". Perhaps this integration is what is involved in the experiences reported at the beginning of this chapter; children, being relatively free of the blocks adults create with restrictive belief systems, are able to more easily perceive these "other realities".

One also hears adults tell of flying dreams, precognitive dreams (ones that come true), being on space ships with ETs, and "going to school" on those ships; however, children have not read the books, seen the movies or been exposed to the information adults have. If indeed these are "only dreams", from what source do the children's minds draw such unlikely scenarios -- the minds of their elders? That theory, if true, would be as paradigm-shaking as visitors from outer space, but would, of course, do nothing to explain precognitive dreams.

If a child is awakened by a nightmare or believes there is a monster in the closet, it's best to acknowledge the experience and talk about it, rather than belittling or mocking them in any way. The child's empowerment is the goal to keep in mind. Remind them how to use the "White Light of Protection". Reassure them however you can, without leading them to erect barriers of fear between types of perceptual experience.

It is well for parents to encourage their children to talk about their dreamtime experiences, and to listen with an open mind. Some "dreams" are glimpses of other realities or dimensions -- or the future!

Reference Books

Dream Game amd Dream Power - Ann Faraday

The Dream & The Underworld - James Hillman (Unique psychological point of view)

The Art of Dreaming - Carlos Castaneda (Riveting tales of alternate realities)

Lucid Dreaming - Stephen LaBerge, Ph.D. (How to do it!)

Extraterrestrials

The following is excerpted from an interview with Amy, age eight:

Caryl: What do they (ETs) look like?

Amy: Well...there's some that are underwater people, and there's some that are just like -- they're like rainbow people, you can walk right through them and they look like rainbows, and stuff like that, there's different kinds.

Caryl: What does the ship look like? Have you ever seen it from the outside or do you just see it from the inside?

Amy: Mm-hmm (yes), sometimes. One time I went up in a ship and I had saw it before I went inside of it. It was like a triangle kind of a ship.

Caryl: Was it real big?

Amy: Mm-hmm (yes), it had lights on the side.

Caryl: So what else do you do on the ship?

Amy: I'll play with the kids, and sometimes I'll go up there and I'll be a teacher for the kids.

Caryl: What do you teach them?

Amy: Sometimes they'll be scared of us, and they'll bring us up there and -- um -- what I would tell them is -- that we are very nice and we will not hurt them and um -- they just would get scared of me sometimes or they'd either run away or they'd kind of float up and go hide.

Caryl: What do the grownups on the ship look like? The people who seemed to be running things, you know?

Amy: Um, there's all different kinds -- um -- I know my brother -- was an alien, he had one of the ships too, but he was still in like that kind of body as he would run it. He still does it sometimes when he's asleep.

Caryl: Your brother would run the ship?

Amy: Mm-hmm (yes). He'd like -- um, help everybody on there ("Brother" is about a year old at the time of this interview -- Amy is apparently talking about his pre-conception or pre-birth activity).

Caryl: When he gets on the ship he gets to be a big person?

Amy: Kind of...I guess I would consider him a grown-up up there 'cause -- you can grow up to a kind of age up there but it depends on what kind of aura you have...Like if -- all the babies up there would have pink 'cause they're just going in, and then the -- um -- I'd say that eight-year olds & nine-year olds and stuff would have yellow and the grownups would have -- white. So what Tommy (her brother) had was yellow so he's in between that right now.

Caryl: Have you seen any other people that have brothers and sisters up there?

Amy: Well, I was gonna have a bigger sister, but she had died in my Mom's tummy and one time when I went up in the ship I got to see her; she would talk to me and she told me why and stuff like that.

Caryl: Why she died? How come she died?

Amy: Well -- um -- turned out she was an alien, she needed to stay in the ship. And then, they sent us Tommy (little brother), so...

Caryl: After that? So, was it a good trade?

Amy: Kind of. I'd rather have a sister.

Caryl: But do you still get to see her sometime?

Amy: (Nods yes) Sometimes she's the one that takes me up into the ships.

Caryl: What's her name?

Amy's Mother: I call her "Tina"...You were in my tummy three months after "Tina" went away...You came in my tummy right away. They would've been, you know, sharing the womb, really.

Caryl: Did you come from somewhere else or did you come from the ship?

Amy: I didn't come from any ship.

Caryl: If you didn't come from a ship, why do you think they take you up on the ships all the time?

Amy: I don't know...maybe in one of my past lives I am gonna be an alien, I don't know!

Caryl: Well, are there lots of different kinds (of ET's) on the same ship?

Amy: Well, most of the time they're all the same on one ship.

Caryl: You go to different ships? You get to like -- go around and have tours?

Amy: Kind of.

Caryl: How do you get up on the ships?

Amy: Aw there's a whole bunch of ways -- sometimes you'll go up alone -- sometimes you'll float -- your body would stay down most of the time and your spirit would just go up, sometimes you'll just start walking and you'd go up into the air, your spirit would -- kinda go up and you'd end up in the ship.

Caryl: But your body stays back?

Amy: Mm-hmm (yes).

Caryl: Sometimes do you take your body?

Amy: Mm-mm (no).

Caryl: But you still look like you so they know what you look like.

Amy: (Nods yes) I do remember doing some stuff up on the ship, I was just kind of learning from them, too, 'cause they'd have me put these crystal shapes into the shape parts (?) and stuff like that, except for they weren't shapes like we have, they're different kinds.

Caryl: Yeah...And do you remember if the crystals did anything when you put 'em in? To the right hole?

Amy: They'd light up.

Caryl: Do they want to know what your life is like here?

Amy: Sometimes they want to know what it's like down here. Sometimes they'd come and visit except for they're in human bodies.

Caryl: Can they just take a human body when they want to, they can just make one?

Amy: Well, they're kind of like costumes.

Caryl: Are they really tight-fitting so it looks really real? Can you tell the difference?

Amy: Sometimes.

Caryl:· Would there be some of them that come on the ships that might be at the grocery store --

Amy: Yes.

Caryl: --or anyplace?

Amy: I remember this one time me and my brother and my Mom went to the grocery store and there was all these people following us. It was so funny -- except for they weren't people. They were -- um -- aliens in people bodies.

Mother: Tell 'em about the bubble ship that had the rooms that looked similar to your house and you could touch the different elements and things, remember?

Amy: Oh yeah -- I remember going up into this one ship was just like a big bubble except for -- um -- the bubble had a thing where the aliens lived, in something that looked like the inside of my house, except I could go through walls and stuff and it was really fun. And -- um -- I'd be able to cook on the stove and stuff, but I'd be able to touch -- um -- flames and stuff and it wouldn't burn me; just -- um -- touch them and actually pick them up and you could actually feel energy from them and stuff.

Caryl: Does all this happen just when you're asleep at night or does it happen during the day too?

Amy: Um, yes, sometimes during the day -- it happens during both.

Caryl: What would you be doing during the day when it happens, like when you're playing outside or something?

Amy: Um -- not really. It'd either be when I am -- if sometimes when I'm playing downstairs, maybe I'm just sitting there and I'm -- um, drawing something I'd just start staring at something and -- um -- then my spirit would go up into the ships.

Caryl: What happens to your body when your spirit goes up into the ships?

Amy: My body, I'd either be -- um -- my body would either be -- um -- drawing or just be staring at something.

Caryl: But it can keep drawing, huh?

Amy: (Nods yes)

Caryl: What else have you seen up there?

Amy: Wel-l-l-l, there's this one time I went -- um -- into this one ship, there were these people but they looked like dolphins. They could talk like people and they could talk like dolphins. They had fins and everything, but they wore real clothes and stuff.

Caryl: Did they sound like dolphins when they talked?

Amy: Mm-hmm (yes). When I went down there they -- um -- had computer-like kind of things and it looked like a big ocean down there.

Caryl: They had computers in the ocean?

Amy: Mm-hmm (yes), and it was kinda -- they just made it look like a big ocean. There was this one computer that had kept the whole ship running and it had a blue light coming out from it, it was a really tiny little light but it shined out really, really big so it made it look like a big ocean and stuff.

Caryl: It was the light that made it look like water?

Amy: Uh-huh (yes), and -- um -- one time I went up to that ship and they had put a new computer in; you touch it and you could, you touch any button you can make -- um -- like, a ghost kind of playmate, just like a spirit.

Caryl: It wasn't real, it was just pretend?

Amy: Yeah, if you would like it to be a boy or something like that, blonde hair or black hair and stuff, you could pick it and you could make up your own things.

Caryl: Did that spirit talk back to you and play with you?

263

Amy: Mm-hm (yes). It's really, really fun.

Caryl: Could you make it do anything you wanted it to do?

Amy: No.

Caryl: Do you go to school, like do you sit in a classroom sometimes and they teach you stuff?

Amy: Sometimes.

Caryl: Is it like school here?

Amy: (Shakes her head emphatically, No)

Caryl: Not at all, huh?

Amy: One time I went up to this one ship and -- instead of aliens [there were] these little tiny, tiny lights. You could barely even see them; they were different colors. When I went up into their ship there was a whole bunch of 'em.

Caryl: Did they talk with you or communicate with you?

Amy: Yeah.

Caryl: In your head?

Amy: Um -- sometimes out loud and sometimes telepathically. (Her tone was rather like, "Don't you know anything?"]

Caryl: It's kinda fun to do it telepathically, huh?

Amy: I like that better...sometimes they'd show me pictures instead.

Caryl: Oh really? Pictures in your head?

Amy: (Nods yes)

Caryl: Are they outside sometimes too, the pictures, where you can look at 'em and flip the pictures?

Amy: (Nods yes)

Caryl: You sound like you sure have an awful lot of adventures. Do you go with them almost every night?

Amy: (Nods yes) (begins to laugh)

Caryl: You hardly have time to sleep, huh?

Amy: (Laughing) Mm-mm (no) -- I remember this one time I went up into a ship and I was laying on the couch and my body was still there and -- um -- there was this -- um -- yellow light that kind of just lifted me up, I was still lying straight, it came up and lifted me up, and it took me through the wall. And I went through the wall and then I went into the ship. I was still -- I think I mighta took my body with it but I'm not sure: so I went up into the ship and it had different sorts of aliens in different rooms. It had a dolphin alien in one room, and it had -- um -- the rainbow aliens in one room and it had all these kinds of aliens but it was in the same ship.

Caryl: That was different then, you don't usually see that?

Amy: (Nods yes) -- And when I got back, I was -- um -- my body was tired and I -- every time I tried to get up and try to, at least just maybe go to get a drink I went eeyeow (indicating slumping down) -- I was so tired!

Caryl: Do you know why you have to go to school every night?   Have they told you why they're teaching you all this stuff?

Amy: Um (pause) -- I don't know.   There's this one time -- um -- I had went up to a ship and my body disappeared...I came back from the ship and I went to go get back in my body and I couldn't find it!   Well -- I just went and laid down on the waterbed and then -- and then I saw my body hiding in the closet, and so I went and I, I jumped back in it.   It was so funny.   I had got up to go and get a drink of water -- and then I went back to bed and I went up in a ship.   And -- um -- my body was still there and then it kinda just -- disappeared.   It was so funny.

Caryl: Sometimes if your Mom's at work can you like go and see her, if you're at home?   Can you go and see, visit, people who are on the earth someplace?

Amy: Yeah, sometimes, in spirit but they won't be able to see me most of the time.

Caryl: When they take you through the walls and stuff, do you feel something?   Does it tingle or...?

Amy: Mm-mm (no)

Caryl: Do you know how to go through walls by yourself?   Can you do it whenever you want?

Amy: Umm -- sometimes.

Caryl: Can you describe what it is you have to do to go through a wall?

Amy: Sometimes I'll -- first I'll see colors and I'll go through the wall...

Caryl: So when you see the colors -- the wall, it's just like -- sort of going through air, huh?

Amy: Mm-hmm. (yes)

Caryl: Is the wall still there, or does it disappear?

Amy: It's gone...Actually "Tina" would come and every time I -- um -- feel sad she'd come and she'd talk to me and stuff. And I'd stay in my room, I'd just lay there and read a book or something, my body would and my -- um -- spirit would be -- running around the house!

Caryl: If your spirit isn't in your body can somebody talk to you and then do you answer them?

Amy: Sometimes.

Caryl: Do you leave your body sometimes at school?

Amy: Yeah. That's a big problem.

Caryl: Teacher doesn't like that very much, huh? What does she say to you?

Amy: Well, most of the time I wouldn't be able to hear her, but I just kind of sit there staring at something, I just sit there going (makes staring wide-eyed face). I wouldn't actually be *doing anything. So she'd be able to tell right away, cuz -- I'd just kinda be sitting there.*

Caryl: Do you get in trouble, or what does she say?

Amy: Sometimes she'll act like she doesn't notice or anything, but sometimes she's very mean...she gets very mad. Her energy will get mad. Every time she'll start being mean -- I'll just shoot out all this love energy, and make a big shield over the whole class. So none of the bad energy can get in to them -- and -- um -- her energy would just kinda get real mad, you'd see all this red stuff shootin' out of her.

Caryl: Do you have other friends in school that can see color around people and stuff?

Amy: (Shakes her head no)

Caryl: No? Do any of the other kids go on ships at night? Do you know?

Amy: Well, normally if they do they get really scared.

Caryl: You don't have any other little friends that you can talk to about it, huh?

Amy: (Indicates no) I wish -- there was somebody -- um -- who wouldn't get really scared. I mean, my other friend -- every time -- um -- I talk to him about it, he just kinda -- looks at me and goes (makes a face) like that -- so he wouldn't know anything what I was talking about.

Caryl: Does he ever go up in the ship with you?

Amy: Sometimes.

Caryl: Does he remember, do you think?

Amy: (Indicates No)

This little girl expressed absolutely no fear of her experiences. Her mother is loving, accepting and supportive. Each morning, she asks the children where they've been during the night and what they've been experiencing. The lines of communication are wide open.

Mark, fifteen, said he doesn't like to telepathically communicate with the UFOs and ETs anymore, because he once inadvertently contacted "the bad ones" and it scared him.

Tammy has been waking up screaming and shaking in the middle of the night since she was about eighteen months old, sometimes with a bloody nose and/or unexplained marks on her body. When Tammy was three, her mother often found her outside in the middle of the night, even though all the doors and windows were locked. When asked where she had been, she would say "flying" or "up in the sky".

The first experience Bobby remembers was at age five when his bedroom filled with blue light. He could "see the little bug people around my bed and they floated me out the window". The next thing he remembers "I was in a room with lots of other kids. We were just waiting for our turn to see the doctor. I wasn't afraid -- I had been there before and knew some of the kids."

A day care provider reported to me that two sisters -- aged two and three -- disappeared from her center. A thorough search of the house, yard and neighborhood turned up nothing. Two hours later the two little girls walked smiling out of the bedroom (the very first place searched). When asked where they had been, they explained they had been "up with their friends playing". They said, "ET came, our bodies got buzzy, we went to sleep and went on the space ship."

One day the same two little sisters were found packing. When asked what they were doing the oldest responded, "I have to get all the pieces of myself and put them together because they need them on the ship so they can have the pieces of myself and put them together so Elyria has more of a piece of me when she is here." The day care provider added that the little girls claimed to be "switching" with duplicates of themselves who live on the ship. She was inclined to believe them because she had noticed that at times the girls seemed quite different, lacking their usual enthusiasm and speaking rather "mechanically". A sensitive herself, she said "The duplicates were cooler and 'squishier' to the touch, had an 'electronic' feel to them and mirror-like eyes."

Millie, five, said going up on the ships was more like an "attunement rather than an abduction."

The writings of Whitley Streiber, Raymond Fowler, Budd Hopkins, John Mack and dozens of other researchers and experiencers have made it clear that SOMETHING is going on out there beyond the fringes of everyday human reality. That "something" apparently includes some sort of agenda involving the manipulation -- or at least the study -- of human genetics. I have found in my research many accounts of children seeing bright lights, and being taken by "friends" of various descriptions, who "float" them up to big space ships. The children report being physically examined or "going to school", after which they are returned from whence they came.

They sometimes wake up in the morning with nosebleeds, bruises or inexplicable marks on their bodies.

Very often, hearing these stories from their kids reminds the parents of their own on-going visitations, some of which may have occurred while the mother was pregnant with the intuitive child. If it's possible to interview the grandparents, one may well find they had similar experiences. There is evidence from many quarters that this phenomenon runs in families.

I have heard the "abduction" scenario described independently by a number of children, some experiencing it as a fearful, terrorizing event, others experiencing it as a natural, normal, "fun" part of life. Upon talking to the parents, I almost always find that the child is mirroring the parent's attitude and perceptions.

Exploration of the subject of extraterrestrial contact has certainly been with us for some time in speculative fiction, TV programs and cinema, even if the mainstream press has, for whatever reason, been reluctant to cover the facts of the matter. America fell in love with the soft, harmless, sweet *"ET"* of Steven Spielberg's 1982 smash hit movie. But a more pervasive image of the space visitors as ruthless invaders -- or at best aloof, Godlike manipulators -- spans the history of literature and film from before H.G. Wells' *War of the Worlds* to *Independence Day* and beyond, including such classics as *The Day The Earth Stood Still, It Came From Outer Space, Invasion of the Body Snatchers, Alien, Close Encounters of the Third Kind, 2001: A Space Odyssey* and -- perhaps most germane to our topic -- Arthur C. Clarke's classic science fiction novel, *Childhood's End.* In general, perhaps because so many people enjoy a good scare, we are sold the view that whoever or whatever these visitors might be and wherever they come from, they do not mean well for the human race! Our children are getting large doses of the ET concept on their Saturday morning cartoons -- *Ninja Turtles, Power Rangers* and many others. The ET presence is used to sell everything from beer and cigarettes, to cereal, cars and telephones. And of course there is now the notorious (and dreadful) "autopsy film" which allegedly depicts the dissection of a deceased extraterrestrial. Regardless of its authenticity, it has brought the ET question into the center of the public spotlight. TV programs such as *Unsolved Mysteries, Sightings* and *The Paranormal Borderline* offer often lurid peeks into various aspects of the anomalous, complete with spooky lighting, skewed camera angles and weird music. Occasionally, a well-researched and informative story in the field of UFOlogy does crop up, but one would have to say this is the exception rather than the rule. And to be sure, rarely if ever is there a serious investigative UFO-related story done on network news programs! That, however, may be changing -- a signal, perhaps, that secrets long hidden will soon be revealed?

Some suggest that all these films and TV shows are part of an attempt to prepare the public for the inevitable announcement that "they" do exist and that at least some elements of the planet's "ruling elite" have had contact with extraterrestrials since 1947 (at the time of the infamous Roswell, New Mexico crash of a UFO) and, some researchers believe, since even earlier in modern history.

Whatever the truth might be, the idea of extraterrestrials interacting with us explodes most popular paradigms of science, philosophy and theology. But until humanity turns the full light and force of its collective consciousness and will upon these strange tales of visitation, it would appear we are condemning ourselves to a Dark Age of denial and missing a colossal opportunity for growth. The intuitive children may be delivering a message of paramount importance for our future.

Reference Books

Ceto's New Friends - Leah Haley (Children's book about ET contact)

How to Catch A Flying Saucer - James M. Deem (Children's book on all aspects of the UFO phenomenon)

Note: Investigate the "youth section" in your public library for books on UFOs and other paranormal subjects. I was amazed how many I was able to find in mine.

Spirituality

Jackie began telling her mom and dad at age three that "God is in everything -- I can see it."

Andy began picking up litter at about age three and making statements like "We have to take care of the earth, so it will take care of us."

Todd, three, stated emphatically to his mother as they left a Christian church, "I can't possibly go back to that church ever again. They don't know what they are talking about. God isn't on a throne some place in heaven. God is the love inside me and you and everybody."

P.M.H. Atwater tells us: "At the age of four...I could clearly see the ether, its tidal forces and wave forms, in the sky and the air around me...Sometimes in play, I would cuff ether's gauzy threads just to see what might happen to the fabric when I did...As an adult, I lost this ability and even forgot all about it."[18]

A three year-old girl told her mother, "You don't have to treat me like an angel." Three years later, she announced, "NOW you can treat me like an angel!"

Dorothy's grandson was born with unusual bumps of cartilage atop each shoulder blade. One day he asked her, "Will I ever get my wings back?" He explained that he had to give his wings up to "have a body." Dorothy always cut wings out of cardboard for her grandson to play with whenever he came to visit her. He put them on and ran around the house pretending to fly.

When Monty was four, his mother would leave him in the care of his two older brothers, aged eight and ten. They didn't pay much attention to him and he was often left alone and frightened. However, he eventually made an interesting discovery: "Something would happen so I knew I wasn't alone. The water would turn on by itself. The TV or radio would come on or something would move in the room. It made me know I was never really alone."

Samantha, five, will suddenly stop playing outside and run over to her mother and say, "An angel just told me to slow down and be careful," or "Jesus just told me he loves me and I should love everybody."

A wonderful story I have heard from several different sources tells of the little boy who went into his newborn sister's room to have a talk with her. His parents overheard him ask her, "Can you tell me about God? I'm forgetting."

Repeatedly we hear from the intuitive children the concept that God is in everything and everybody. Perhaps it is because of their expanded vision that they are able to see this "God Force" as energy exuding from everything. Some say their "friends" tell them or that they "learned it in school". Whatever the source, such an idea naturally leads them to respect all life and nature, creating a way of being in the world that de-emphasizes the differences among people and precludes belief in the superiority of one group over another. Imagine a world in which everywhere one looked, one SAW God! If that couldn't put an end to war and the other myriad cruelties to which humans subject one another and their home planet, I cannot imagine what would. While we can't know for certain the source of this "hard-wired Nirvana" in the intuitive children, we can agree that a better metaphysics for

275

the longed-for "New Age" of peace and enlightenment cannot be found. Indeed, this is metaphysics made physical, empirical, real; spirituality that requires no priestly intermediaries or religious structures. It is, in short, a vision highly threatening to those who wish to maintain the status quo. It's utterly liberating.

But it's certainly not anything new; this way of seeing the world may be safely said to be part of the core mysteries of all the world's religions, and many metaphysical treatises of modern times urge us to develop such a vision. To have our children coming into the world constantly and literally immersed in its divinity can only bode well for our future -- if they can maintain that ability into adulthood!

Again, from many sources, we hear the message that humanity is on the verge of a great transition, one that is -- for lack of a better term -- spiritual in nature. The ancient mysteries long held in trust by shamans, priests and secret societies are emerging more and more into general consciousness, more easily accessible than ever before to any seeker. As mentioned earlier in these pages, planet Earth is increasingly seen as an entity unto herself, of which all creatures living upon her are a part, and that entity is undergoing some sort of fundamental change. The mystery of Consciousness itself seems to lie at the core of that change -- a mystery perhaps still somewhat beyond human understanding, but certainly not outside our experience! Are the intuitive children harbingers of that transformation of consciousness among humans, part of the beginning of the next circle in the spiral of our spiritual growth? This is what my intuition, experience and research are telling me.

In Wambach's study, more than 80 percent of her hypnotized subjects said they chose the 20th century in which to be born because it would be characterized by a new development of spiritual awareness, a coming together of people to transcend their individuality through the realization that they are linked on higher planes. Although mentioning earth changes, they mostly spoke positively of future events. Some recalled being eager to be born and claimed they were here to assist in a new development in mankind's history.[7]

When asked why they were on Earth, they responded that they wanted to learn to relate to others and love unconditionally, without being demanding or possessive. 28 percent said they had a role in teaching mankind to understand his unity and to develop his higher consciousness. Many emphasized the Golden Rule.[7]

The Prodigies that Robyn Quail and I interviewed almost all told me that they feel as though they're here on a "mission" of some sort. Some feel they must help humankind develop spiritually, or be of assistance during the coming earth changes. Others feel they must develop the technological breakthroughs they've been given -- technology usually of an ecologically beneficial nature. Almost all feel they've been given vital information of some kind to share with the rest of us. Will these new little ones provide us with previously obscure insights into our spiritual nature? As they say, "Out of the mouths of babes...!"

Reference Books

The Game of Life - Florence Scovel Shinn (Simple, practical lessons in life -- wonderful!)

The Celestine Prophecy and *The Tenth Insight* - James Redfield (visions of the "New Age")

Living In The Light - Shakti Gawain (Lessons in life)

Handbook To Higher Consciousness - Ken Keyes, Jr.

Cosmic Consciousness - Richard M. Bucke (Mystical experience and the human mind -- first published almost 100 years ago -- a classic!)

Mountains, Meadows & Moonbeams - Mary Summer Rain (Great story book to teach metaphysical principles to a child)

All I See Is Part of Me - Chara M. Curtis

Guess How Much I Love You - Sam McBratney

We Are All Special - Arlene Maguire

Fairies, From A to Z - Adrienne Keith

When I Get Bigger - Mercer Mayer

A Journal and Play Book, A Place to Dream While Awake - Sark (children's activity book)

The Missing Piece Meets the Big O - Shel Silverstein

A Child's Gift of Lullabies - Aaron Brown (melodies for children)

Children of Light - Jan Royce Conant - Obtain directly from the author at Three Bridges Road, East Haddam, CT 06423 (203) 434-9030 (Children's book)

Color

Lannie, three, was in the grocery store with her psychic grandmother when a man came up to her and tried to touch her cheek. Tammy yelled, "Don't touch me, you're black!" (The man was Caucasian.) She and her grandmother could see his aura and there was a large black cloud all around him. According to her grandmother, Lannie has always had the ability to see auras. As a very young infant she would smile and gaze around people's head and reach out toward their faces, as if touching a cloud around them. One day Lannie was with her grandmother in a store where they were taking aura pictures. Her grandmother asked her if she wanted her picture taken. She replied, "I don't need a picture. All I have to do is look in the mirror!"

Randy, nine, came up to my display table at an event and said, "I see color around people, but I don't understand what I see and everybody here says you can help me; will you?" We had a very enlightening conversation (for both of us!). He said, "You know, little kids see color all the time, but their parents say, 'no you don't' so they forget how. I was lucky, my parents told me I could, so I still can and I draw pictures of what I see. Want me to draw your picture?" After analyzing his drawing, I knew what he was seeing and why -- he was right. Before he left he said, "Do you have any pain in your body?" I told him my low back hurt a little. He put out his hand to my back and the pain was instantly gone. He exclaimed, "How's that? My Mom taught me that trick. One day she had a sore throat and told me to put my hand on it and it got better and I've been doing it ever since. Anybody can do it, if they try."

Dana says she can always tell when her Mom or Dad is mad because "they get all red". She's been telling her Mom what color she sees around her every day since she was about three, and she "can see color around everybody, even plants and animals."

At the age of four, Jerry was having what appeared to his worried parents to be "fits". Jerry explained to his therapist that sometimes at night he went "so far out" of his body that he would be at "too high a frequency" when he tried to come back (hence the "fits"). He had to work to calm his energy. To aid that process, he had color-coded his various bodily systems: red for the circulatory, yellow for the endocrine, green for the respiratory, blue for the nervous system. He said he was learning to "integrate my human self."

Becky, four, says she can see colors coming out of people's mouths as they talk -- "it sort of looks like bubbles".

One of the most basic and frequently reported abilities of intuitive children is that of seeing auras (the electromagnetic energy field around a person). They perceive the aura as cloud-like colored energy around a person, animal (usually around the head) or plant. Sometimes they only see a small band of white light surrounding the body. Since they're very sensitive to the "feeling" of different colors, it's extremely important that their caregivers be aware of the effects of color, so that they can help the children understand what they're seeing and feeling, and be able to make necessary and appropriate adjustments to environmental and clothing colors.

Color affects everything that we do in life; from the clothes we wear, interior decoration and the food we eat, to our physical and emotional health and even our education. All children are dramatically affected by color, but the intuitive children even more so, due to their hypersensitivity.

Everything in our Universe is energy, vibrating at different speeds, rates of vibration or frequencies. Scientists have classified these various wavelengths on the electromagnetic spectrum to help us understand this principle. X-rays, television waves, radio waves, and microwaves, as well as the seven colors of the rainbow (the so called "visible light spectrum") all have characteristic frequencies.

Colorology is based on the principle that each of the seven colors of the rainbow carries a certain frequency or rate of vibration, and our physical bodies are able to "tune in to" or receive that frequency. Within our bodies we have seven major endocrine glands. These endocrine glands regulate the functioning of our bodily systems, i.e., reproductive, circulatory, respiratory, etc. Endocrine glands secrete hormones, and if they secrete too much or too little of these hormones, physical and/or emotional dis-ease can result. Since everything is energy in one form or another, it follows that the seven major endocrine glands and the molecules of which they are composed are, like everything else, vibrating at particular frequencies. Researchers such as Valarie Hunt and Christopher Hills have discovered that each of the seven endocrine glands vibrates at the same frequency as one of the seven colors of the rainbow.

We can, therefore, introduce color to our physical bodies by various methods and directly affect the vibratory rate of these endocrine glands and the amount of hormones they secrete, thereby influencing all of our bodily functions and systems and improving our physical health. Color also influences our feelings and emotions by stimulating the area of the brain which vibrates at the frequency of that color, producing a particular emotional response.

Because we are alive, we vibrate, and this vibration creates an electromagnetic field around us called an aura. In its elementary form it can be perceived as simply a white glow around the body; however, some people are able to see the more expanded aura, with all its colors. Due to the intuitive child's ability to see beyond the visible light range on the electromagnetic spectrum, s/he can often see auras, thereby discerning if a person is happy, sad or even sick.

I believe we are all born with the capacity to see color around people, but often due to parental failure to encourage and validate announcements such as, "You sure are blue today, Mom," we repress and eventually lose the ability. Many parents can recall their infant children gazing around their heads, apparently seeing something. These babies are seeing the aura, and if parents would validate the experience for them by asking, "What are you seeing, what color is it?" even before the child can talk or knows what "color" means, they will be encouraged to retain the ability, as well as much of their other natural "psychic" abilities.

Young children are hyper-responsive to the colors red and orange. It can make them hyperactive, agitated and angry. We need all of the colors of the rainbow somewhere in our lives. However, red and orange do not belong in or on a child's bed, or any place where it can be seen from the bed. I would also think twice about dressing a child -- an intuitive child, particularly -- in red or orange, unless s/he was extremely lethargic.

Allow the child to choose his or her own colors, particularly in clothing, whenever possible. Children usually have an instinctive understanding of what color they need.

Some children know intuitively what the aura colors "mean"; most don't, however, and are very curious. Learning the characteristics of each color enables the intuitive child to understand what physical and emotional conditions are indicated by the colors s/he is seeing. S/he gains external validation for an intuitive experience, as well as help in any healing efforts, because s/he now know what areas of the body require attention.

I strongly urge everyone to learn the principles of Colorology, both for themselves and for their children. It's safe, simple, effective and inexpensive and the intuitive children respond particularly quickly to it.

Karyl has told me repeatedly that color is truly the key to understanding not only how our physical and emotional bodies operate, but also how to help create physical and emotional health and balance. She says that as Mother Earth changes frequency in the transition from the indigo to the violet band in her "Spiral of Life" (or from the third to the fifth dimension, in another metaphor), we must continually balance our chakra systems using color. This will enable our current physical, three-dimensional bodies to make the transition. She says Colorology is a very ancient science that has been used throughout the ages to heal and balance. It's time for humanity to remember how to use the science of color in their everyday lives.

I have frequently seen a vision of what I was told is "the Spiral of Life"; It looks like a colossal, whirling fog composed of individual specks of energy. I was shown that at the base of the spiral is the color red; the vibration "raises" as it moves through all the colors of the rainbow -- orange, yellow, green, blue and indigo to violet, which is the highest frequency and shortest wavelength. (My readings indicate that the Millennium Children are coming in on the indigo or violet vibration!) The energy that makes up this Spiral has been called many things through the ages by those seeking to understand who and what we are: Chi, Qi, Prana, life force, spirit, soul, Christ consciousness and God, to name a few.

We each have a vibratory rate or signature, at which we alone vibrate, somewhere within this spiral. This signature is as unique to each person as his or her fingerprints. We begin our human adventure in third-dimensional reality in the red frequency range, moving through the seven colors as we gain in frequency or vibration. Through the accumulation of life experience, we grow in self-awareness, Cosmic Consciousness, spiritual mastery -- whatever you want to call it -- until we fully comprehend that we are one with Source, and can live that realization in every moment.

DNA is the blueprint from which the physical body is created. It's found in every cell of the physical body. It's donated half from your mother and half from your father, and spirals together to create the instructions from which your unique physical body develops. We choose parents whose particular DNA combination will create the frequency or "Life Color" the soul desires to best facilitate its journey back to Source.

As we move through the colors, learning lessons, overcoming physical and emotional challenges, and developing special gifts and talents, the Life Colors fade one to the next. Our spirit, soul or essence retains the memory of its previous experience. This information is always available to us on the subconscious level and sometimes even consciously.

The energy fields we know as bodies are constantly seeking a state of dynamic balance within their particular Life Color vibration. Mood changes, various emotional states, illness and health are some of the ways we experience this constant play of energy seeking balance.

Although the fundamental Life Color remains the same throughout life, we also move through all the colors in each lifetime. These are the stages of life: we are "red" in infancy, as we get used to being in the physical body and learn to use the senses. In the orange phase, we go beyond our own bodies to the social stage, to see who else is in our world. Yellow is when we develop our intellectual capacity -- going to school. The green stage is when we learn about love and matters of the heart. Blue is the creative stage, when we figure out how we're going to support ourselves, and learn to communicate our needs and desires. Indigo usually occurs in mid-life, when we realize the answers are not "out there" and begin looking within. Violet is the stage of spiritual maturity, in which we see that we are a part of a much larger "something". Although this amazing Universe is made up of huge complexes of spirals within spirals within spirals, all interacting to create what we call our lives and our world, the Life Color spiral is, I feel, a key to knowing who we truly are.

The Life Color shouldn't be confused with one's "favorite" color. Your favorite color represents physical and emotional issues you have chosen to work on at this moment in your life. Colors you dislike represent those issues you are not willing to deal with right now, physically and/or emotionally. You're likely to have problems or imbalances in both or either areas. These "tastes" change throughout your life as you work through the issues they represent. Knowing the characteristics of your favorite and least favorite colors provides insight into what areas of life you're working on -- or ignoring. And understanding your Life Color provides insight into your role in this "game of Life" and the lessons that come along while playing it.

Reference Books

Colorology: The Science of Color - Caryl Dennis (A simple, yet scientific explanation of how color affects you and how to use it practically in your life.)

What's Your Color - Caryl Dennis (Booklet describing the Life Colors)

Nuclear Evolution - Christopher Hills

Resources

Rainbows Unlimited, 1245 Palm St., Clearwater, FL 34615, 813- 441-2270. (Offers a complete line of color therapy products)

Recreation & Creativity

Roberta, three, stunned her parents -- especially her mother -- when she climbed up on the piano bench and began playing a tune the mother had often played while pregnant with Roberta.

Mark's drawings were never childlike. He always colored within the lines and began drawing people and animals at the age of two.

Play is the first way we learn. It's how we create our ability to create! It's been observed that children who aren't played with don't learn to play, and are at risk at every level of their mental development. Again, we see how important appropriate models are in the process of moving from child to adult.

The "win or lose" model, like so many products of the dualistic world view, isn't helpful in creating mentally healthy people. There's nothing to learn from losing except how to be a loser -- a lifelong habit, with its accompanying frustration, stress and pessimism, may be the result. "Winning" at the expense of another only breeds arrogance and an unreal and unnecessary distance between the "I" and the "other". To foster the feeling of identity with creation which the intuitive child may exhibit to a marked degree, noncompetitive and creative play is far more useful. Here is where the imagination -- our everyday link to the Infinite -- can be freely developed. Things that a child can take apart and put back together in creative ways -- "real world" things -- are most desirable, and of course items such as clay, plain paper, fingerpaints, colored pencils, construction paper in a variety of colors, pieces of fabric, wooden sticks or blocks and other such materials stimulate the imagination and are beneficial.   Lots of movement is essential: Rahima Baldwin Dancy points out that "A young child's earliest play involves movement for the pure joy of it."[17] Her book *You Are Your Child's First Teacher* has an abundance of ideas and resources for introducing creative play into a child's life.

In general, the more children can be stimulated and encouraged to use their imagination, the greater the benefit to their overall mental abilities at present and in the future. Storytelling, as opposed to television, offers a good example of what I mean. Many experts in child development warn of the dangers to children's minds posed by television. Because TV provides the brain with both auditory and visual information, the creative process (imagination) is literally "put to sleep" -- there's just nothing for it to do! Some studies have shown that the content of a program is irrelevant for the child under seven years old; its neurological effects are the same regardless of what the child watches. What is significant is that habitual TV watching literally causes imagination to atrophy. Storytelling, on the other hand, requires that the listener supply images to go with the words. The imagination gets lots of practice in creating worlds! Pearce tells of the little girl who preferred radio to television because "the pictures are so much better." Enough said!

Intuitive children are often "bookworms" and love to stay inside, reading and learning. As important as such activities are, it's also important that they be encouraged to get outside for the proverbial "fresh air and sunshine". Trips to the zoo, the beach or the park will offer opportunities for both learning and exercise. Also, because they're often fascinated by the sky, a telescope can be a magical gift for the intuitive child.

And don't forget to dance! Singing, dancing and playing musical instruments are very important in healthy child development. Children are naturally musical; they love sounds. They love to hear them and make them -- with their voices or by banging a spoon on a cooking pan. Once your child becomes verbal, s/he will love to sing with you, even more so if you add gestures and movements to match the words, like the classics, "I'm A Little Teapot" and "Ring Around the Roses".

And speaking of art, a simple way to monitor a child's emotional state -- especially the sometimes moody intuitive child -- is to observe his creative work. If, for example, a child uses a lot of black and brown in his art, or draws frightful, menacing figures, it could be a sign of distress, alerting a caregiver to keep an eye out for other signs of emotional disturbance. Of course, talking with the child about the artwork can be most informative, and helpful to the child.

The bottom line is that play is a vital part of the relationship between parent and child, as well as an essential tool in mental development. A home without the laughter and joy engendered in free play is no home at all.

These children -- and most other children as well -- also require time for contemplation and meditation. Some may dismiss it as "day dreaming", but meditation may be how the intuitive child connects to Spirit and/or his source of information. For any child these interludes offer an opportunity to use the imagination.

It is best, whenever possible, to follow the intuitive child's lead as to when, where and what activity is appropriate for him or her.

Reference Books

You Are Your Child's First Teacher - Rahima Baldwin Dancy

Getting To Know Kids In Your Life - Jeanne McSweeney & Charles Leocha, World Leisure Corporation, 177 Paris St., Boston, MA 02128, 617-569-1966 (Book of provocative questions to ask a child)

Resources

Real Goods, 555 Leslie St., Ukiah, CA 95482-5507, (800) 762-7325,   (Creative games, toys and crafts)

A Happy Life, Jill Stevens, Two Wing Publishing, 1635 S. Rancho Santa Fe, San Marcos, CA 92069, (619) 471-1418 (Imagination songs for children)

Zoobooks, P.O. Box 85384, San Diego, CA 92186, (800) 992-5034 (Magazine for children with a scientific bent or a love for animals)

HearthSong, 156 N. Main St., Sebastopol, CA 95472, (800) 325-2502   (Imaginative toys and crafts)

Whole Child, P.O. Box 100, Campbellville, Ontario LOP 1BO, Canada (800) 387-2888 (Toys for creative play)

Back to Basics Toys: Games & Hobbies, 31333 Agoura Road, Westlake Village, CA 91361, (800) 356-5360   (Toys and games)

Magic Cabin Dolls, P.O. Box 1996, Peoria, IL 61656, (888) MC-DOLLS (Handcrafted natural fiber dolls and doll kits)

Zephyr Press, P.O. Box 66006-C, Tucson, AZ 85728, (520) 322-5090 (Books for "new ways of teaching for all ways of learning")

The Heritage Key: An International Children's Catalog, 6102 E. Mescal, Scottsdale, AZ 85254, (602) 483-3313 (Collection of multicultural books, toys and dolls from around the world)

Music For Little People, 605 S. Douglas St., El Segundo, CA 90245, (800) 727-2233 (Instruments and kid's music)

Animalearn: The Magazine For Kids Who Love Animals, 801 Old York Rd. #204, Jenkinstown, PA 19046, (215) 887-0816

Website

Gordon-Michael Scallion will have a website offering children's stories available February 10, 1997 -- www.DREAMVOYAGER.com

Conclusion

Danielle, six, was receiving counseling at school because of her "defiant" attitude. One technique the counselor used was to have Danielle make a list of things that made her unhappy. She told her parents that she didn't understand why the counselor "got so mad" when she asked him to do the same thing (she could see by the color of his aura he was unhappy). "I'm not a germ," she said, "I'm a person." Everyone wants respect!

Marianne, two, was having a dramatic temper tantrum. Her mother calmly stopped her, told her to look into her eyes and tell her what was the matter. She exclaimed, "This body is too little and I don't want to be here!"

In her book *Future Memory,* P.M.H. Atwater finds it "fascinating that between the ages of four and five is when most childhood cases of alien abductions and alien sightings are reported to occur; when a large percentage of early childhood cases of the near-death phenomenon happen...and when kids commonly report paranormal activities like out-of-body experiences, flying dreams, disembodied voices, spirit visitations, and heightened intuition."[18] There would appear to be what might be called a "window to the paranormal" in the development of most if not all children. Those that I have dubbed "intuitive children" seem to have that window open from birth, and are able to go back and forth through it at will -- whether they have appropriate models to "imprint to" or not. That is not to say, however, that their connection to Spirit is indestructible. Like everyone else, they will "forget" if encouraged to do so by negative reactions from their elders or, when they get into school or other social interactions outside the home, by their peers.

My motivation for writing this book is to help these intuitive children to develop their abilities to the fullest, and hopefully save them from at least some of the torment many of the Prodigies endured at the hands of the ignorant and uninformed. Whether extraterrestrials are telepathically "coaching" humanity with information and technology and/or manipulating our DNA; whether all this high strangeness is simply the next step in the evolution of the human psyche; or whether we are unknowingly accessing other dimensions in some as yet unimagined way, it seems certain that Homo Sapiens are at a crucial point in the journey of Life, and that these special children may have been appointed "Keepers of the Flame" that will light our way through the difficult years to come. Can we afford to ignore that possibility?

I believe that on some level, one agrees before the fact to take on the responsibility of parenting one or more of these "millennium generation" intuitive children, with the concomitant rewards, challenges and possibilities. Intuitive children require special attention, education, understanding and most of all lots of unconditional love and acceptance. The parents' attitudes about, perspectives on, and reactions to what their children say and do are pivotal in the realization of their full potential. It should be remembered that they may be able to "read" others' thoughts, emotions and body language. Denial, lies or half-truths will only confuse and upset them. Dealing with "inner child" issues is of great help to anyone, but especially to the parent of an intuitive child.

"Sasha", in *Preparing for Contact,* tells us:

> It is in the subconscious that you store your childhood and past-life pain. This old pain is what forms your belief systems. When these beliefs are changed, your entire life experience changes with it.

Go within, as deeply as you can. Find your own demons, fears and that part of you that is not you but merely a reflection of your programming from this life and other lives. Do not abolish these things; befriend them. Look into the mirror of your soul to see all that is there -- the light, the love, and the ugliness. When you can befriend all of that, you will have gotten to the level of the unconscious. Doors will begin opening quickly. You will have begun the integrative process within your consciousness. That place is so powerful! And is your true state of being."[7]

And, P.M.H. Atwater in *Future Memory*:

All of us become like children when we begin each new progression from one level of experience to another, from one plane of existence to another, until we successfully integrate our experiences in preparation for our goal of soul maturity.[18]

A part of one's parental responsibility is to educate oneself as much as possible relative to the ideas and experiences intuitive children have, so that one can calmly, rationally and intelligently discuss any matter with them. Open communication is essential to help children integrate into consensus reality without being consumed by it.

Respect, which of course we all want, seems to be extremely important to the intuitive children. Many of them feel and think like adults and do not understand why they aren't being treated like adults. Self-esteem can also be a problem for these children, because they feel so different from their peers and often face ridicule.

A recent study showed that unimaginative children are far more prone to violence than imaginative children, because they're unable to imagine an alternative when they confront a situation that's threatening, insulting, unpleasant or unrewarding.[3] The importance of stimulating the imagination cannot be overestimated.

These children must to be taught boundaries, psychic and otherwise. If they're telepathic, they often believe everyone is, and thus feel vulnerable to unwanted psychic intrusions. They can be taught -- as I pointed out in the chapter on psychic abilities -- to imagine a "white light energy field" around themselves, to prevent others from reading their thoughts.

Our minds are capable of creating miracles. All we need do is realize it and use the energy of will to direct our thoughts and mental energy. The study of multiple personality disorders offers insight into the mind's power. One personality may be allergic to strawberries and be suffering an attack of hives; another personality comes in who isn't allergic and the hives disappear immediately. One personality can be blind and the other sighted. One can be deaf and the other not.

Pearce tells a wonderful story about a child who severely cut his hand. His father instinctively said, "Let's stop the bleeding together." They focused their energy on the wound, and the bleeding stopped almost immediately.[4]

Young children believe their parents are omnipotent; therefore, all they may need is modeling to bring forth potential healing abilities. Should a child become ill, the parent can assure him or her that they both have the personal power to heal, and then devote full attention to that healing. Through continual suggestion, reassurance, and reaffirming of this power and its availability to the child, the parent communicates the idea that the child controls his/her own healing, and that mind has dominion over the world.

Because we are alive, we vibrate and emit life energy from our bodies. We can project that energy onto another person, thereby sharing our energy with them. Love magnifies this power. In the Bible it is called laying-on-of-hands. It is not a mystical ability, it is simply the inherent power of Life. We have an unlimited amount of this healing energy to share with our children, and they can share theirs with us, as well.[1] Intuitive children are often consciously aware of their natural ability to heal, and able to use it with spectacular results, as some of the stories in this book will attest. How they can attain this consciousness -- let alone the ability itself -- with no one modeling the behavior for them, is a question that will perhaps be answered one day by the children themselves.

The frustration for some intuitive children of being in this confining, confusing, 3-D frequency can result in temper displays. Their frustration is best acknowledged, discussed and then redirected in a more positive direction. Music, movement and art can often be used effectively in these cases.

One little girl could not understand why her teacher would not let her take a rest whenever she felt tired. This need has been described variously by intuitive children as wanting to "make a connection", "recharge my battery", "go home" or "go to the ship". The children apparently require more than just a nap. It would be well to honor that need whenever possible.

Finally, they need as much touching, hugging and unconditional love as you can offer -- just like any other kid!

From *Future Memory:* "...[O]ur true future is in remembering who and what we really are, and then behaving accordingly.

Once so 'reborn', regardless of how, we are called upon to return to society not as reformers but as transformers, preparing the way so that others can awaken as well."

I think that's a pretty good description of the mission that the Millennium Children -- of whatever age -- have accepted. May they succeed beyond any of our wildest dreams.

Reference Books

You Can Heal Your Life - Louise Hay (Inner Child)

Women Who Love Too Much - Robin Norwood (Great book for men and women about relationships)

Love Is Letting Go of Fear - G. Jampolsky (Inner Child)

Men Who Hate Women & The Women Who Love Them - Susan Forward (Relationships)

Smart Women, Foolish Choices - Drs. Cowan and Kinder (Relationships)

Your Inner Child of the Past - W. Hugh Missildine

The Family - John Bradshaw

My Mother, Myself - Nancy Friday (Inner Child)

I'm OK - You're OK - Thomas Harris, MD. (Inner Child)

Say Goodbye to Guilt - G. Jampolsky (Inner Child)

Love & Addition - Stanton Peele (Inner Child)

Resources

Happy Dreams Tapes, 800-345-8515 (Self esteem audio tapes)

Notes

1. *Colorology, The Science of Color*, Caryl Dennis (Rainbows Unlimited, 1990)

2. *Bonds of Fire*, Alice Rose, Ph.D. (Secret Heaven Books, 4651 Roswell Rd., Suite I-801, Atlanta, GA 30342, 1996)

3. *Evolution's End*, Joseph Chilton Pearce (HarperCollins Publishers, 1992)

4. *Magical Child*, Joseph Chilton Pearce (E.P. Dutton, 1977)

5. *The Secret Life Of The Unborn Child*, Thomas Verny, M.D. (Summit Books, 1981)

6. *Preparing For Contact*, Lyssa Royal & Keith Priest (Royal Priest Research Press, 1994)

7. *Life Before Life*, Helen Wambach (Bantam Books, 1979)

8. *Children of the Blue Ray,* Gordon-Michael Scallion -- *Earth Changes Report*, 1992 article, Matrix Institute, Inc., P.O. Box 336, Chesterfield, NH 03443, (800) 628-7493

9. *Immunization: Theory vs Reality*, Neil Z. Miller, (New Atlantean Press, 1996)

10. *DPT: A Shot In The Dark*, Harris L. Coulter and Barbara Loe Fisher (Harcourt Brace Jovanovich, 1985; Warner 1986; Avery Publishing Group, Inc. 1991)

11. *Toxic Psychiatry*, Peter Breggin (St. Martin Press, 1991)

12. *How To Raise A Healthy Child...In Spite Of Your Doctor*, Robert S. Mendelsohn, M.D. (Ballantine, 1984)

13. *When Children Don't Learn*, Diane McGuiness (1985)

14. *Attention Deficit Disorder, Hyperactivity & Associated Disorders*, Wendy S. Coleman, M.D. (Calliope, 1993)

15. *Having Twins*, Elizabeth Noble (Houghton Mifflin, 1990)

16. *Primal Connection*, Elizabeth Noble (Simon & Schuster, 1993)

17. *You Are Your Child's First Teacher*, Rahima Baldwin Dancy (Celestial Arts, 1989)

18. *Future Memory: How Those Who "See The Future" Shed New Light On The Workings of the Human Mind*, P.M.H. Atwater (Birch Lane Press, 1996)

19. *Vaccines: Are They Really Safe and Effective* - Neil Z. Miller (New Atlantean Press, 1996)

The Laws Of Manifestation

Decide what you want.

List the properties and qualities of what you desire to manifest.

Creative a visual representation of your desire, such as a "treasure map".

Create positive affirmations to say throughout the day.

Imagine how it will *feel* to have what you desire. The more emotion you can attach to your desire the better.

Focus energy and attention on your "properties and qualities" list and/or visual representation several times a day -- particularly upon awakening and just before going to sleep.

Always add, "This or something better" to your request.

Be thankful for the perfect manifestation of your desire for your highest and best good.

ABOUT THE AUTHORS

Caryl Dennis

In 1987 she began receiving telepathic transmissions concerning Colorology and Cosmology, which resulted in her first book, *Colorology: The Study of the Science of Color*. Her desire to discover who was communicating with her led her to research the UFO phenomenon. In 1991 she compiled *The UFO Reference Book*.

For the last few years she has been investigating the *Vanishing Twin Phenomenon*, which she came upon in the course of research involving extraterrestrial contactees who became geniuses. Through this research she discovered she herself is a twin, and has since had direct communication and contact with her "missing" twin sister, Karyl. Caryl travels extensively with her partner, **Parker Whitman,** consulting, researching and lecturing on both the subjects of Colorology and UFOlogy. She is also an intuitive counselor.

Parker Whitman

has for thirty years explored the subjects of nutrition, metaphysics, and the generally strange. He has a Bachelor's degree in English from the American University in Washington, D.C.

Books and Products

Colorology: The Science of Color	$ 16.00
The UFO Reference Book	16.00
What's Your Color?	7.00

The Life Colors explained

Body, Mind & Spirit	
Healing Rainbow Card	3.25

5" x 7" frameable card with envelope

Rainbow Cellophanes	12.00

Five colored cellophanes for solarizing water

Rainbow Overlays	12.00

Seven 8 1/2" x 5 1/2" colored overlays for better reading

Rainbow Slides	12.00

Seven 35mm slides for use in a slide projector

Rainbow Gels	24.00

Eight 8 1/2" x 11" gels for use with lights

Body Poster	10.00

8 -1/2" x 11" laminated full color anatomy chart

Positive Energy Purple Plate	13.00

Prices include shipping. Florida residents add 7% sales tax.
Send check or money order to:
Rainbows Unlimited, 1245 Palm St., Clearwater, FL 34615